POSTCARD HISTORY SERIES

Corning

ON THE COVER: This 1920 multi-view postcard shows Corning's five largest schools. All five of these postcards are shown in full size with captions in chapter 2. (Author's collection.)

ON THE BACK COVER: See page 59. (Author's collection.)

POSTCARD HISTORY SERIES

Corning

Donald Carapella Jr.

ARCADIA PUBLISHING

ISBN 978-0-7385-7202-4

Published by Arcadia Publishing
Charleston, South Carolina

Printed in the United States of America

Library of Congress Control Number: 2009926118

For all general information contact Arcadia Publishing at:
Telephone 843-853-2070
Fax 843-853-0044
E-mail sales@arcadiapublishing.com
For customer service and orders:
Toll-Free 1-888-313-2665

Visit us on the Internet at www.arcadiapublishing.com

This is dedicated to my father. We enjoyed sharing and studying history together. Although I am no longer the junior Donald, I will always be Donald Junior.

Contents

Acknowledgments

I am very thankful to the many people who helped make this book happen. Diane Gardner let me borrow postcards that I did not have. The Southeast Steuben County Library in Corning has shared many historic facts by letting me read through old city directories. The friends of the library hold a great book sale twice a year, where I have purchased many local history books and old local newspapers. I am thankful for the people that saved all these postcards since they were made; they were archivists without knowing it.

I have great respect for my family. Thanks to my mom, my sister, and her family for letting me visit their casa in the tropical paradise they live in. I love Corning and being part of it, but after a cold New York winter, nothing feels as good as the sun in the warm Sonora Desert. My respect extends especially to those who came before me, including my Italian grandfather, who was a World War I veteran; he came to Corning in the mid-1920s. Lastly, it also includes my dear father, who went to heaven in 2008. This book is for you dad. See you when I get there.

My love of history and collecting began at an early age. When I was about seven, my father got me interested in the old and foreign coins that he had collected throughout his life. We sat down together and sorted them out by date and put them into folders. Because of him, I started collecting postcards about 15 years ago. I was attracted to the hobby because a picture can be worth a thousand words and tell a story. I also like the hobby because hundreds of postcards can be stored in one album. This book illustrates about 200 postcards and took me years of searching to accumulate. Unless otherwise noted, everything pictured in this book is from my collection.

Introduction

Located on the Chemung River in Upstate New York, the Corning area is considered to be very historic. Before European settlers came to this country, it was inhabited by Native Americans. In the 17th century, the Corning area was in the southern part of the Seneca Nation, which was part of the Iroquois Confederation. The first white people to visit this area explored the land around what became Athens, Pennsylvania, in 1615.

Erastus Corning was a wealthy industrialist, investor, and politician. Corning and some associates from Albany formed a company called the Corning Company. In the 1830s, his company bought 340 acres of land in the area that later took his name. The group also sponsored the Blossburg and Corning Railroad, which was one of earliest railroads in this area.

Friedrich Wilhelm Augustin Steuben was born in Magdeburg, Prussia. He was from a military family and was an officer by age 17. He eventually became a staff member in Frederick the Great's headquarters. In 1777, George Washington had him come to America, where he eventually was remembered as the person who shaped the Continental army into a formidable fighting force that proved capable of defeating the British. Steuben County was created in 1796 and today is one of 62 counties in New York State. When it was first created, Steuben County was larger than now at about 50 square miles and probably had fewer than 600 citizens. Today the county population is almost 100,000. Indiana also has a county named after Steuben, and some town and city names are derived from Steuben.

In 1833, the Chemung Canal was finished, and it connected the Chemung River to Seneca Lake. Corning had a dock where boats were loaded to be sent down river to the canal. The Chemung Canal made it possible to enter Seneca Lake, the Erie Canal, and then west to the Great Lakes or east to New York City. This was a new trade route for lumber and produce from this area and coal from Pennsylvania. The canal was used until 1878 when it was not needed because the railroads had taken over the transportation needs of the community.

In the post–Civil War 1860s, the railroads grew. The Blossburg and Corning Railroad was busy in Corning. In the 1870s and 1880s, the Fallbrook Company built tracks and operated trains from Corning south to Williamsport. In the 1890s, the Fallbrook Railroad Company was a key player in the local economy. The Erie Railroad, New York Central Railroad, and the Delaware, Lackawanna, and Western Railroad were all important in 20th-century Corning.

The rise of industrialism in the United States from the 1870s through the dawn of the 20th century was happening in Corning. Entrepreneurial businessmen in Corning started companies such as the Corning Stove Works, the Payne Foundry, and Maltby's wholesale grocery business. In 1868, a glass factory was built in Corning because of the low prices and the availability of raw materials and coal. It later evolved into the Corning Glass Works, which to is today called Corning Incorporated. The Corning Glass Works opened the glass center in the 1950s. Today it is still a destination for tourists and is now called the Corning Museum of Glass.

Like most other small cities of its time, Corning had social organizations such as the Mason's, the Odd Fellows, and the Elks. Schools, churches, people, and all the above subjects can be remembered by collecting postcards and historic items.

One

Transportation

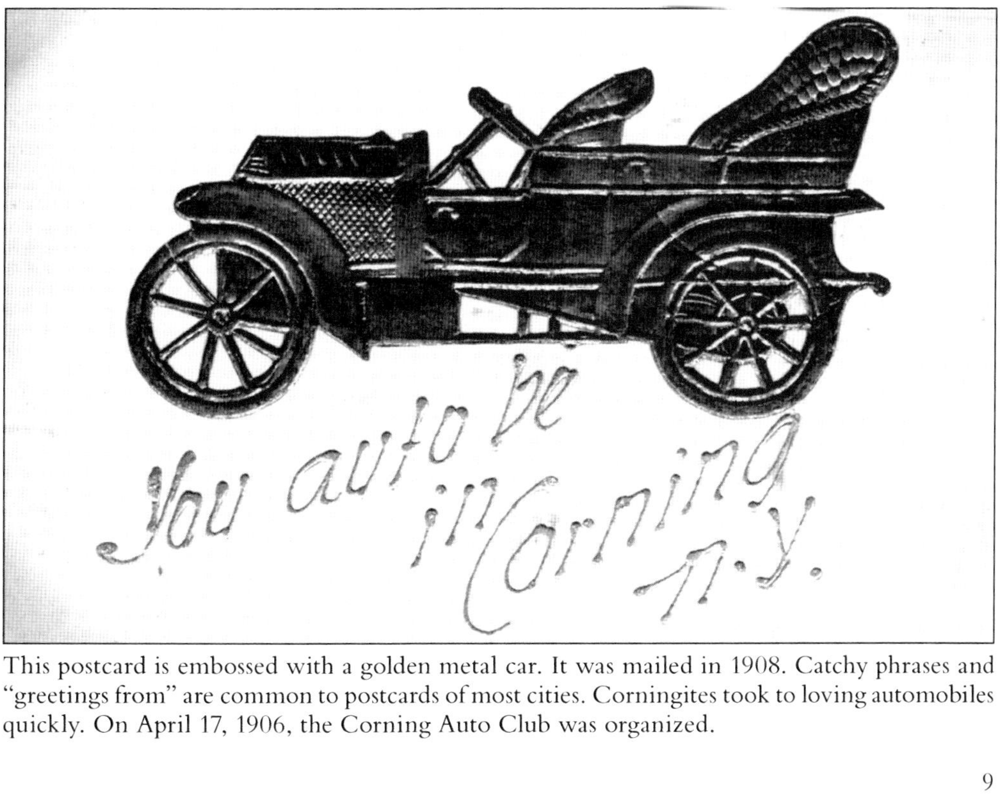

This postcard is embossed with a golden metal car. It was mailed in 1908. Catchy phrases and "greetings from" are common to postcards of most cities. Corningites took to loving automobiles quickly. On April 17, 1906, the Corning Auto Club was organized.

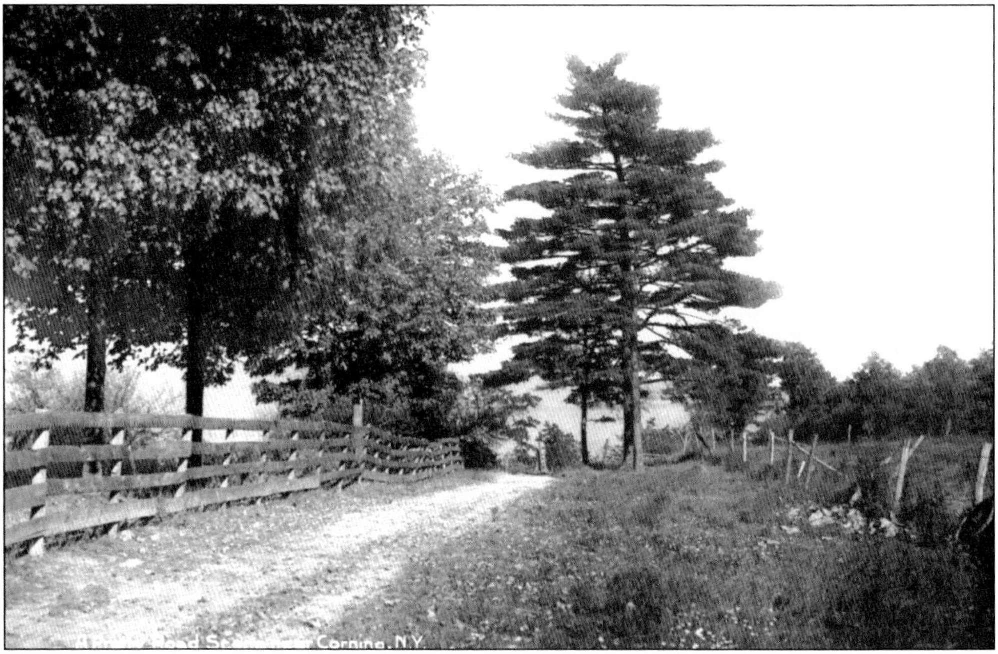

This postcard from 1907 shows what a country road outside of Corning looked like. They were built with a horse and buggy in mind but had automobile traffic in the future.

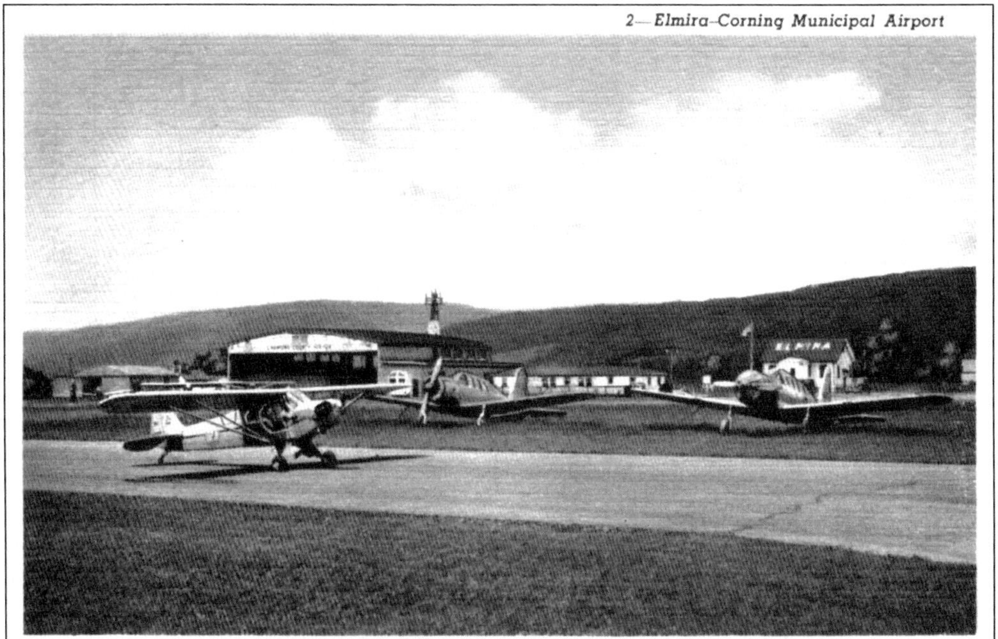

Corning and its neighbor Elmira share this airport. It is now called the Elmira-Corning Regional Airport. This site started out in 1933 when American Airlines built this early version of the airport. After World War II, the airport changed and grew into what it is today. Elmira is visible on top of the house on the right. This postcard is from the late 1940s.

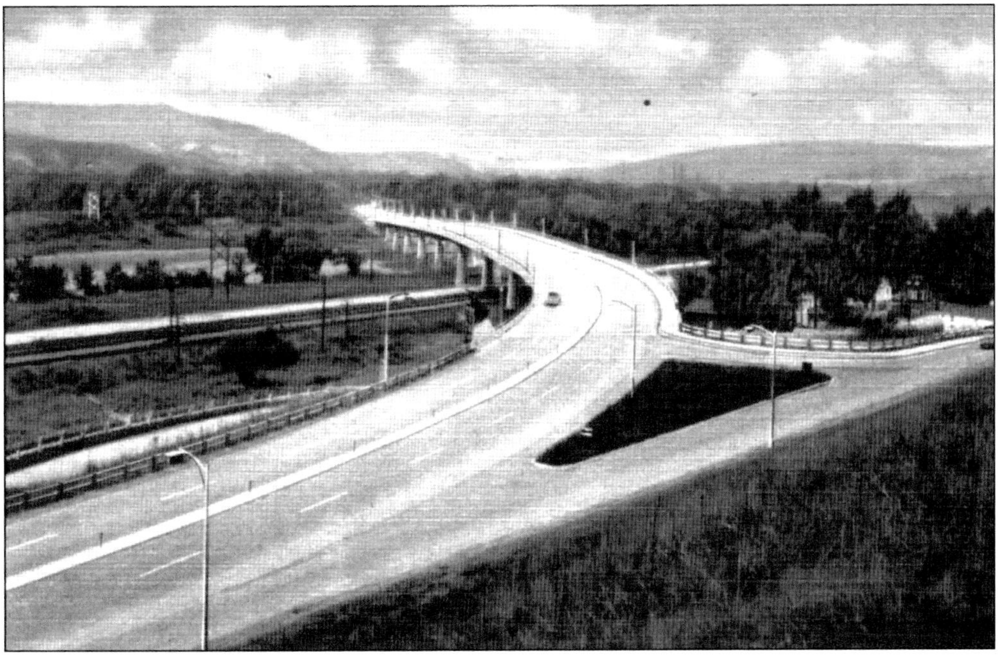

Before this bridge was built in the 1950s, Market Street went over a bridge into Gibson. Gibson was a bigger town than now, having had several stores on its main street. On the left side of this postcard across the river, a structure from Dension Park can be seen.

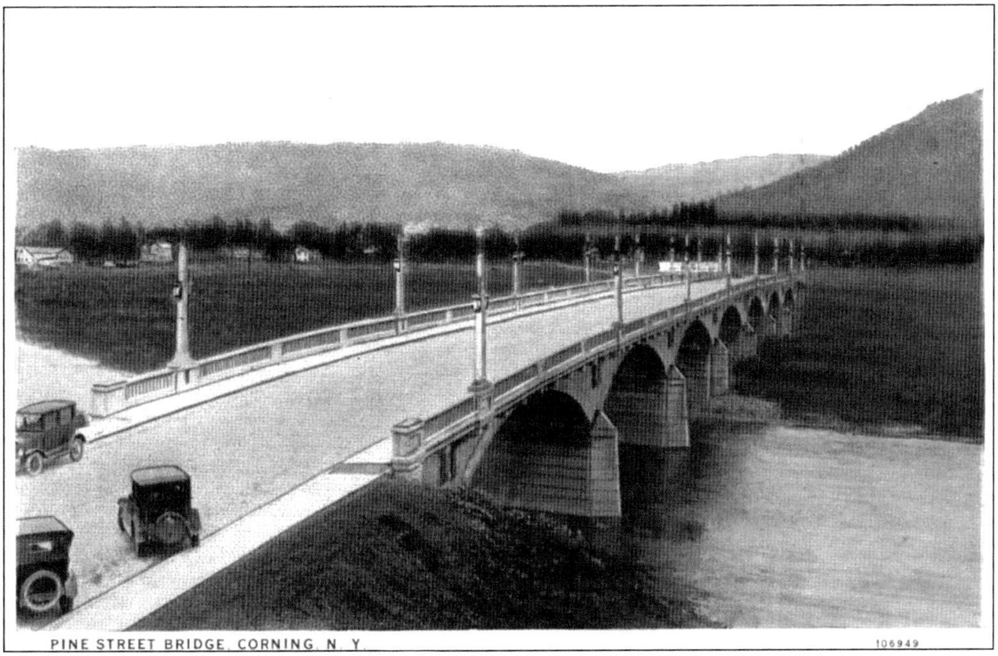

The Pine Street bridge and the Bridge Street bridges were the main ways to cross the river until the late 1970s, when a new bridge was built to replace the Pine Street bridge. With that, the street that was on the north side of the bridge changed as well. The new Centerway Street was one block east. On the bridge, a plaque can still be seen.

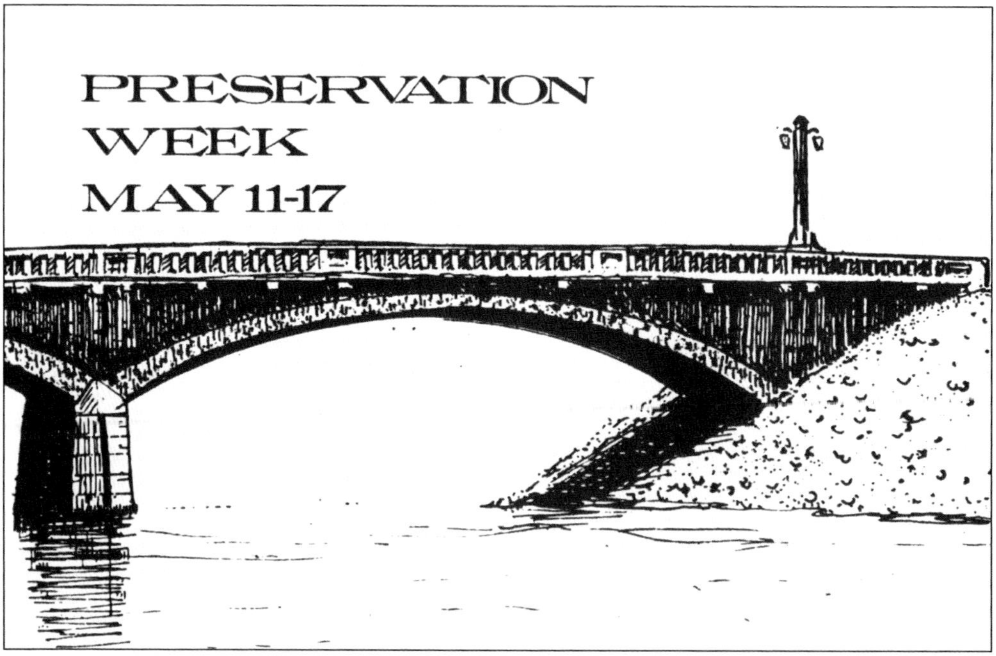

This bridge was built in the 1920s and was restored and open to pedestrians in 1980. On the south side of the bridge there is now a park. On the north side, the dyke along the river has a walking path going west that provides great scenery and can be taken all the way to the Patterson Bridge.

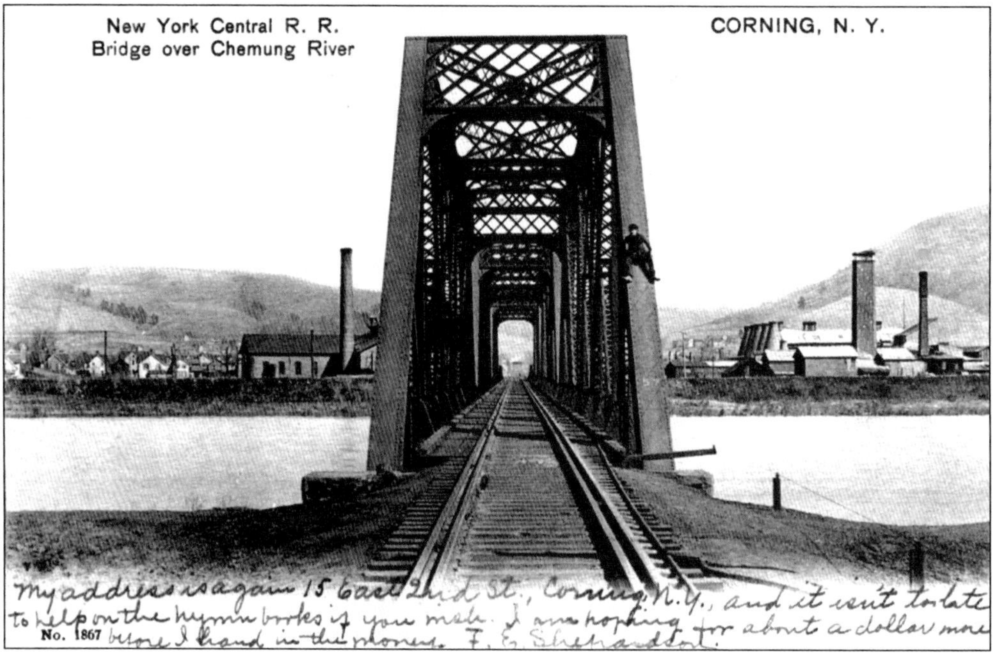

The New York Central Railroad bridge connected north-side tracks to the south side. On the right side across the river is Corning Brick Works. This postcard was mailed on January 10, 1910, with a message from the sender talking about owing money for hymn books.

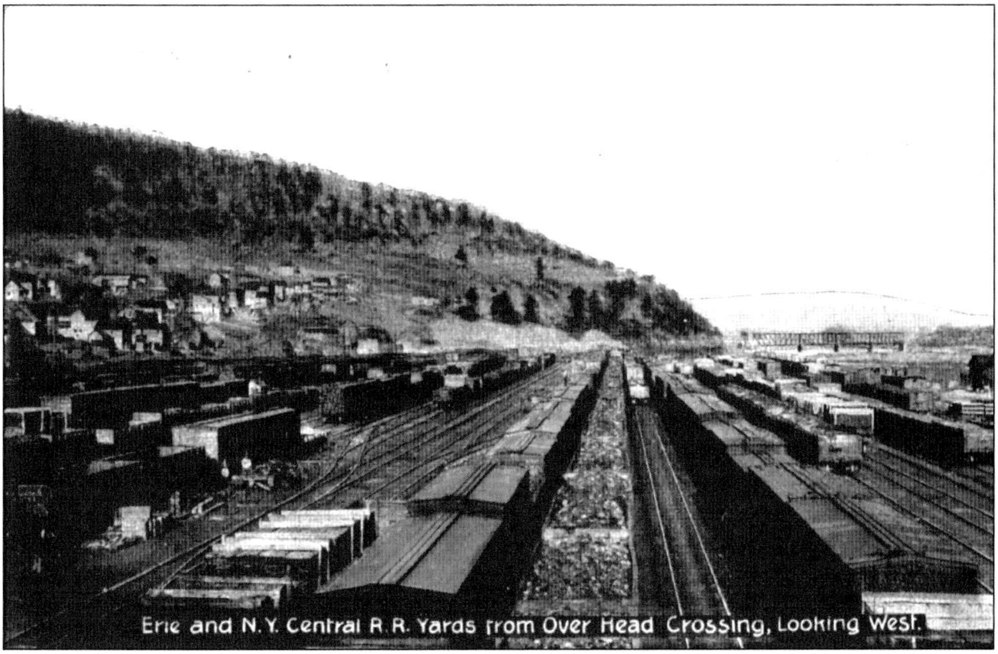

The Erie Railroad and New York Central Railroad yards were in the area of Corning where Wegman's Grocery store is today.

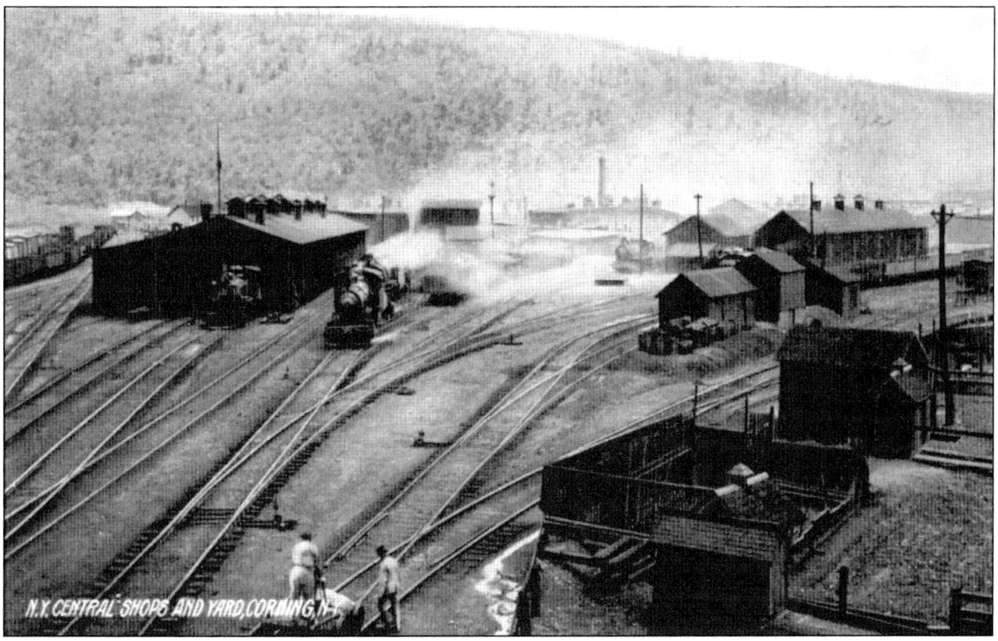

The New York Central Railroad shops and yards were used to repair the railcars and engines.

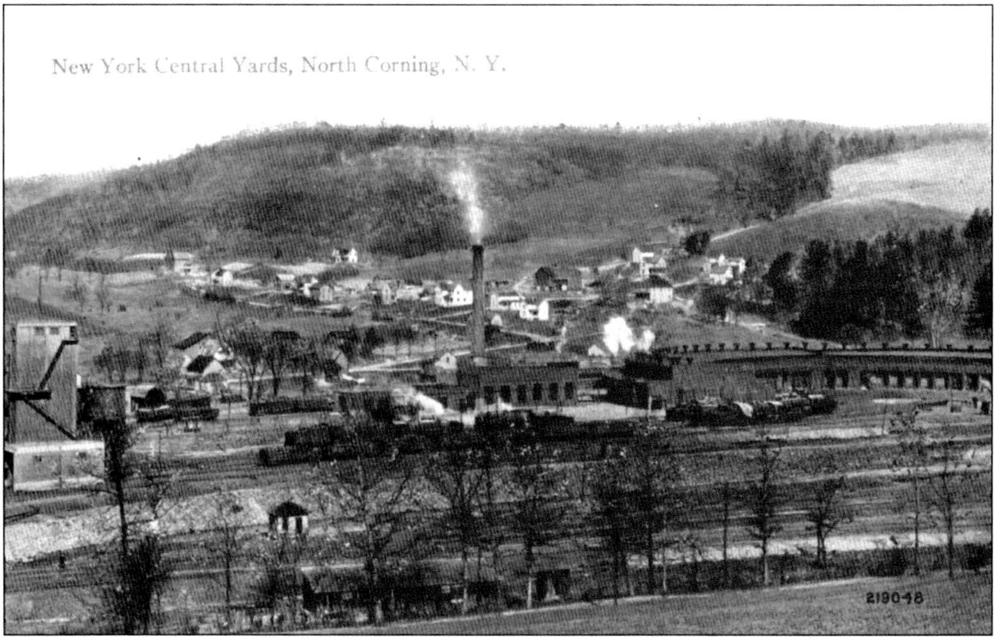

The New York Central Railroad yards of North Corning were built in 1909 and 1910. They were thoroughly equipped with machine shops, a 100-ton per hour coal hoist, and a roundhouse. This was in the part of Corning where Highway 414 begins today. By the 1950s, these buildings were torn down.

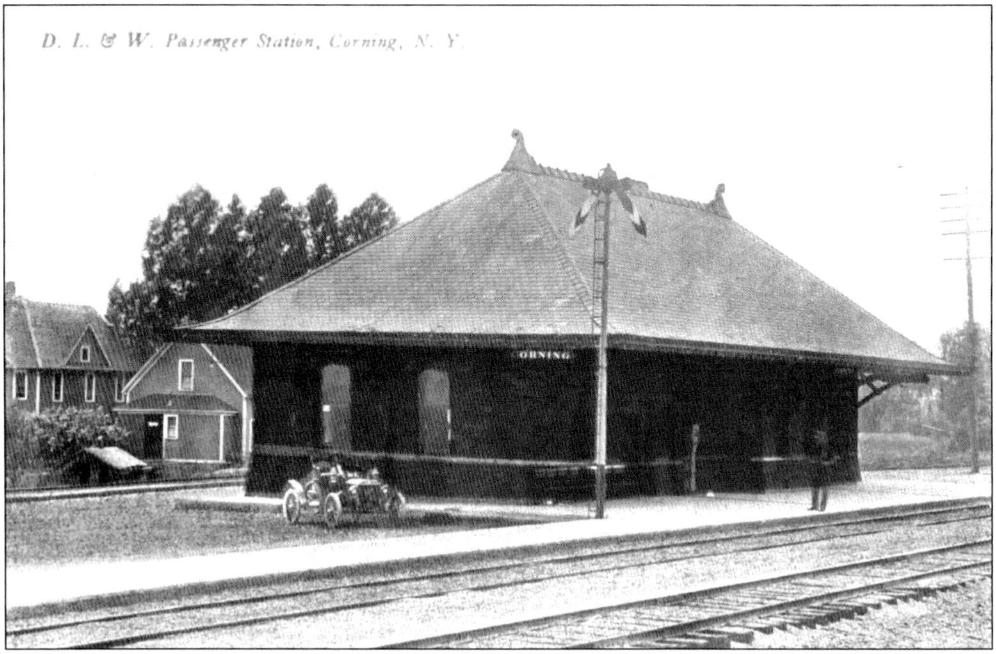

The Delaware, Lackawanna, and Western Railroad had been doing business in Corning since about 1880. This station opened in 1902 and remained a passenger train station until about 1970.

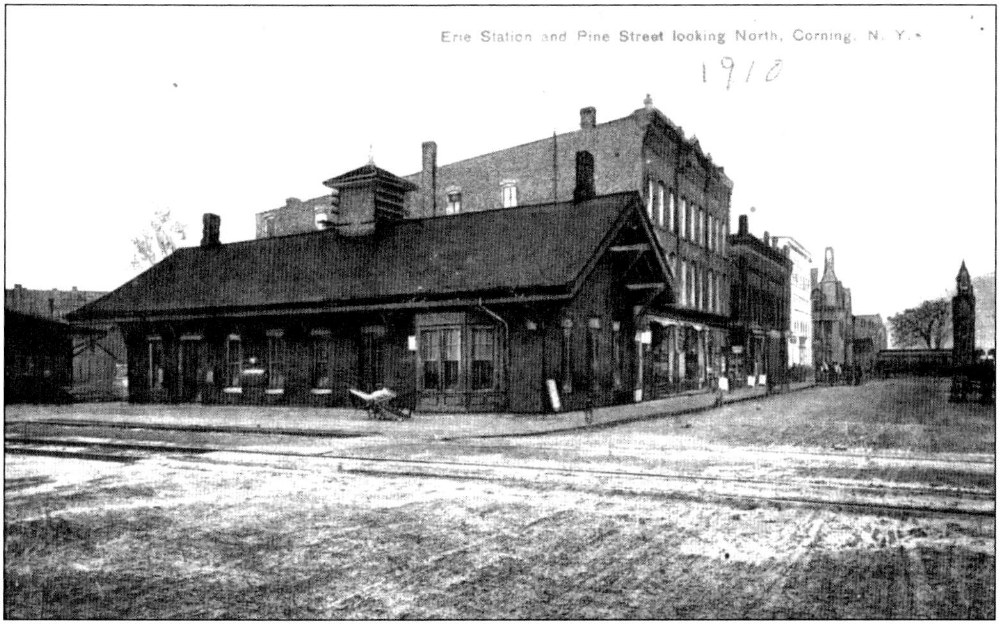

On July 9, 1860, passenger trains began stopping at the new Erie depot on the corner of Pine Street and Erie Avenue. The St. James Hotel opened on January 31, 1906. This postcard shows how the station was conveniently located in the center of town.

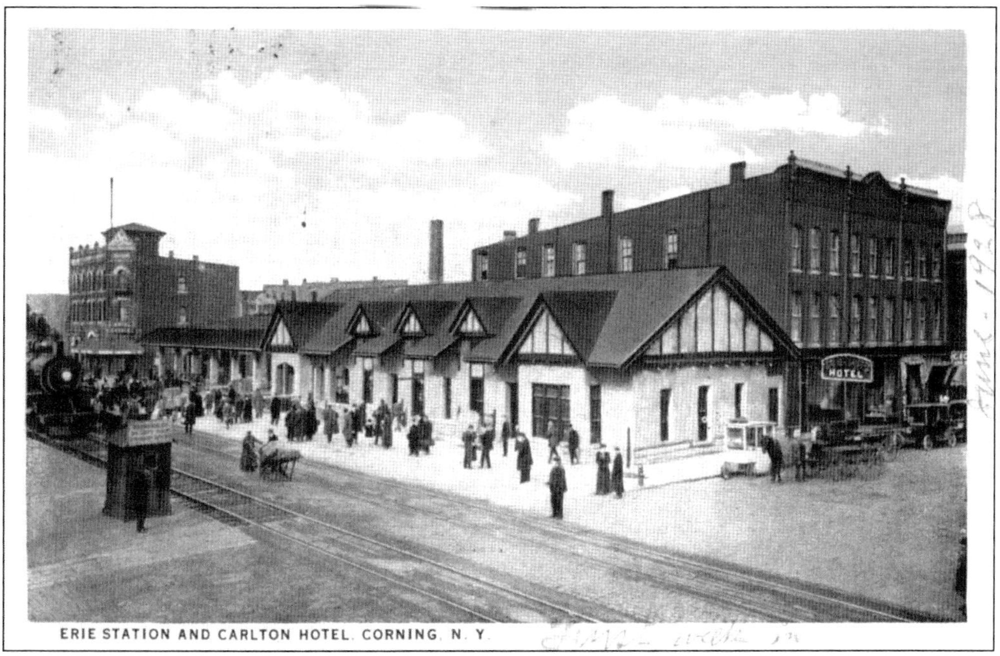

The sender of this postcard wrote the date June 1928 on the right side of this postcard. The Carlton Hotel came after the St. James Hotel and was there through the 1920s. Looking west, the three-story building is Casale's Hotel.

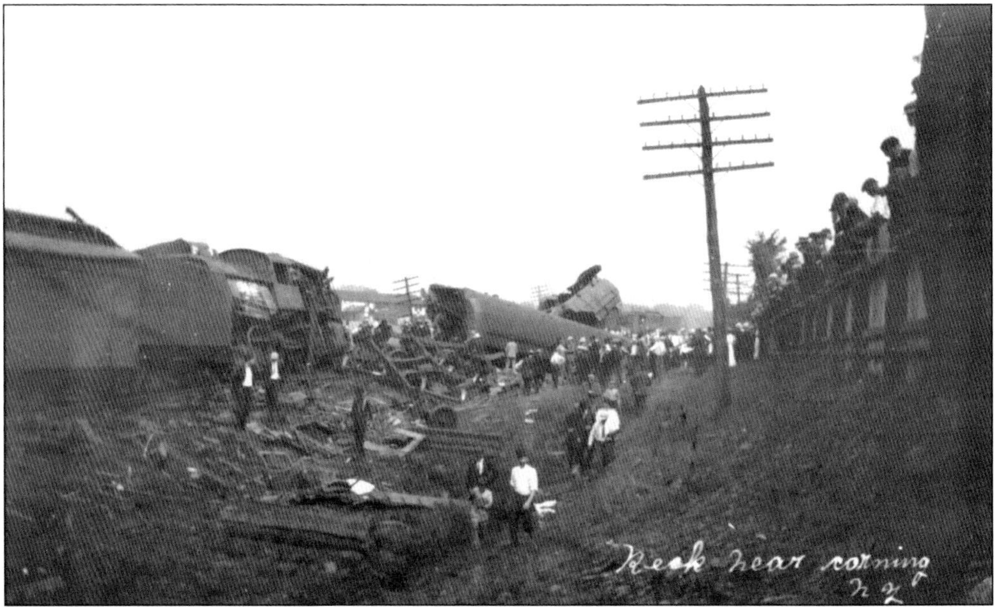

These July 4, 1912, postcards illustrate the worst rear-end train collision in the Corning area to date. The No. 9 train was composed of seven sleeping Pullman cars, a buffet car, and two coaches and was headed toward Buffalo with holiday travelers from Elmira, Scranton, Binghamton, and Brooklyn. As the engineer neared the Gibson station, he saw the stranded cars on the track, slowed, and came to a complete stop. He then got ready to help push the stranded cars to a side track.

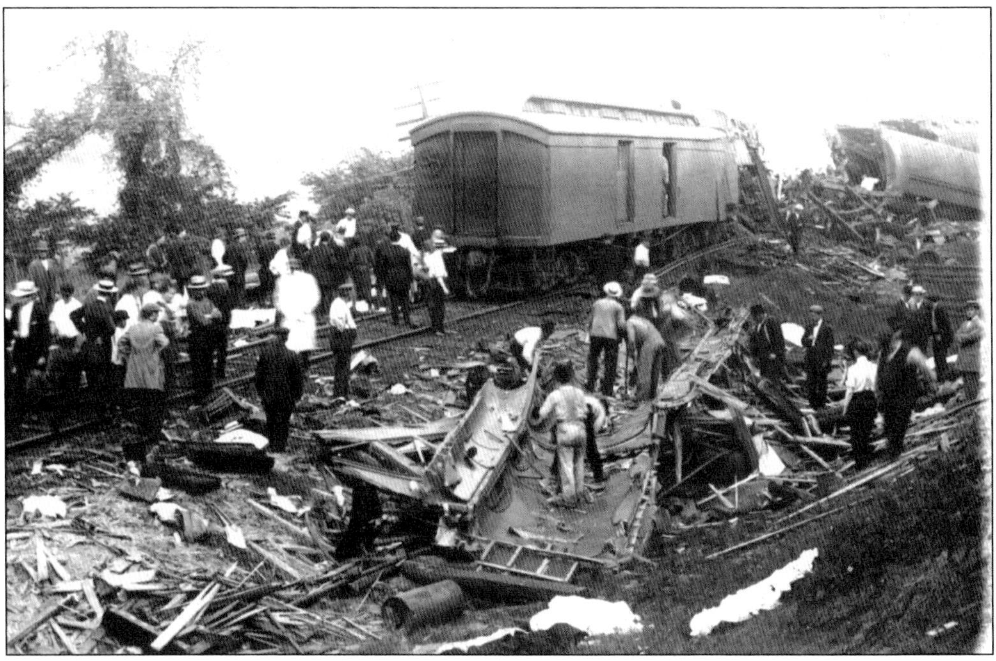

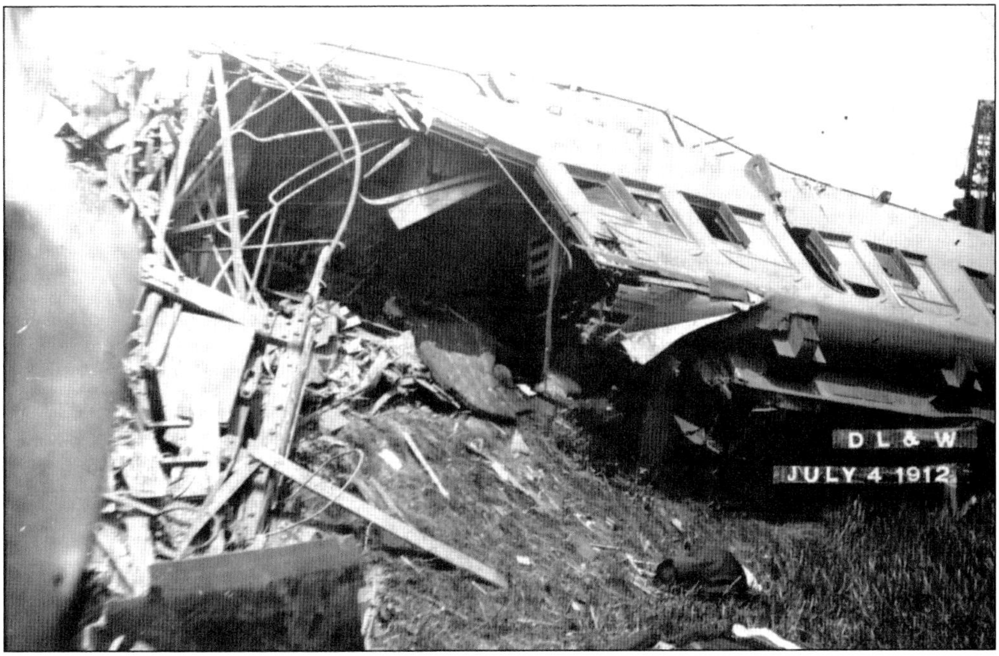

A little after 5:00 a.m., the Delaware, Lackawanna, and Western Railroad left Elmira with the mail and Fourth of July travelers. A thick, early morning fog formed from the Chemung River. The No. 11 engineer missed the warning signs and ran into the No. 9, pushing that train into cars from the 393. This terrible accident left 39 people dead and 88 injured. This postcard marked "DLW" shows passenger cars from the train that jumped the tracks when the engineer threw it into reverse after seeing the train not moving ahead.

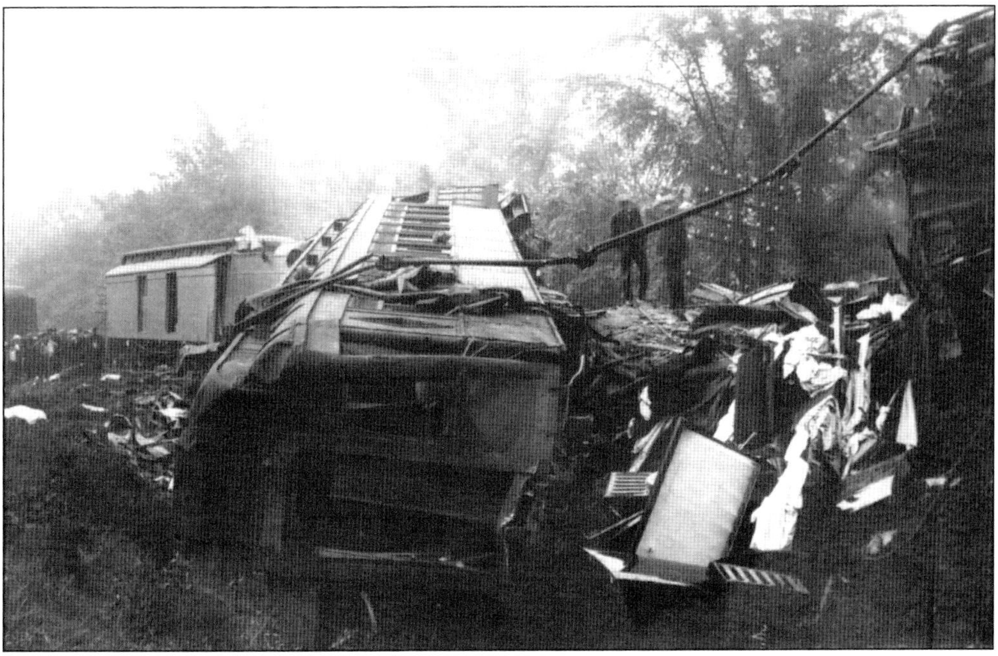

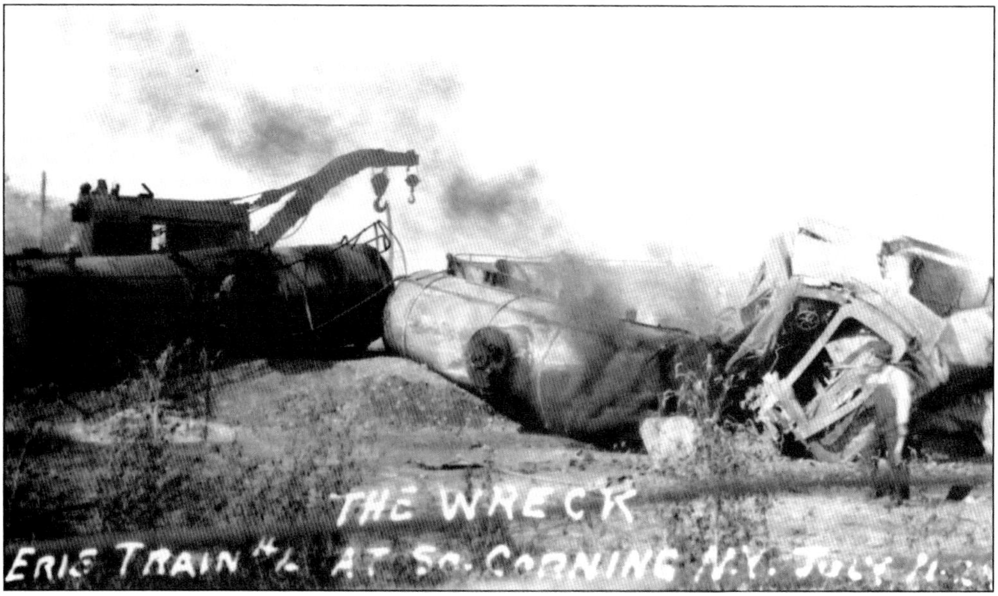

This train wreck happened on July 11, 1929, in South Corning. The Associated Press reported that five people were burned to death and that a sixth was probably fatally burned as the passenger train ploughed into a tank car on the westbound lane that had left the tracks when the two trains passed. The report went on to say that coal from the passenger train set the tank car ablaze. The fire spread rapidly to the baggage car, two mail cars, and a passenger car.

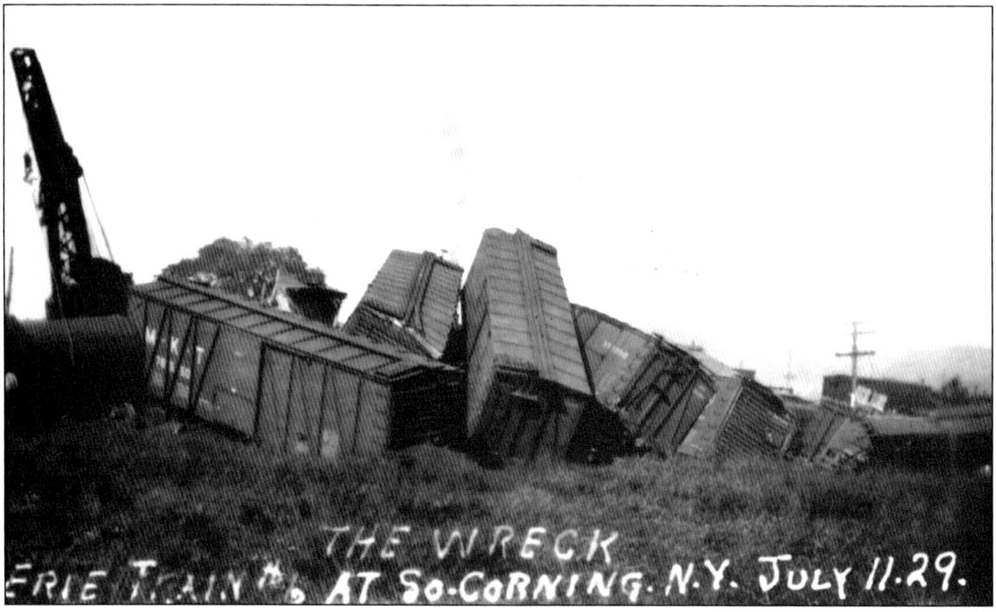

Two

Churches and Schools

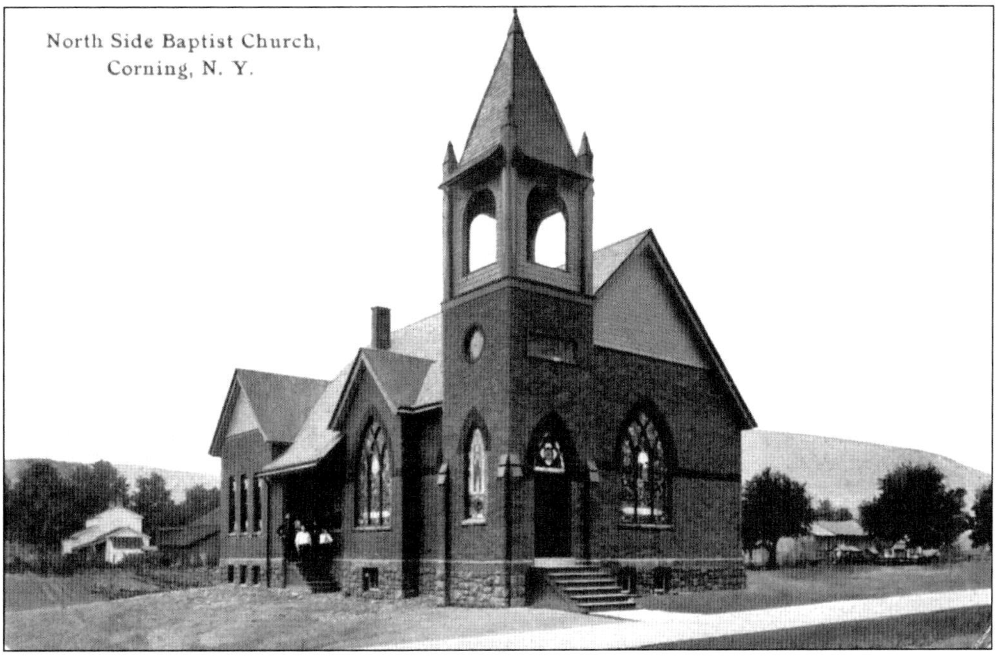

The North Side Baptist Church was founded by Baptists who lived on the north side and wanted a church closer to home. It started in 1902 with 42 people. Thirty-five of them came from the Baptist church on the south side. The Reverend George Laughton was the first pastor, serving from October 1902 through 1904. After additions were built, the church is bigger now and is still in use.

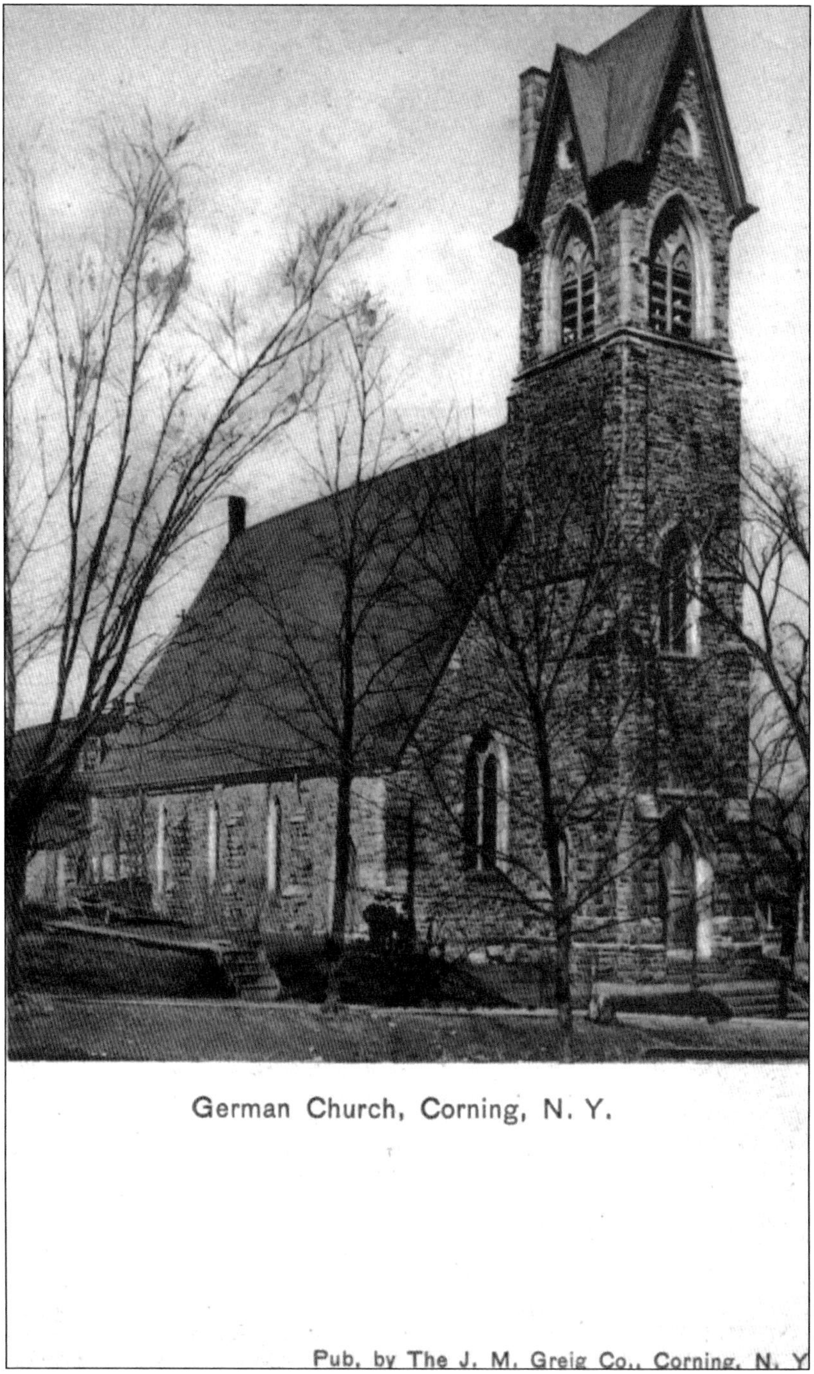

The German Evangelical Church was located at 71 West First Street. Its cornerstone was laid in 1895. German Protestants established the first German Evangelical congregation in 1895 in the former Christ Episcopal Church on the corner of Erie and Walnut Streets. When that building was taken down, its walls were used to construct the new church. In the 1930s, it became the Seventh-day Advent Church. From the 1950s through the 1970s, it was known as the Redeemer Evangelical Lutheran Church.

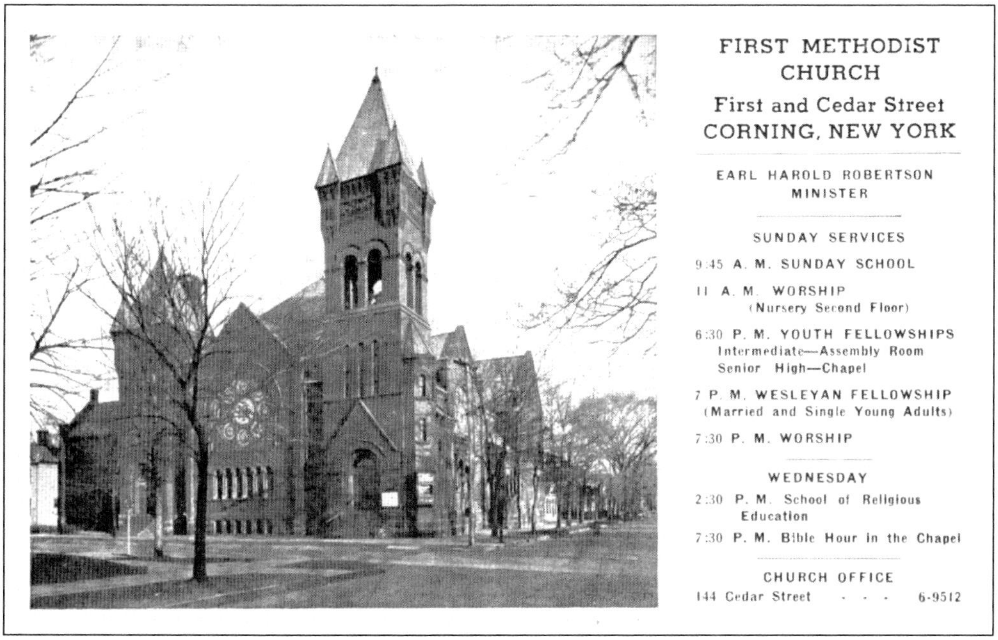

The First Methodist Church was built in 1893 and dedicated on June 4, 1894, on the corner of First and Cedar Streets. It was designed and built by H. G. Tuthill at a cost of $40,000, which included a good pipe organ. This postcard was mailed in 1952. The church is still in use today.

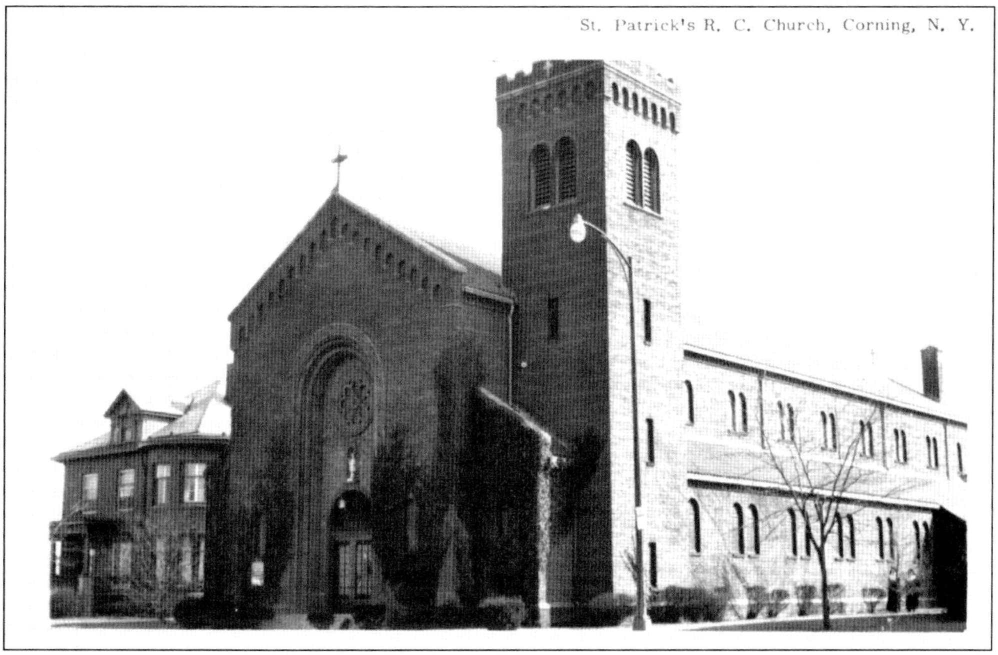

St. Patrick's Church was built in 1903 and had a school that started at the same time. A new school building was constructed in 1960. The whole lot is for sale in 2009.

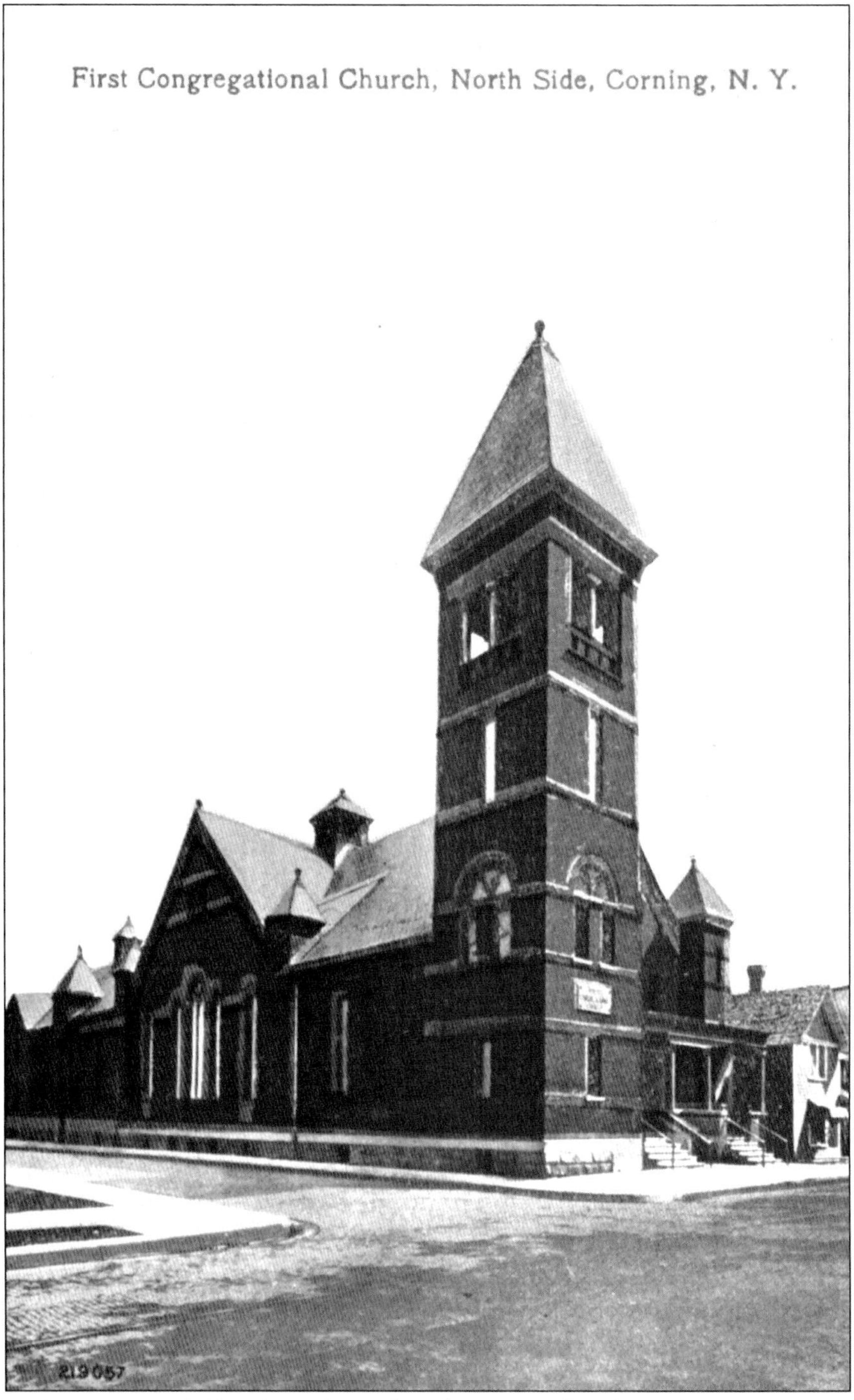

The First Congregational Church was located on the corner of Bridge and Ontario Streets. It was dedicated on May 13, 1897, and cost about $21,000 to build. Andrew Carnegie donated $1,200 towards the cost of the $10,000 pipe organ. The church remained open until 1958, when part of it was torn down. There is currently a Curve's business and parking lot located there. What remained of the church was extensively remodeled and is now used as office space.

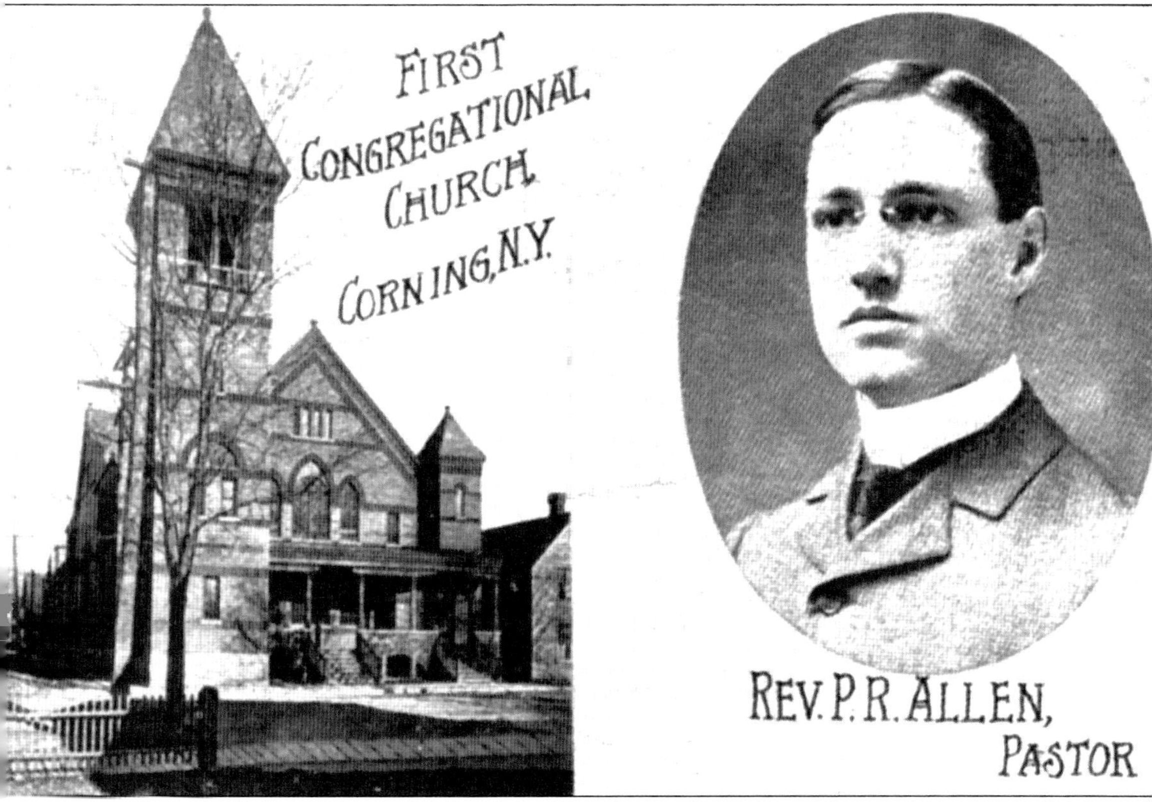

The 1905 and 1907 Corning city directories give the address of Rev. Paul R. Allen as 207 Bridge Street. The 1910 census records show him at age 34 living in Chenango County with a daughter named Elizabeth. The 1913/1914 directory gives Clinton J. Taft as pastor of this church. Taft was from Broome County and had a wife and two daughters. A postcard like this would have been used by the pastors and the church for official business.

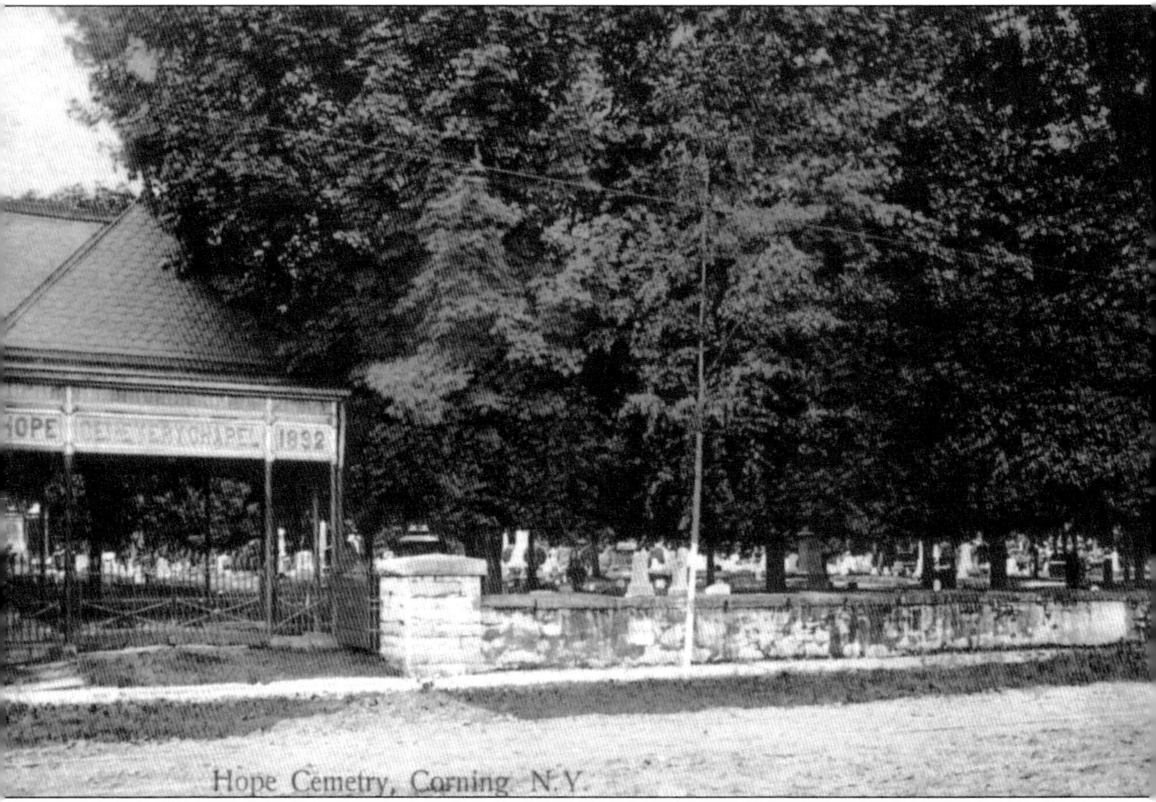

Hope Cemetery was started in the 1890s. When it was first opened, horse-drawn carriages hauled a wagon though the gates to the chapel, which was built in 1892 at a cost of $7,000. The cemetery and the chapel are still there, but the chapel building has not been used in a long time.

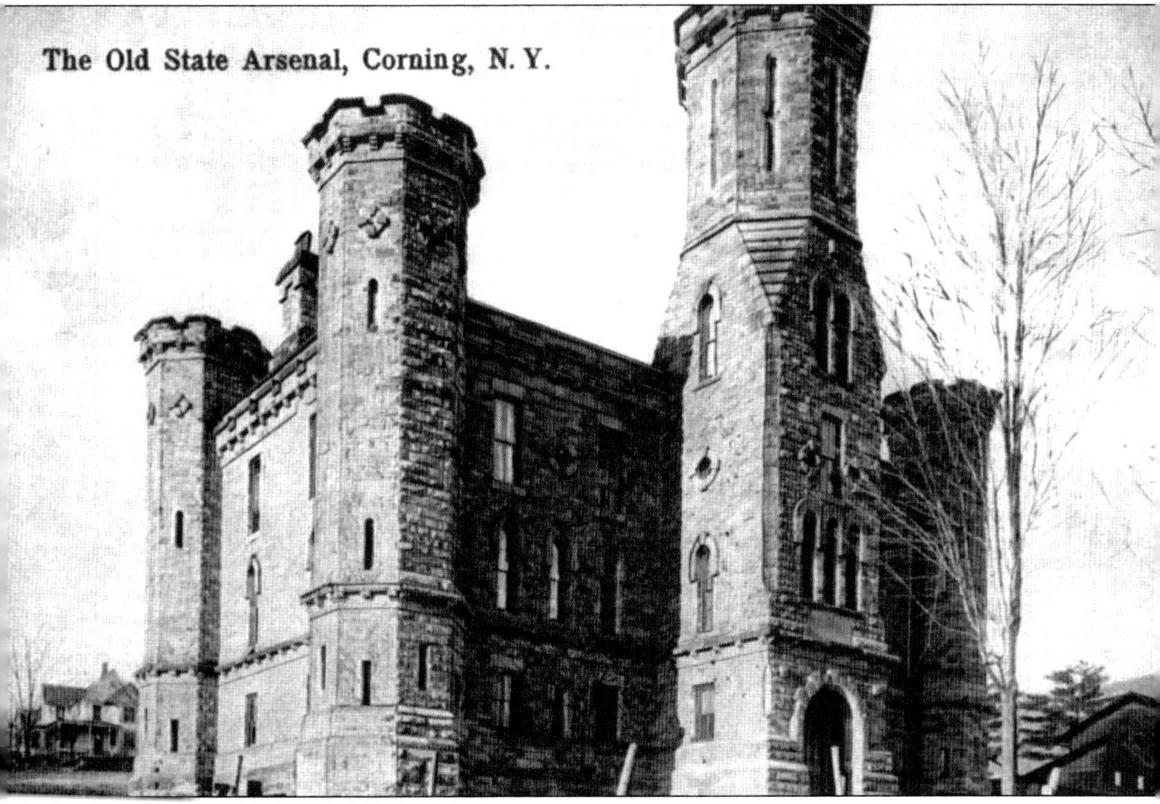

The old state arsenal was built by an act of the New York State legislature. Assemblyman Col R. B. VanValkenburgh had a lot to do with having it located in Corning. State legislators appropriated $14,000 but did the job for $12,000. After completion, it was used for storage of ordinances and served as headquarters for 60th Regiment of the New York State Militia's Company C and Company D.

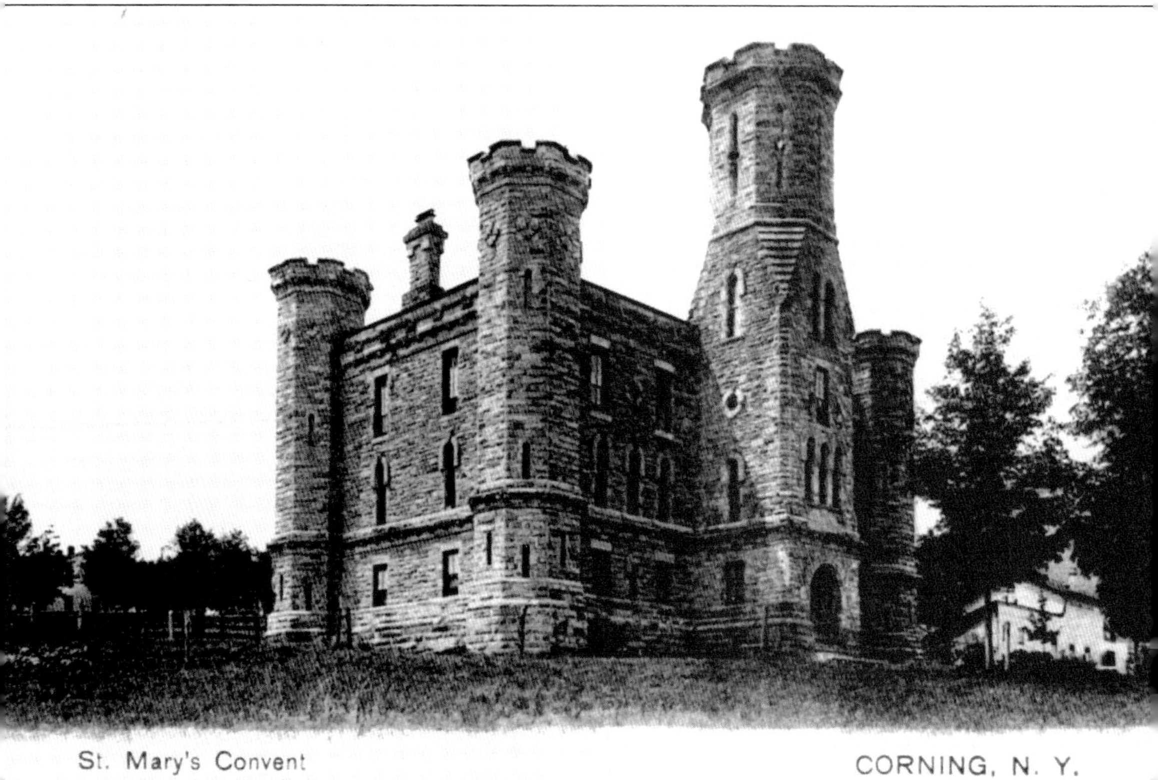

In 1873, the state decided to sell the arsenal building. Plans for a business located there failed, and St. Mary's Church bought the building. From about 1875 to 1906, it was used as an orphanage. In the 1960s, it was torn down to make room for what are now the Castle Garden Apartments.

St. Mary's school was built in 1881. It was the first parochial school in Corning.

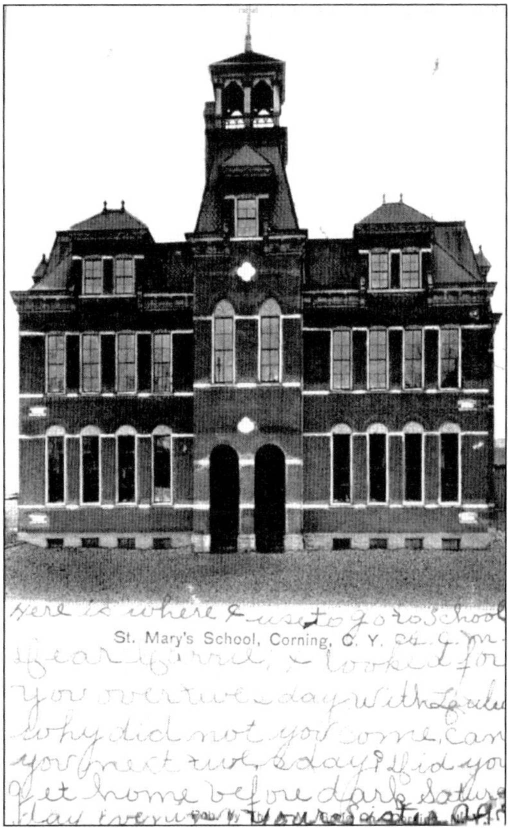

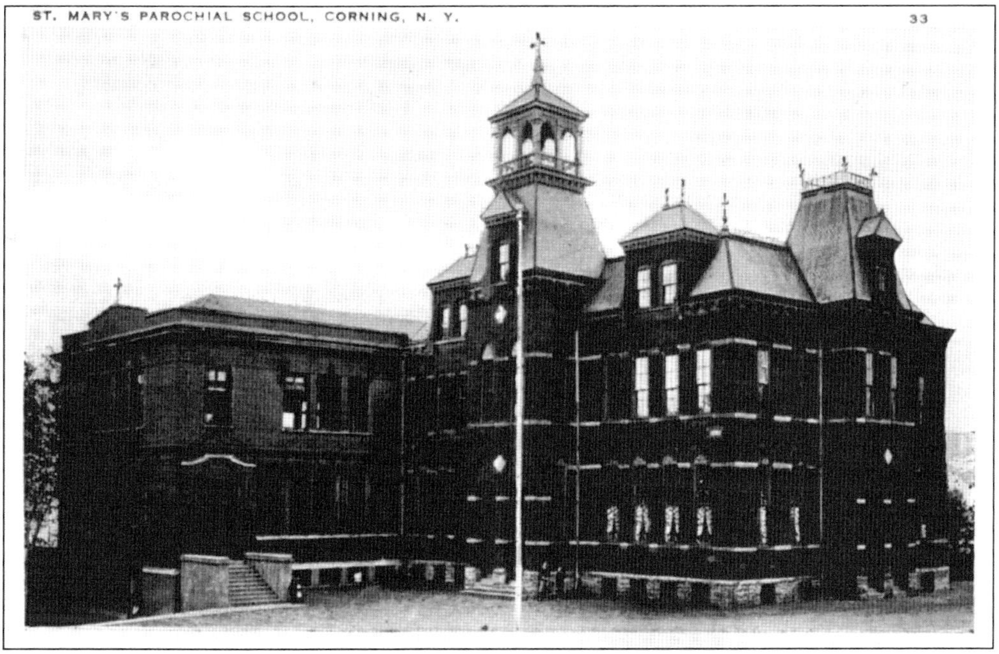

In 1912, an addition was put on this building. It included a gymnasium, a basketball court, and a swimming pool.

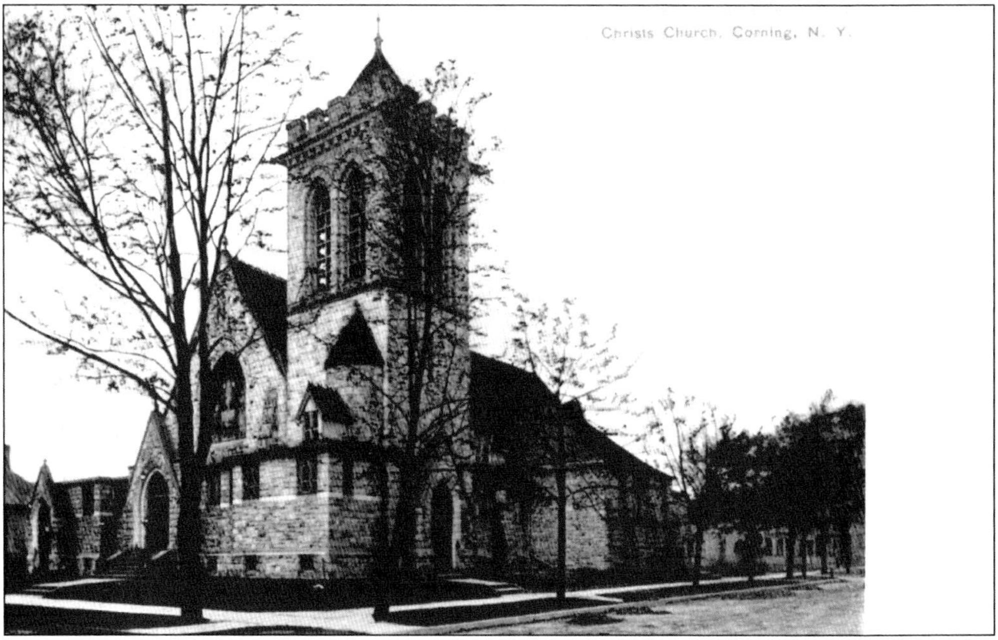

The Christ Church (Episcopal) was built with stone from a local quarry. The structure cost more to build than most other area churches, with more $60,000 being spent.

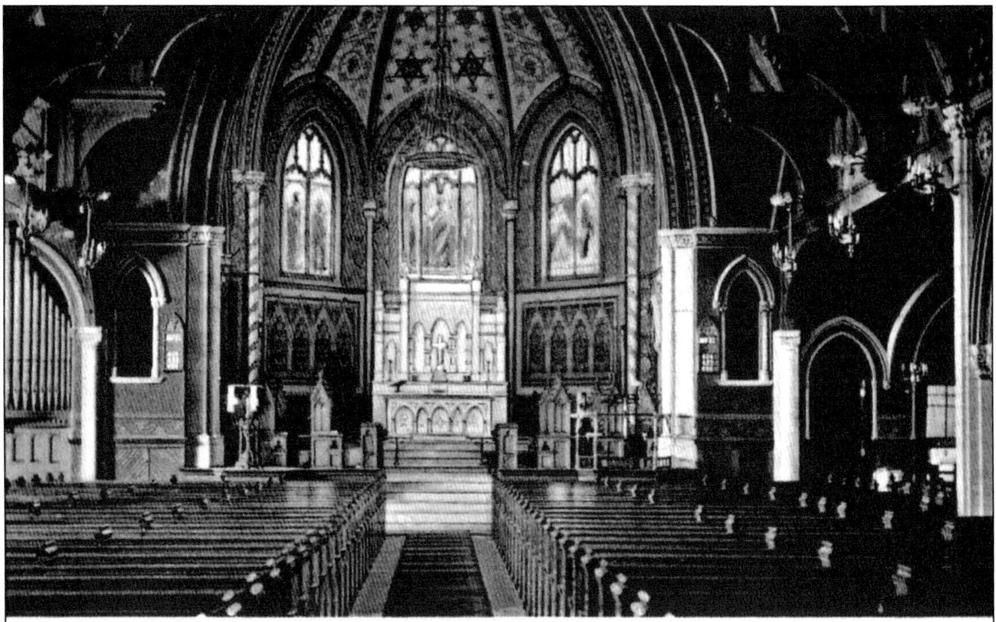

The fine decorations of the church included stained-glass windows from Tiffany and Company. Pentagrams can be seen above the windows. In 1910, a fire damaged part of the church and Tiffany and Company made $15,000 in repairs, including six new stained-glass windows. This postcard was mailed in 1909 to a wife or girlfriend in Virginia.

This is a small art deco dance card booklet. The date was April 20, 1938. Class officers, patrons, and patronesses are listed, as well as 20 numbered lines for dances in case someone was that popular.

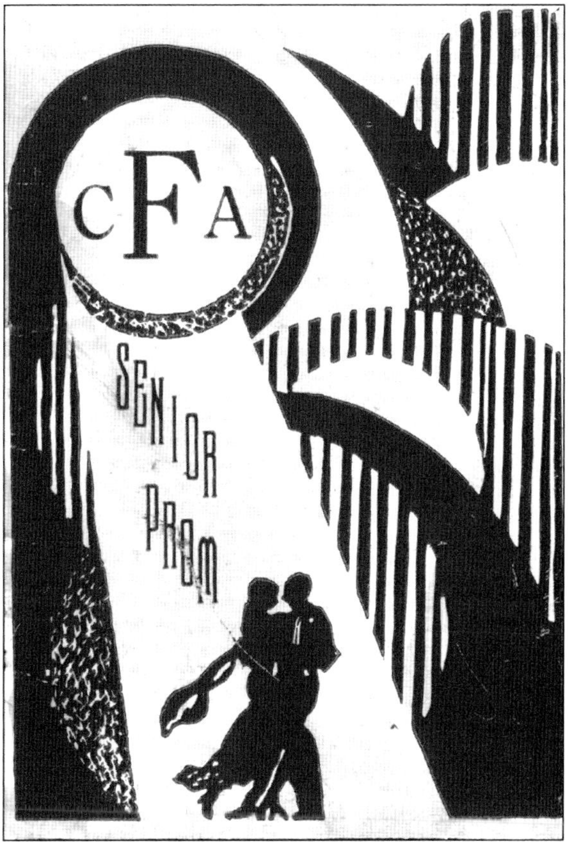

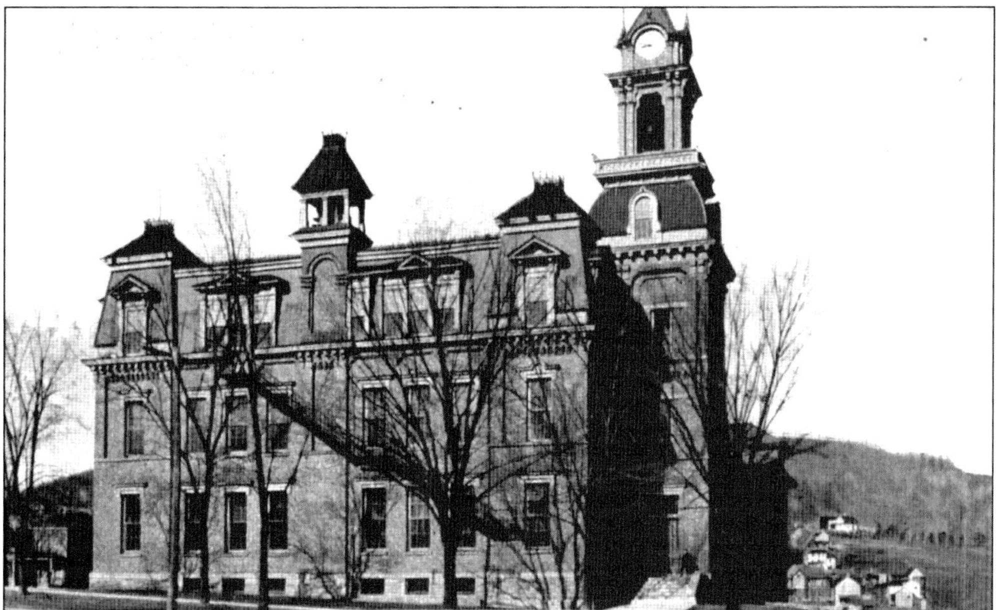

This school was built in 1873 on the corner of Walnut and Third Streets. The highest tower had a massive bell weighing 2,500 pounds.

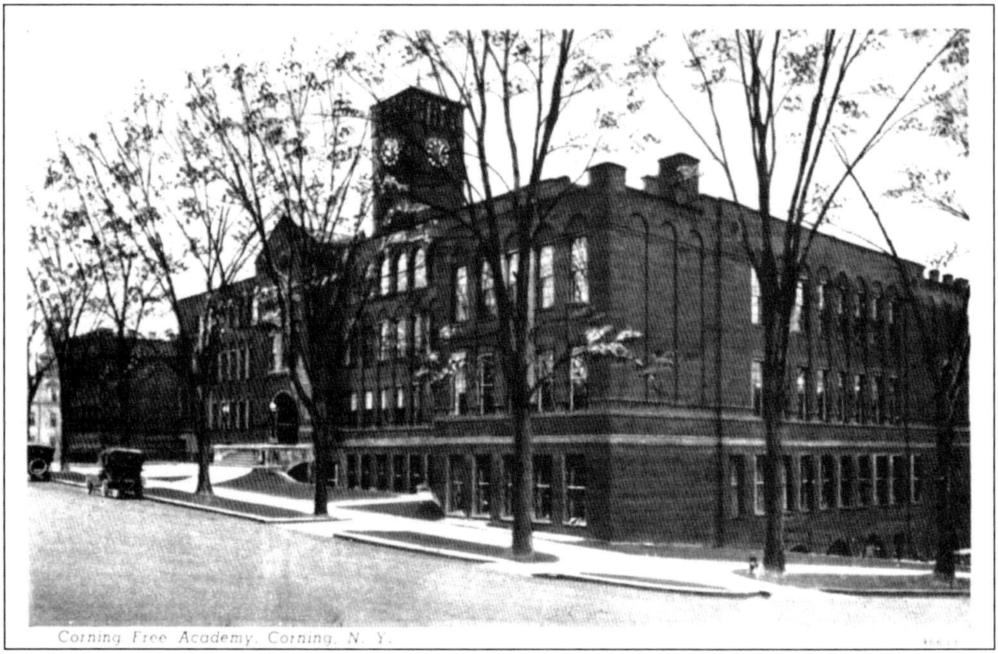

This version of Corning Free Academy was built in 1923 and still looks the same today. People can still see boy and girl icons above different doors for them to enter.

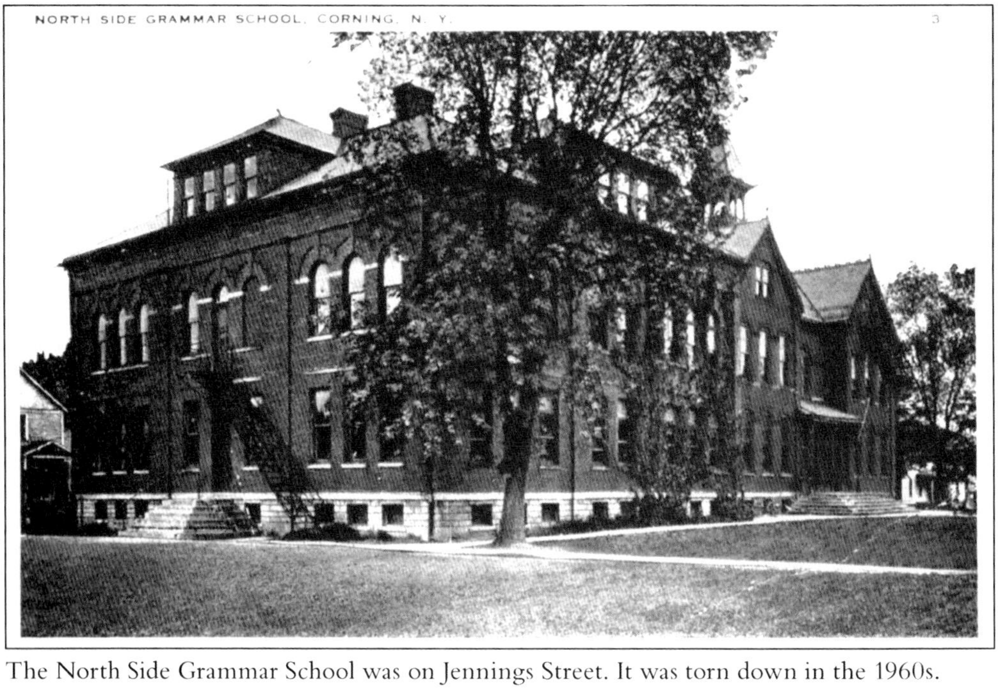

The North Side Grammar School was on Jennings Street. It was torn down in the 1960s.

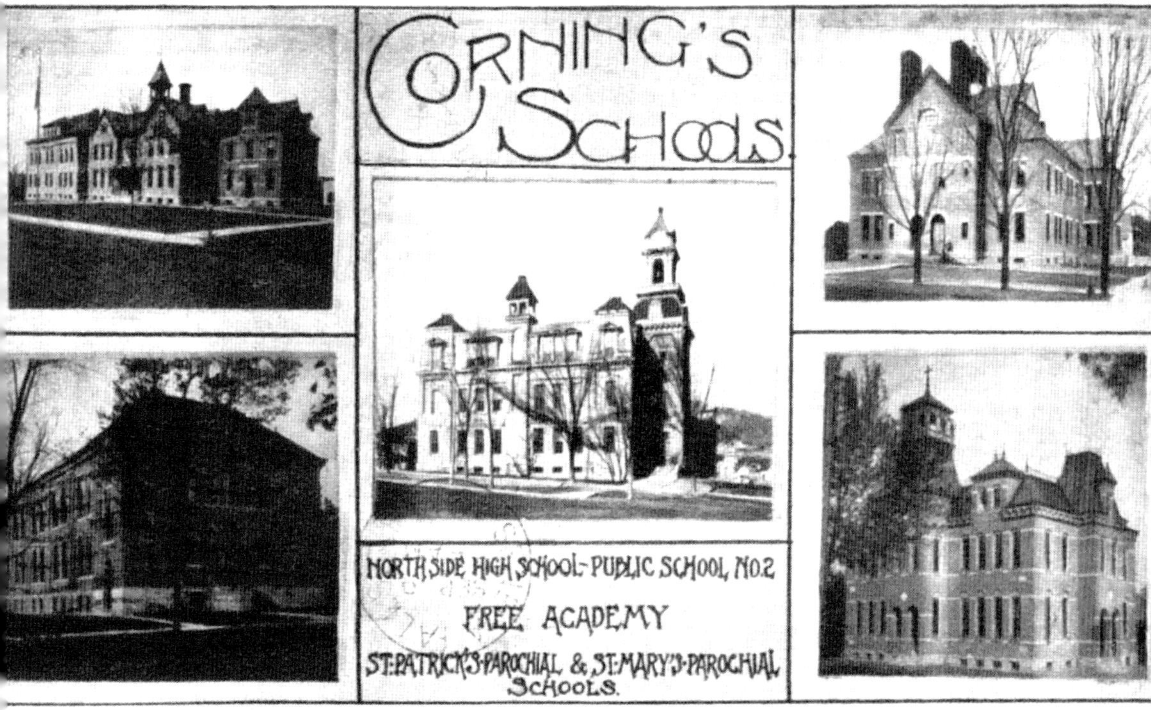

This multi-view postcard shows images of five early Corning Schools. St. Patrick's Parochial School is on the lower left corner. It is the only school on this postcard that does not have its own postcard in this book. This postcard was made by the N. E. Paper and Stationary Company in Ayer, Massachusetts, and is unusual because it is about three-eighths of an inch longer than most other postcards.

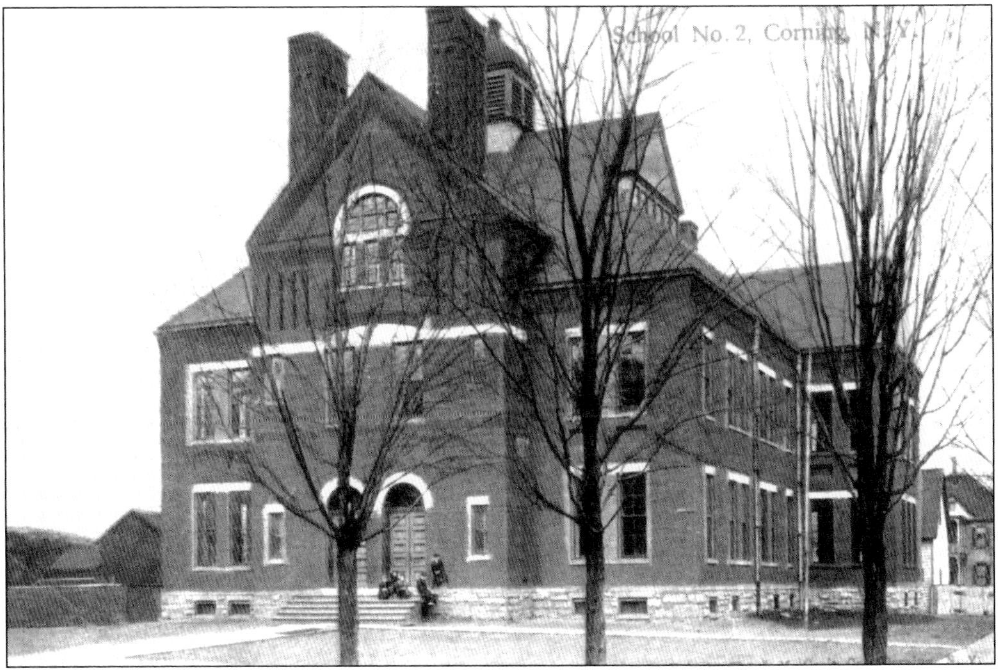

School No. 2 was built in 1883 at 291 East First Street. In later years, it was used as offices for the Corning City School District. Today it is called the Alternative School for Math and Science.

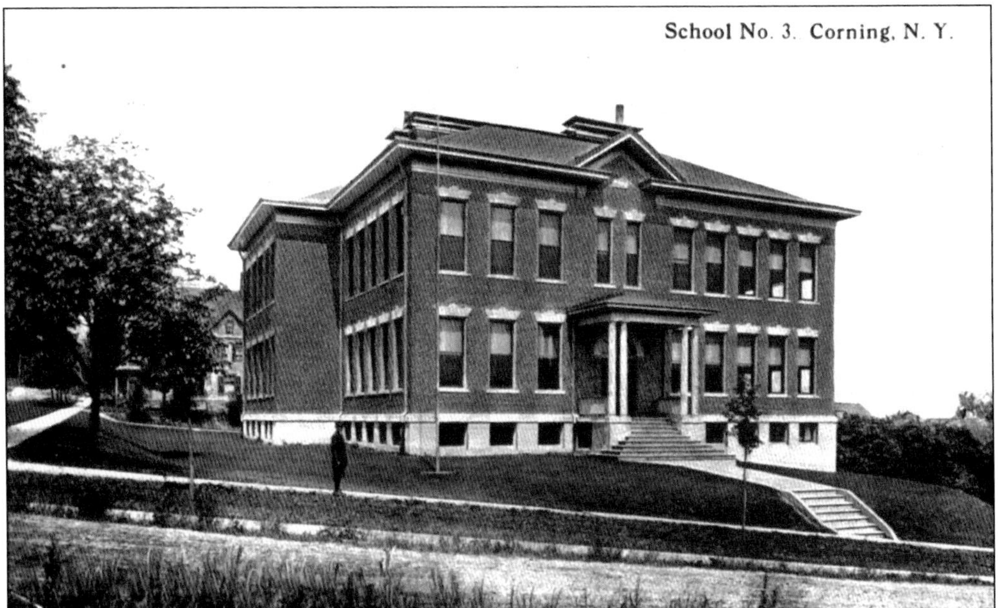

School No. 3 was at the corner of Chemung and Fifth Streets. In the beginning of the 21st century, this building went under major renovations, being made into condominiums. The date 1909 from when this building was constructed can still be seen on the top front in stone.

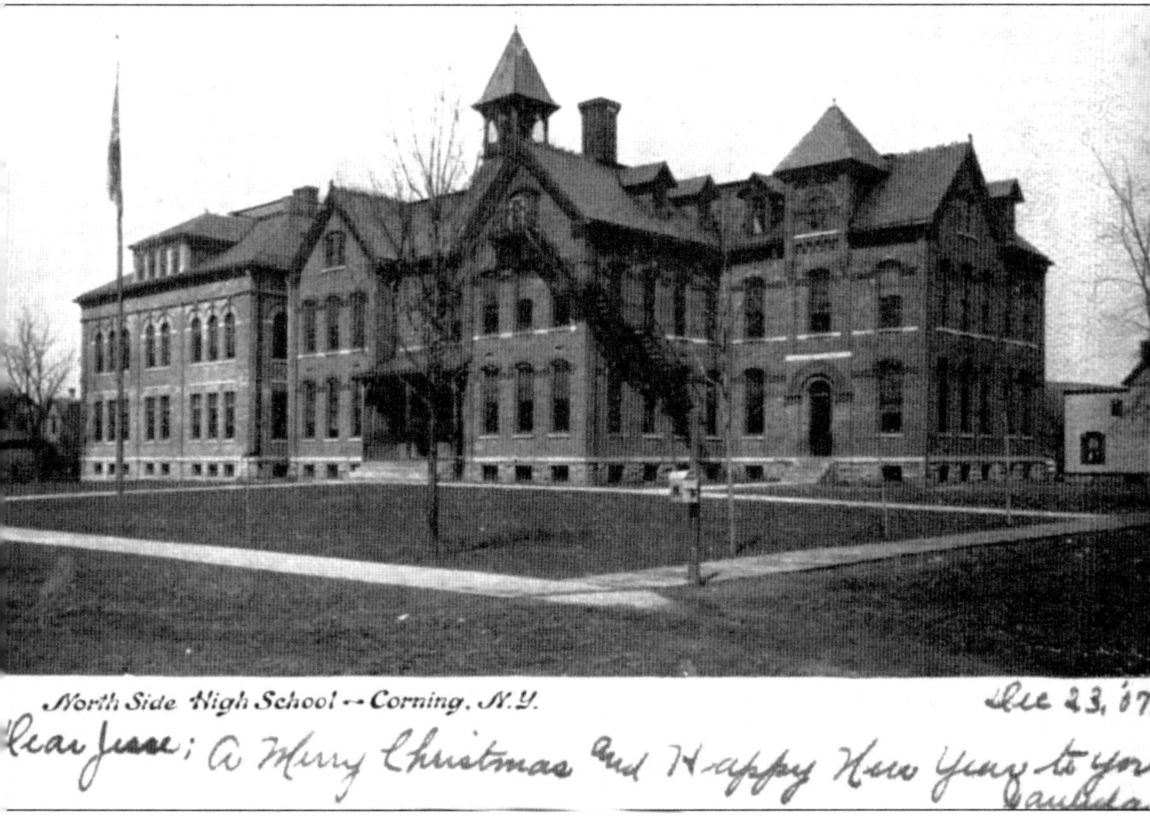

Christmas and happy New Years greetings were written on the front of this postcard December 23, 1907. This was how the North Side High School looked from 1896 to 1908. From about 1890 to 1895, only the center part of this building was the school. It was remolded in 1895, adding the east wing, and the west wing was built in 1897.

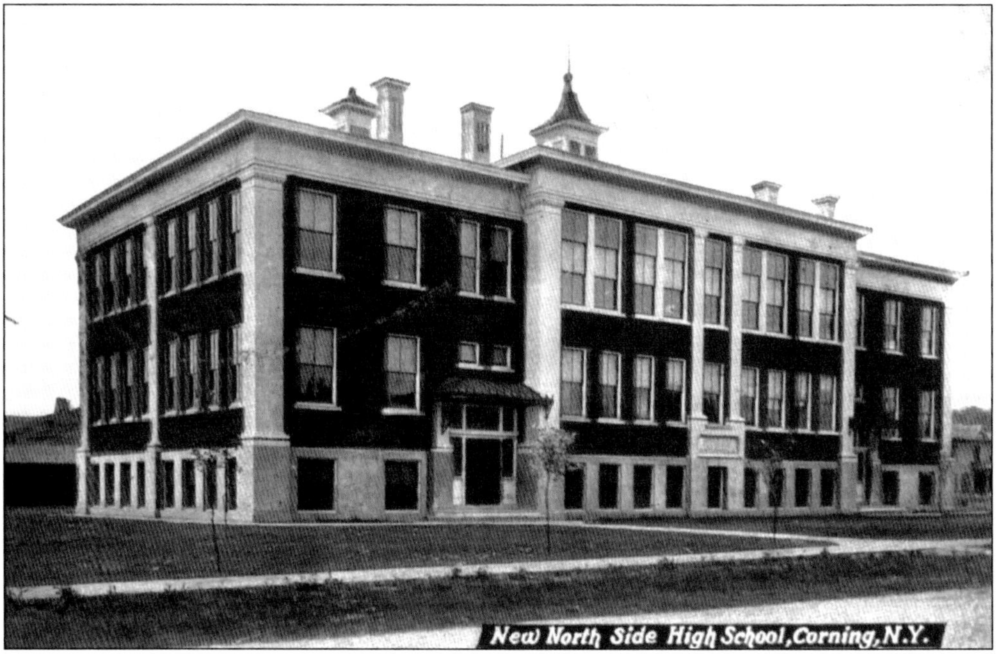

This is how the new North Side High School looked, starting in 1908. This postcard was mailed in 1911. That year, Margaret Kelly and George Richard were class valedictorians.

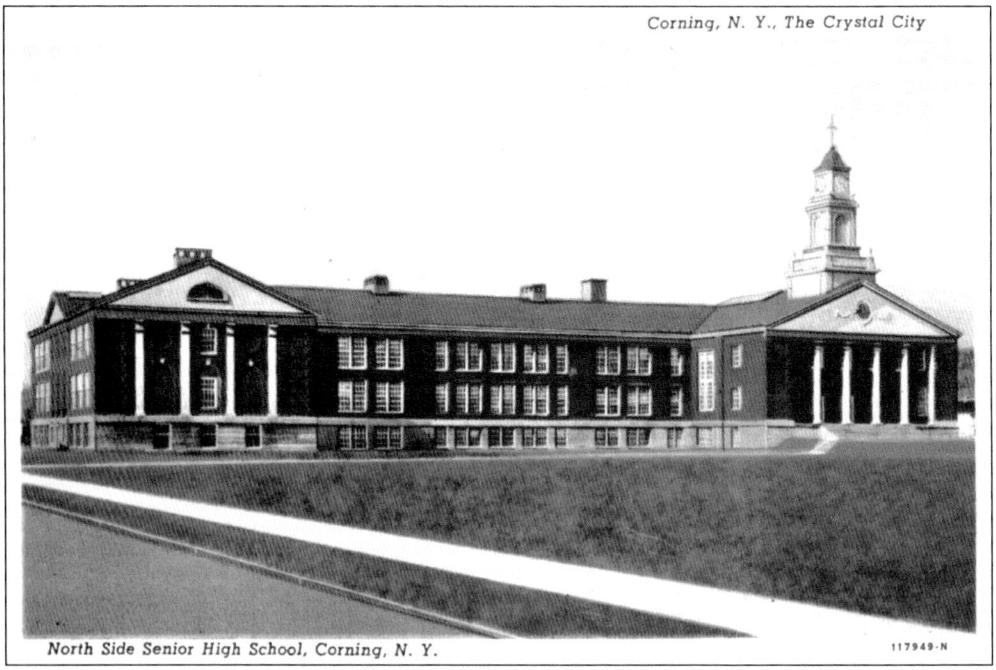

This is how North Side High School has looked since 1927. When East High School opened, this was used as a junior high school.

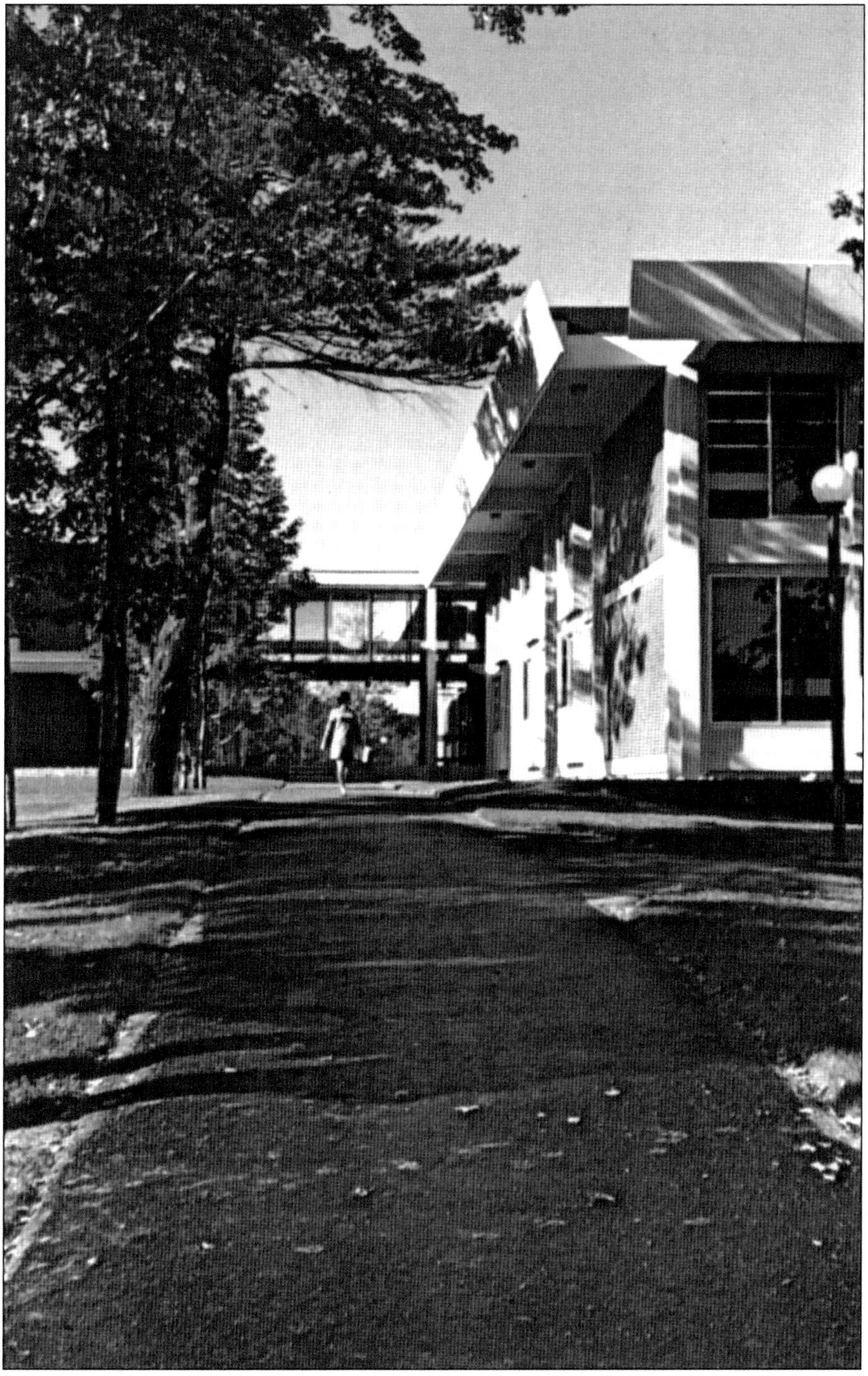

In 1956, New York State approved plans for a new Corning Community College. Classes began in 1958 at the old school No. 3 on Chemung Street. The new campus was opened on Spencer Hill in 1963. This late-1960s postcard shows two of the early buildings: one was used for admissions and the other was for classes. Since then, there have been several additions to the campus. Today the college covers 550 acres and has eight buildings, plus an observatory and planetarium.

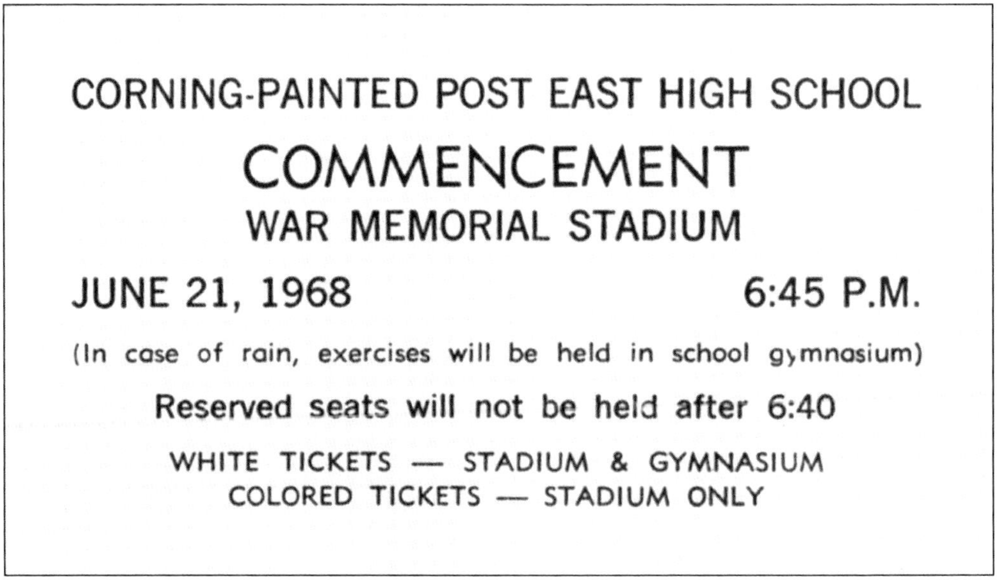

CORNING-PAINTED POST EAST HIGH SCHOOL

COMMENCEMENT

WAR MEMORIAL STADIUM

JUNE 21, 1968 6:45 P.M.

(In case of rain, exercises will be held in school gymnasium)

Reserved seats will not be held after 6:40

WHITE TICKETS — STADIUM & GYMNASIUM
COLORED TICKETS — STADIUM ONLY

In 1968, the East High School senior class officers were Tom Mourhess (president), Pat Boland (vice president), Ann Marie Louiz (secretary), and Nancy Slater (treasure). That year, 301 seniors graduated. East High School was opened in the fall of 1963 and had its first graduating class in June 1964.

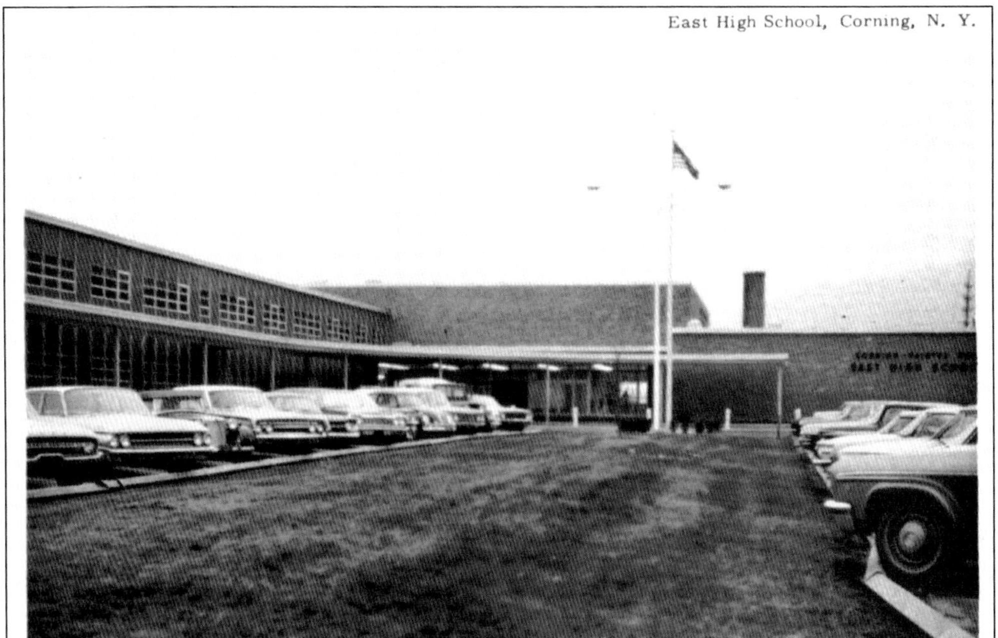

Three

Businesses and Glass

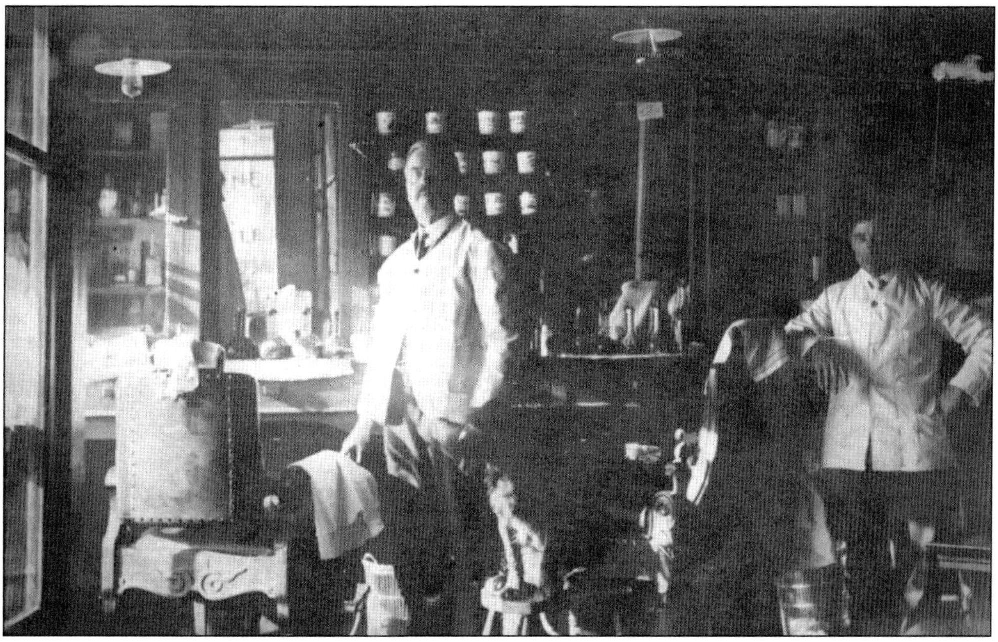

This barbershop interior postcard was mailed from Corning in February 1910. Behind the barber on the left are personalized shaving mugs. For years, the local barbershop was a kind of clubhouse for working-class men. Those who could afford it had their occupation, name, or initials painted on their own shaving mug. Highly sought after today are the shaving mugs that had occupation-related topics, such as fireman, carpenter, and railroad worker.

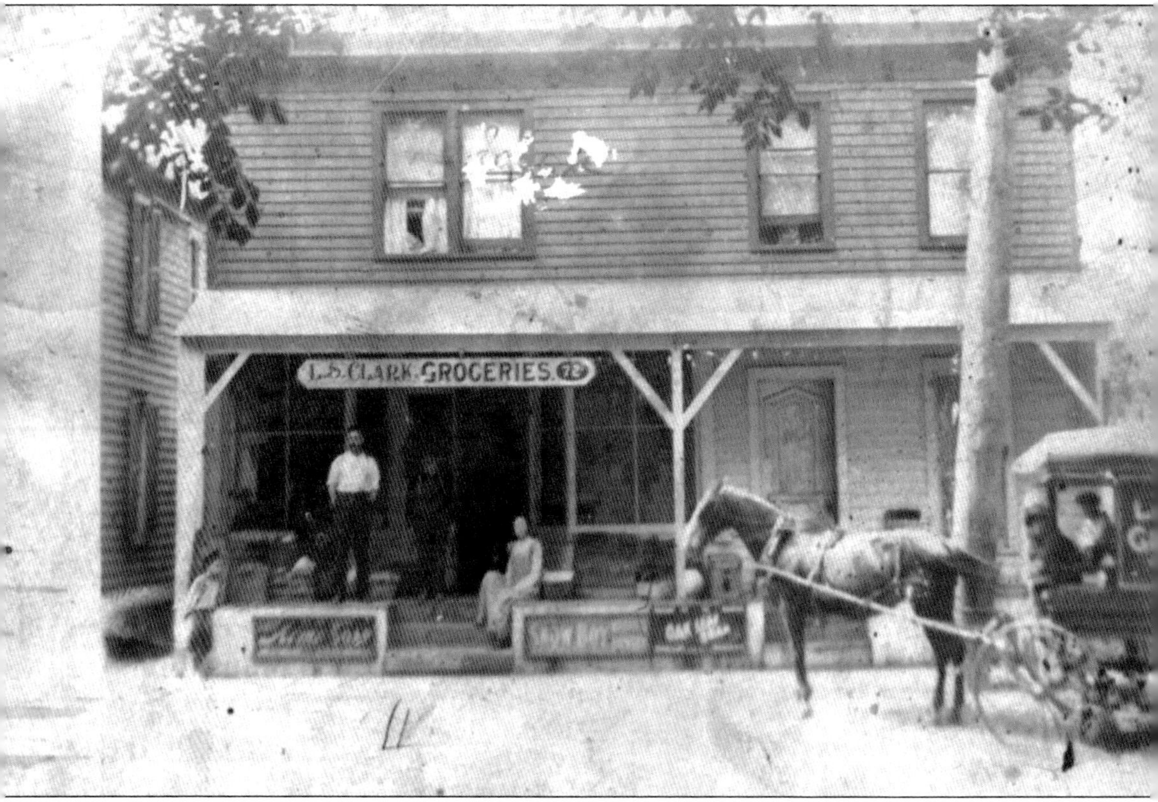

This postcard was mailed in 1906 and shows L. S. Clark Groceries. The store was owned by Lewis S. Clark and was located at 72 William Street. Clark lived upstairs with his wife and son. He retired about 1924, and this store was then called Cash Food Stores. In front of the store are advertisements for soap. Acme, Snow Boy, and Oak Leaf must have been the leading brands of soap at that time.

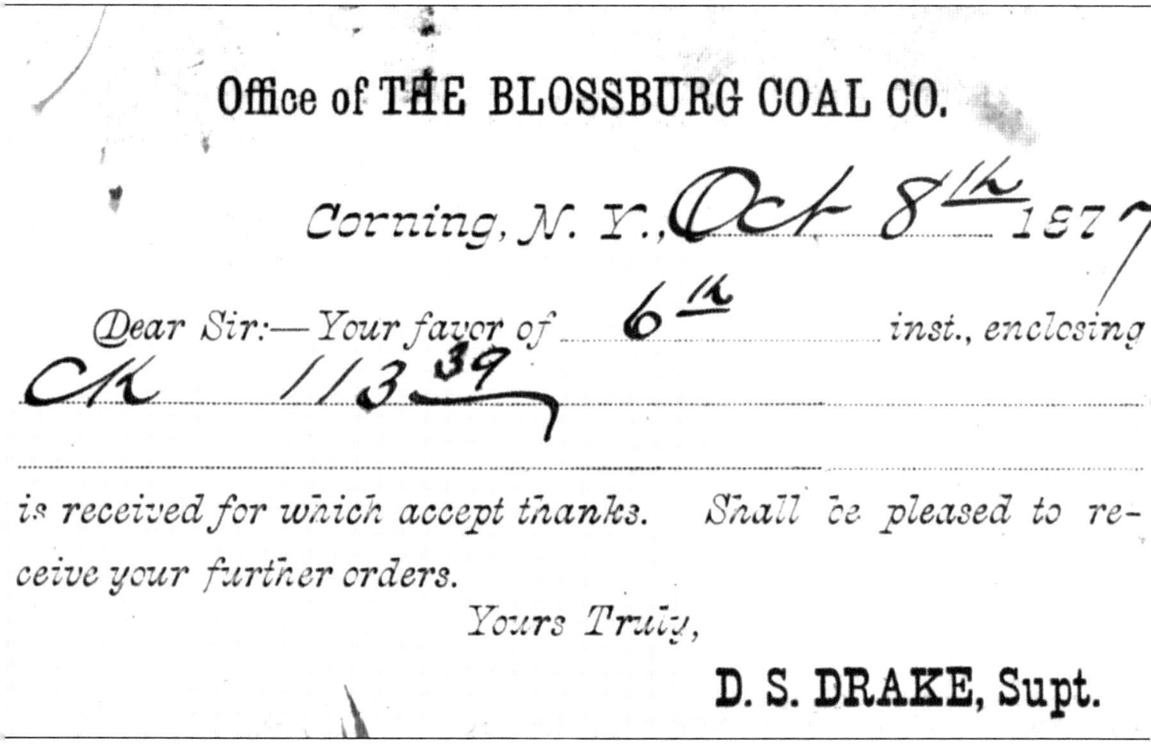

Office of THE BLOSSBURG COAL CO.

Corning, N. Y., Oct 8th 1877

Dear Sir:—Your favor of 6th inst., enclosing

Ck 113 39/

is received for which accept thanks. Shall be pleased to receive your further orders.

Yours Truly,

D. S. DRAKE, Supt.

The Blossburg Coal Company was formed in 1866. It shipped coal from mines near Blossburg, Pennsylvania, to Corning and other places. This postcard was mailed in 1877 to Gillett and Company in Elmira. Starting in 1877, Gillett was a maker of augers and auger bits. Before 1877, the well-known Milton Nobles and the Nobles Manufacturing Company manufactured draw knives at that site. Milton Nobles is remembered as a great toolmaker and holder of several patents.

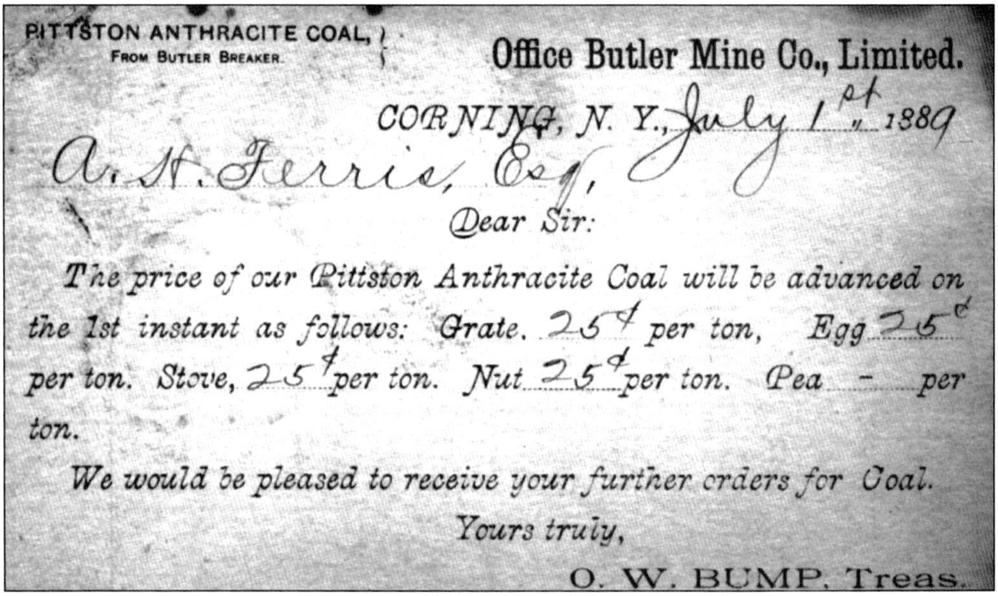
PITTSTON ANTHRACITE COAL, FROM BUTLER BREAKER.

Office Butler Mine Co., Limited.

CORNING, N. Y., July 1st 1889

A. H. Ferris, Esq,

Dear Sir:

The price of our Pittston Anthracite Coal will be advanced on the 1st instant as follows: Grate 25¢ per ton, Egg 25¢ per ton. Stove, 25¢ per ton. Nut 25¢ per ton. Pea - per ton.

We would be pleased to receive your further orders for Coal.

Yours truly,

O. W. BUMP, Treas.

The Butler Mine Company Limited is listed as being in the Drake Block in the 1895 city of Corning directory. The company mined and shipped coal. A. Houghton Jr. is listed as being chairman. This postcard was mailed in 1889 to Batavia and mentions the price of the firm's anthracite coal being raised to 25¢ a ton.

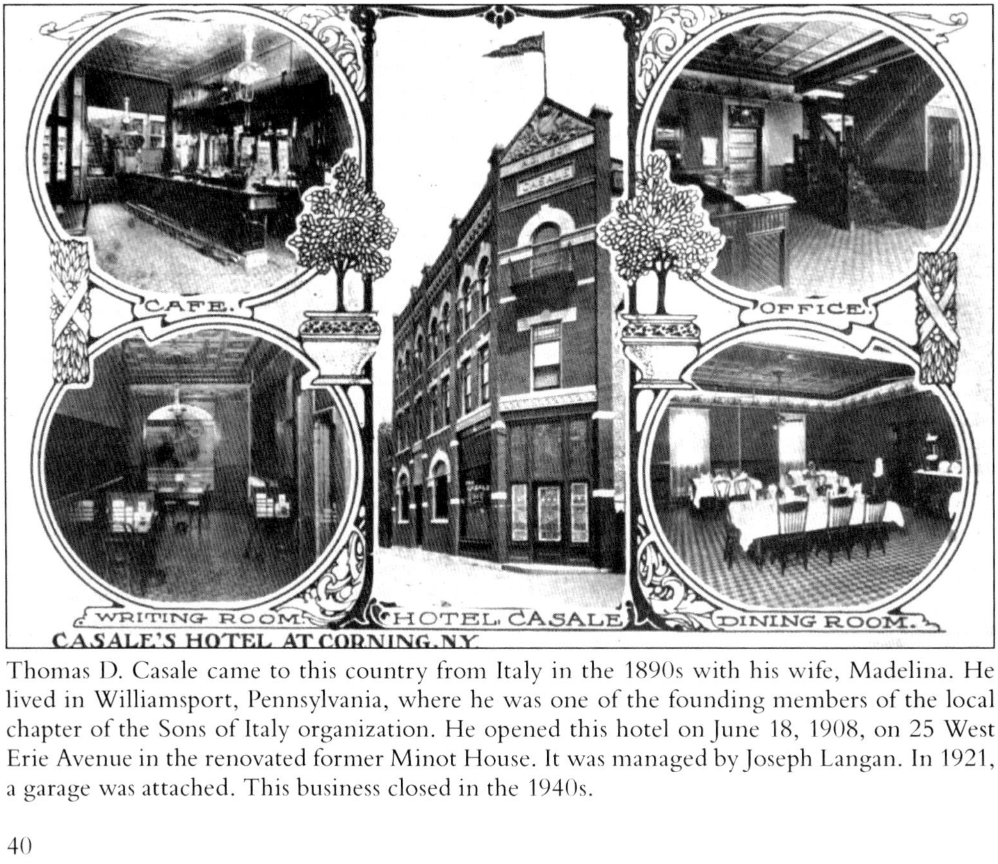

Thomas D. Casale came to this country from Italy in the 1890s with his wife, Madelina. He lived in Williamsport, Pennsylvania, where he was one of the founding members of the local chapter of the Sons of Italy organization. He opened this hotel on June 18, 1908, on 25 West Erie Avenue in the renovated former Minot House. It was managed by Joseph Langan. In 1921, a garage was attached. This business closed in the 1940s.

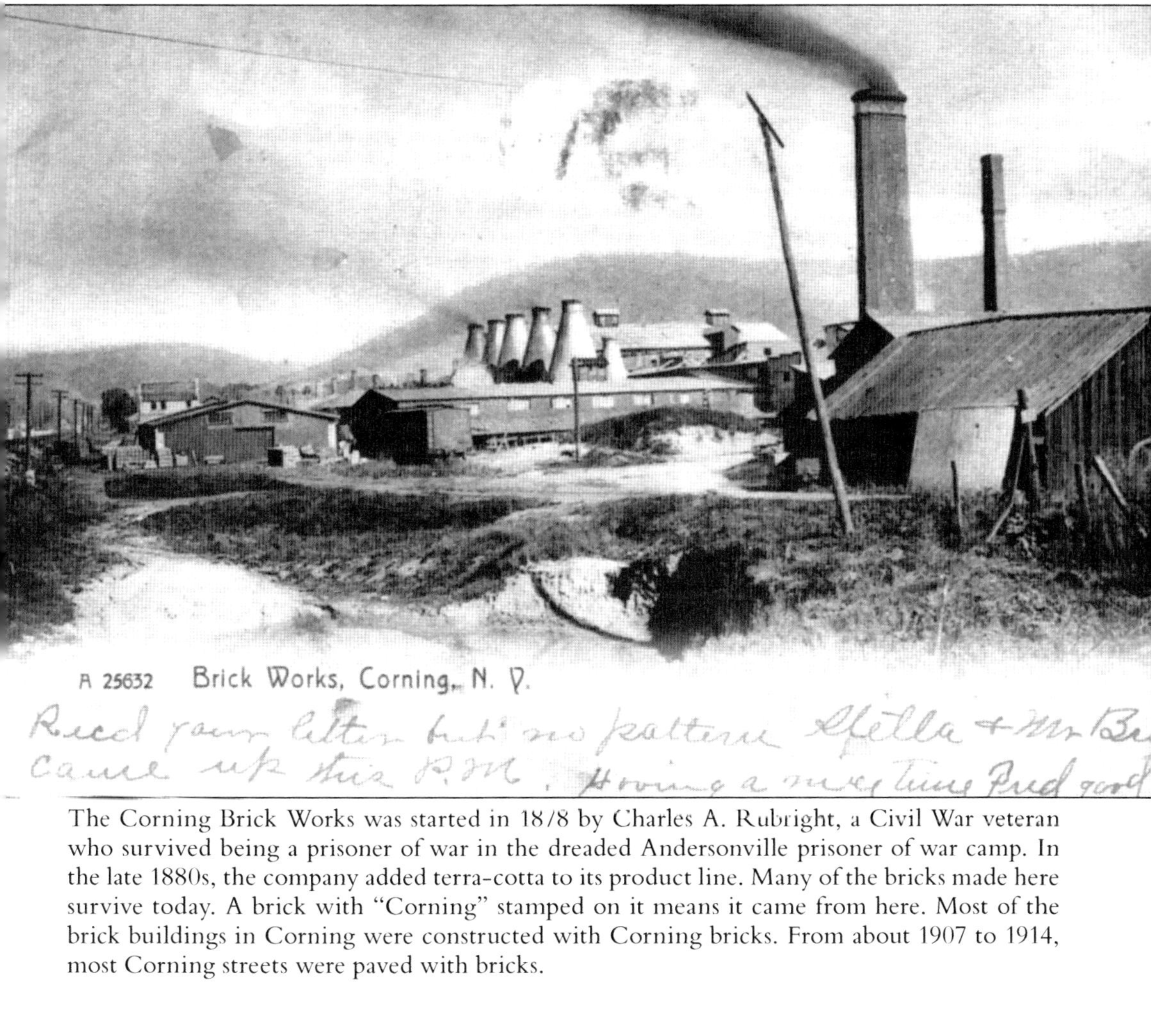

The Corning Brick Works was started in 1878 by Charles A. Rubright, a Civil War veteran who survived being a prisoner of war in the dreaded Andersonville prisoner of war camp. In the late 1880s, the company added terra-cotta to its product line. Many of the bricks made here survive today. A brick with "Corning" stamped on it means it came from here. Most of the brick buildings in Corning were constructed with Corning bricks. From about 1907 to 1914, most Corning streets were paved with bricks.

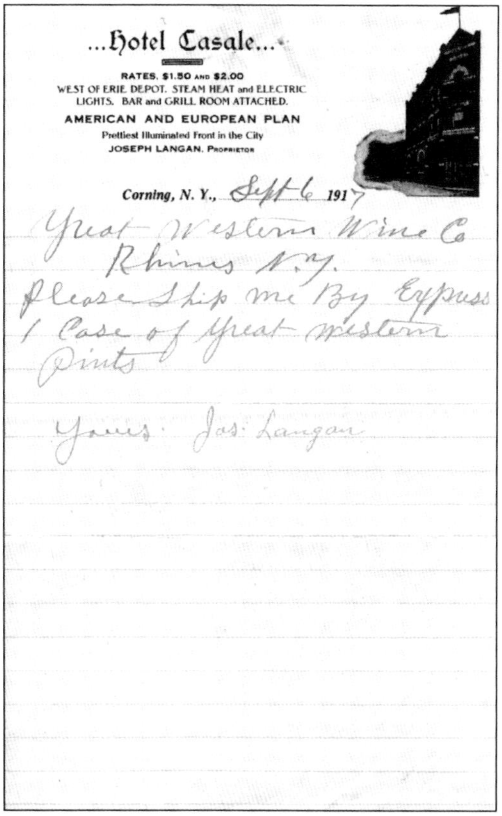

...Hotel Casale...

RATES, $1.50 AND $2.00
WEST OF ERIE DEPOT. STEAM HEAT and ELECTRIC LIGHTS. BAR and GRILL ROOM ATTACHED.
AMERICAN AND EUROPEAN PLAN
Prettiest Illuminated Front in the City
JOSEPH LANGAN, PROPRIETOR

Corning, N. Y., Sept 6 1917

Great Western Wine Co
Rhiems [Rheims] N.Y.
Please Ship me By Express
1 Case of Great Western
Pints

Yours: Jos: Langan

Like many other businesses of the time, the Hotel Casale had illustrated letterhead that was used for correspondence. This one was mailed to the Great Western Wine Company, which was started in the 1860s. The wine company has had different owners and today goes under the name Pleasant Valley Wine Company. Notice the rates for staying at the hotel.

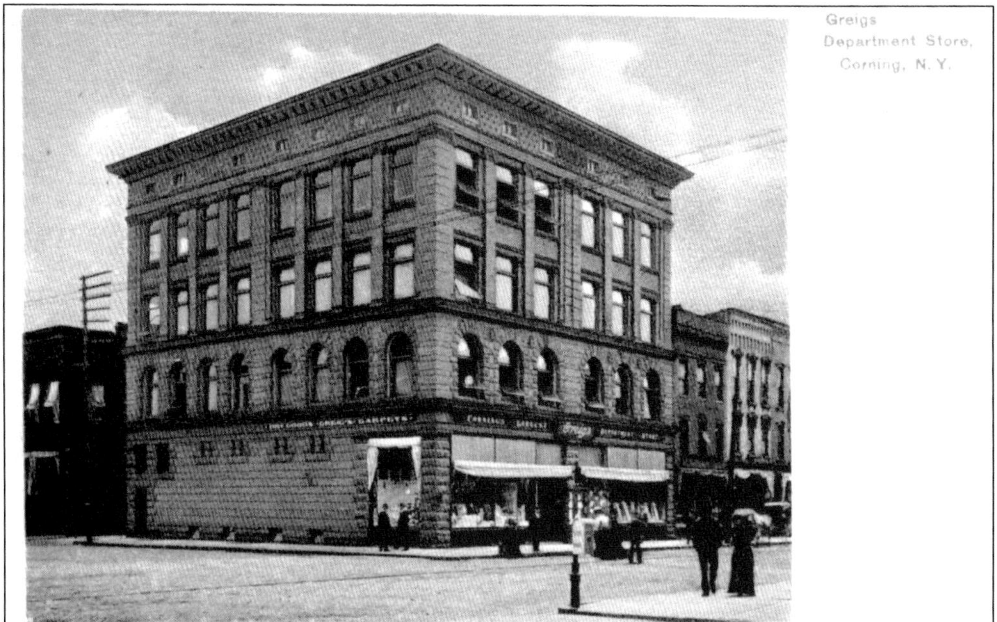

Greig's first store was located at 1–3 Market Street until 1910. The third location was called Greig Specialty Shops on Market Street and sold women's wear from about 1917 to 1918. (Courtesy of Diane Gardner.)

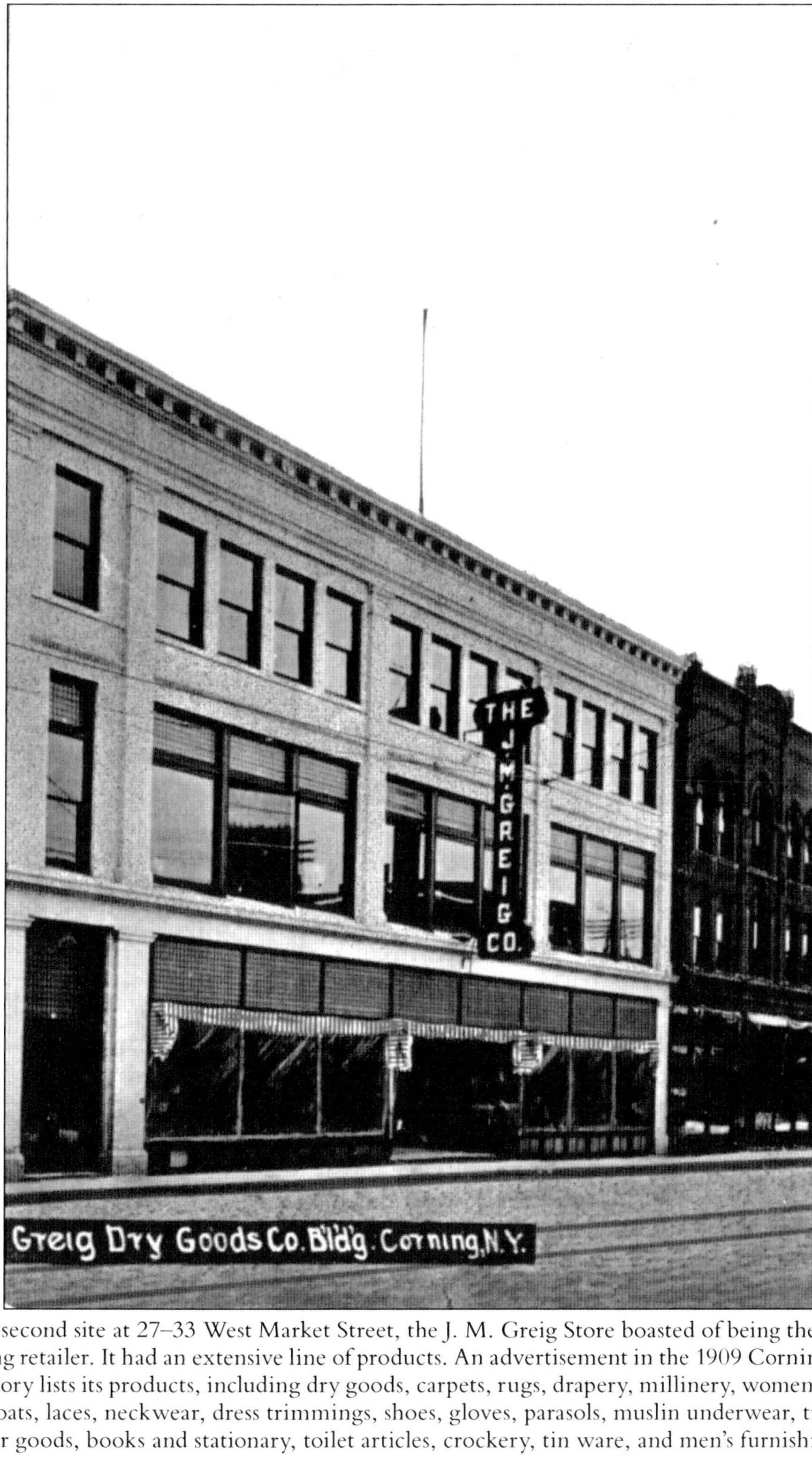

At its second site at 27–33 West Market Street, the J. M. Greig Store boasted of being the city's leading retailer. It had an extensive line of products. An advertisement in the 1909 Corning city directory lists its products, including dry goods, carpets, rugs, drapery, millinery, women's suits and coats, laces, neckwear, dress trimmings, shoes, gloves, parasols, muslin underwear, trunks, leather goods, books and stationary, toilet articles, crockery, tin ware, and men's furnishing.

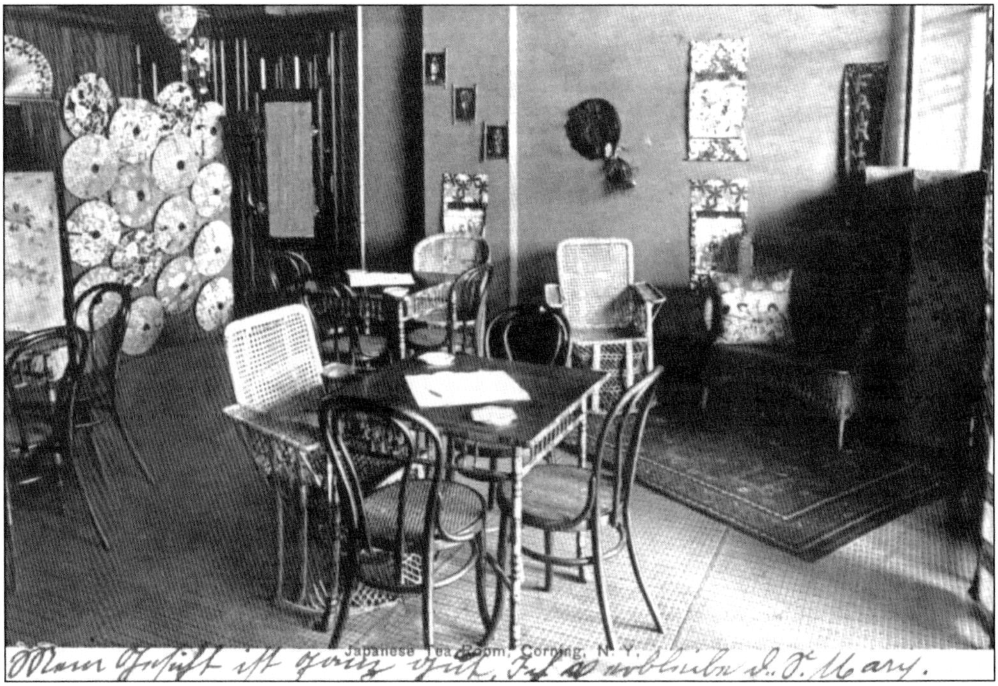

Before coffee gained the popularity of today, people drank more tea. This postcard shows the Japanese tearoom in Corning. Wicker chairs and Japanese-themed decorations create the atmosphere.

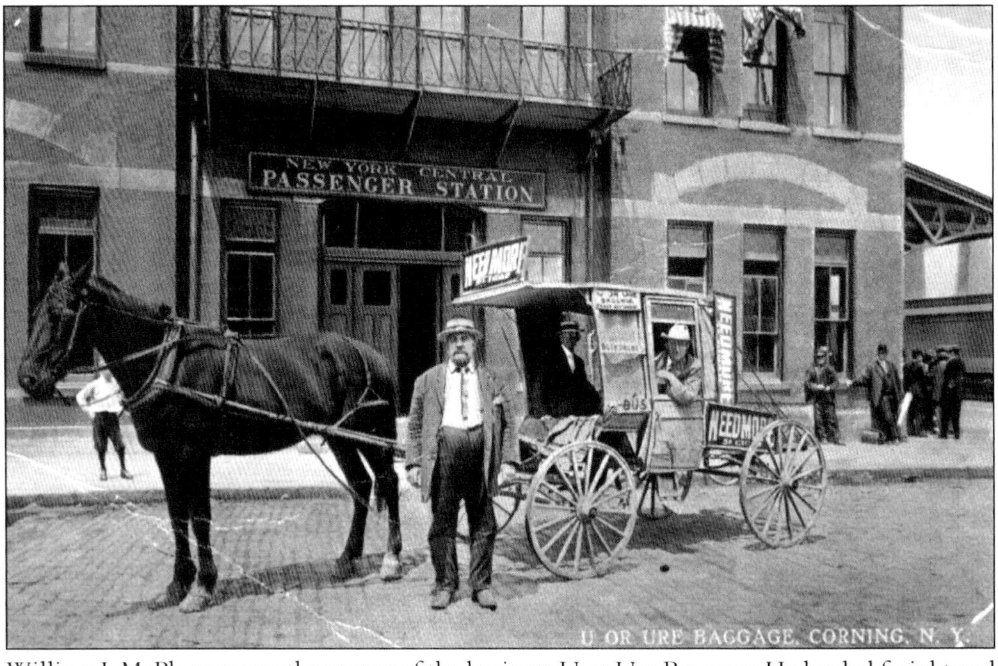

William J. McPherson was the owner of the business U or Ure Baggage. He hauled freight and gave people rides from before 1901 until 1918.

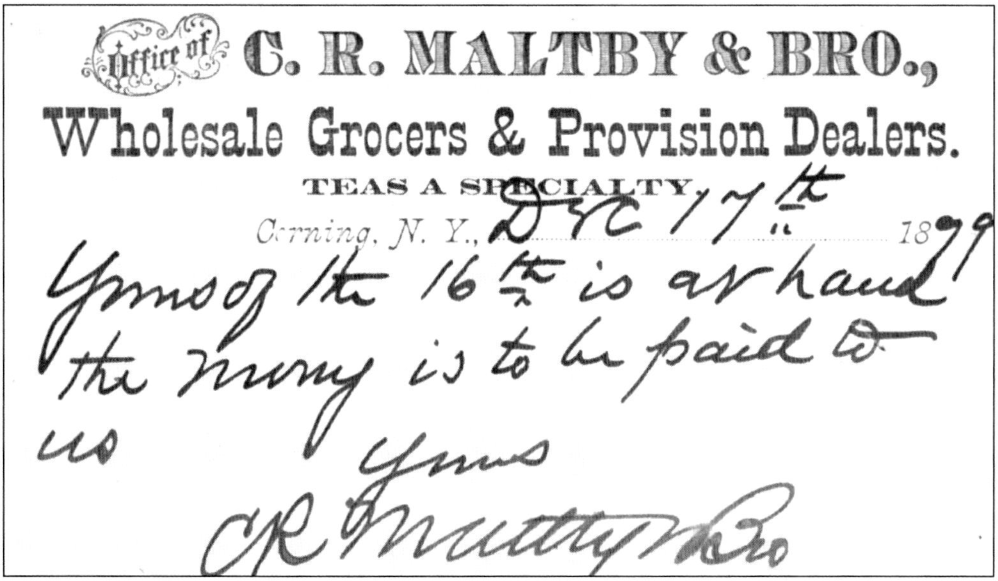
Office of C. R. MALTBY & BRO.,
Wholesale Grocers & Provision Dealers.
TEAS A SPECIALTY.
Corning, N. Y., Dec 17th 1879
Yours of the 16th is at hand
the money is to be paid to
us Yours
C R Maltby & Bro

Charles R. Maltby entered into the grocery business in the 1860s. Soon after, he changed from a retail grocer into the wholesale grocery business. His brothers Jerome and Erastus became his partners. This postcard was mailed in 1879 to an H. Sherwood and Son in Wellsboro, Pennsylvania.

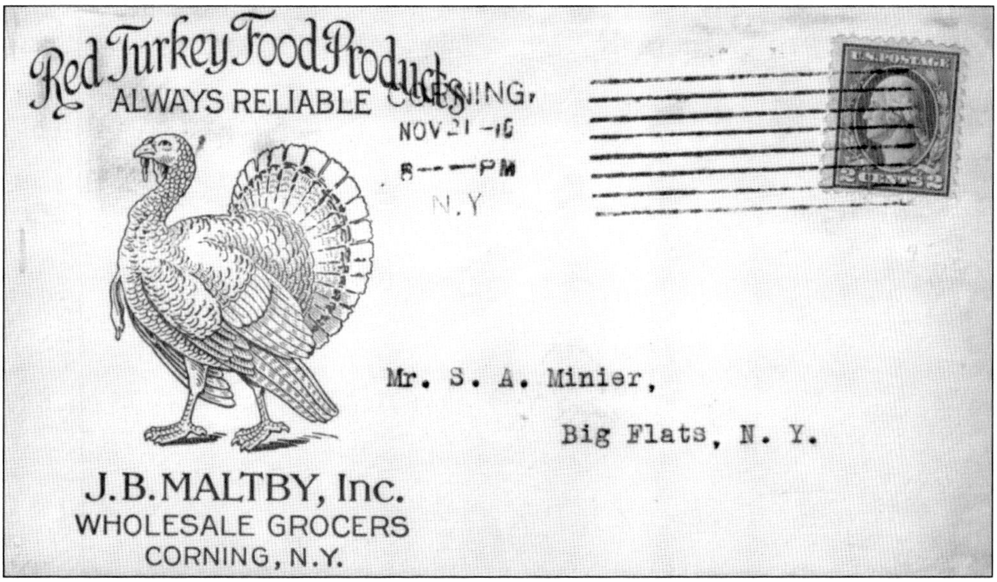

This illustrated envelope advertises the Red Turkey brand of food products. This included Maltby's own roasted coffee, which sold really well from around 1910 through the late 1930s. In 1916, when this was mailed, the business was called J. B. Maltby, Inc. The Minier family, who received this business letter, has a long history in Big Flats and still has a grocery business there under the family name.

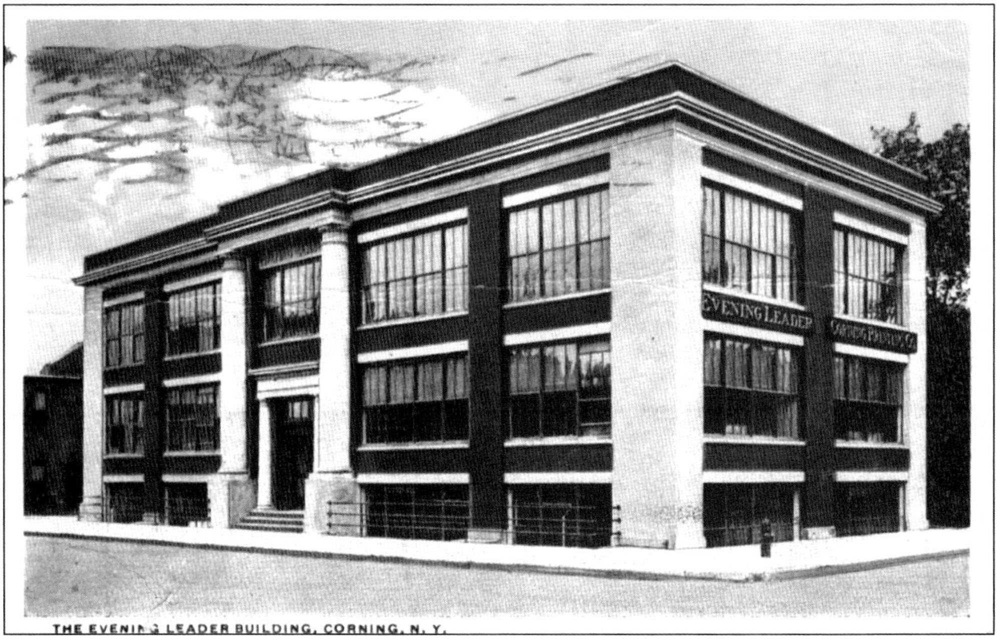

The *Evening Leader* is today the main newspaper of Corning. It was preceded by the *Corning Journal* and the *Corning Sun*. This building was constructed in 1916 on the northeast corner of Walnut Street and Erie Avenue, now Denison Parkway. The *Evening Leader* building was razed to make way for a new J. C. Penney Company store. The newspaper then constructed a new, modern one-story home at the corner of Centerway and East Pulteney Street.

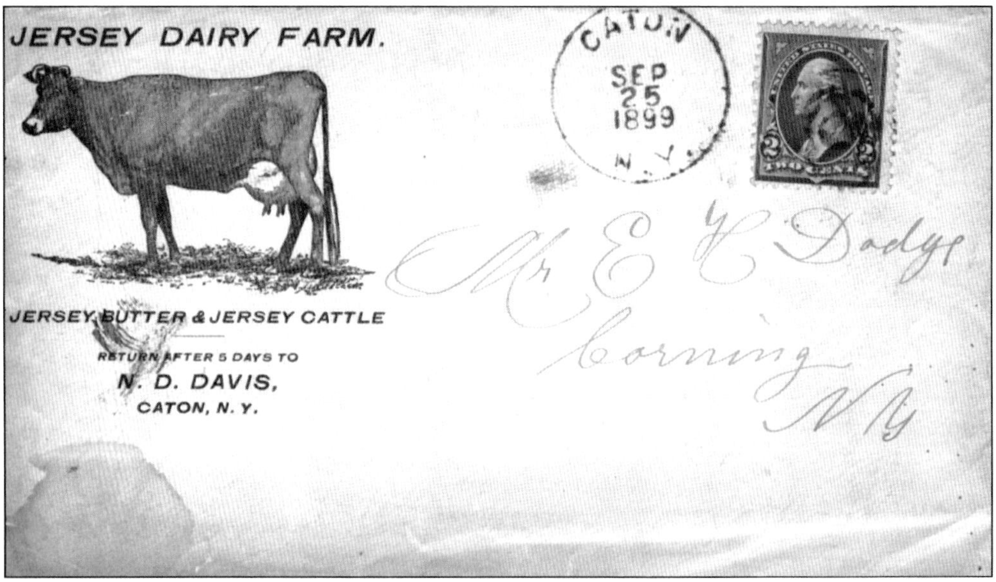

This illustrated envelope and its contents were mailed from Nelson D. Davis, who was one of the earliest dairy farmers in Caton. He came from Massachusetts and started dairy farming in Caton in the 1860s. He and his wife, Julia, had five children. Inside of this envelope were documents concerning the sale of Jersey cattle to Edwin H. Dodge, who lived on the Hornby Road.

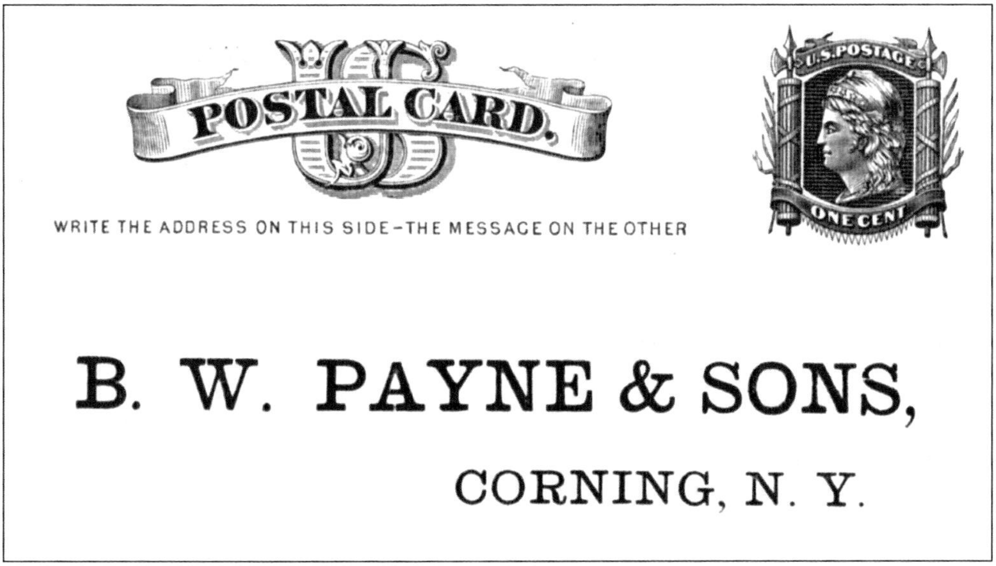

B. W. Payne and Sons was established in Corning in 1840. It made engines, boilers, and heavy machinery, including one of the earliest non-releasing rotary valve engines. In 1883, better shipping facilities offered in Elmira enticed the company to move there. When Benjamin W. Payne died, his two sons, Benjamin N. Payne and David W. Payne, carried on, concentrating on high-speed engines and getting out of the boiler business in the late 1890s.

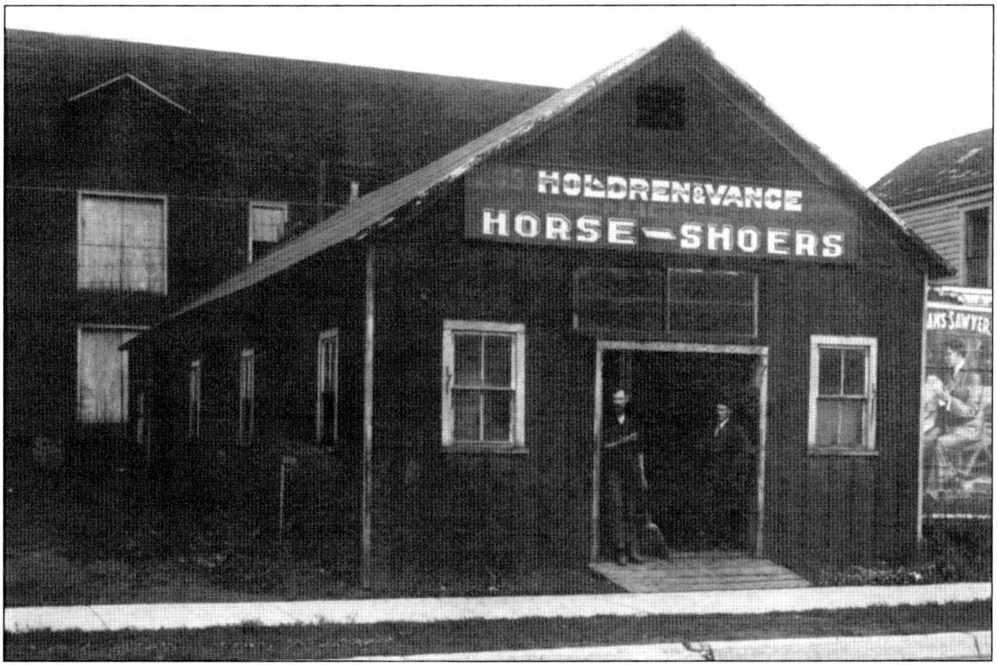

"Corning, N.Y. Market St. 1912" is written on the back of this postcard. John R. Holdern and William H. Vance had this blacksmith shop at 209 East Market Street from about 1905 to 1912. After that, the shop was owned by Vance and William H. Mann in 1913 and 1914 and then Fred Moore in 1915 and 1916.

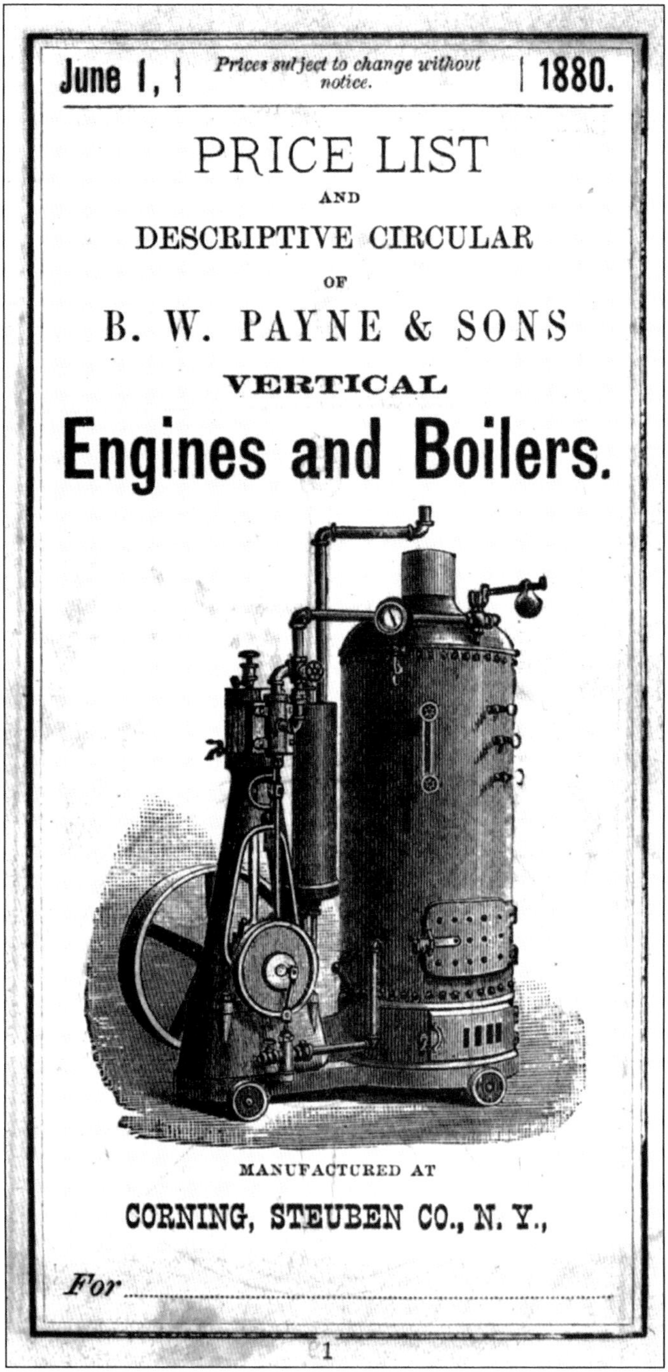

June 1, | *Prices subject to change without notice.* | 1880.

PRICE LIST

AND

DESCRIPTIVE CIRCULAR

OF

B. W. PAYNE & SONS

VERTICAL

Engines and Boilers.

MANUFACTURED AT

CORNING, STEUBEN CO., N. Y.,

For ....

1

This is a small 20-page price list booklet. On the cover is a picture of a vertical engine with a wrought-iron boiler. The engines came in five different sizes, from 3 to 16 horsepower, with costs from $250 to $800. Half of the pages describe how to operate the engines and boilers and the usages of such items. The booklet claims the three-horsepower engine could power a 28-foot steam yacht. Other uses for the engines mentioned by satisfied customers included a band saw, a thrasher, a newspaper printer, and even a cotton gin in Georgia.

Stephen T. Hayt was a politician who was present at Abraham Lincoln's inauguration. He was a member of the New York State senate's 27th district from 1864 to 1866 and a delegate to the Republican National Convention from New York in 1860, 1868, and 1884. The Hayt mill was rebuilt into the Corning Glass Works Memorial Clubhouse, and the building is still on Market Street and remembered as the clubhouse.

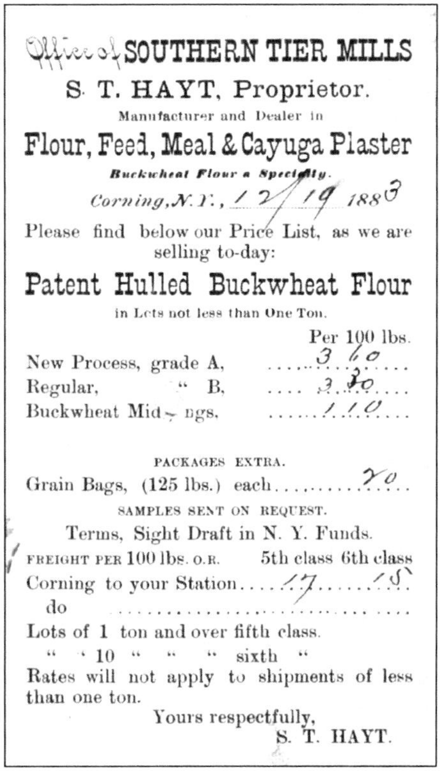

Office of SOUTHERN TIER MILLS

S. T. HAYT, Proprietor.

Manufacturer and Dealer in

Flour, Feed, Meal & Cayuga Plaster

Buckwheat Flour a Specialty.

Corning, N. Y., 12/19 1883

Please find below our Price List, as we are selling to-day:

Patent Hulled Buckwheat Flour

in Lots not less than One Ton.

	Per 100 lbs.
New Process, grade A,	3.60
Regular, " B,	3.30
Buckwheat Middlings,	1.10

PACKAGES EXTRA.

Grain Bags, (125 lbs.) each 20

SAMPLES SENT ON REQUEST.

Terms, Sight Draft in N. Y. Funds.

FREIGHT PER 100 lbs. O.R.	5th class	6th class
Corning to your Station	17	15
do		

Lots of 1 ton and over fifth class.
" " 10 " " " sixth "
Rates will not apply to shipments of less than one ton.

Yours respectfully,
S. T. HAYT.

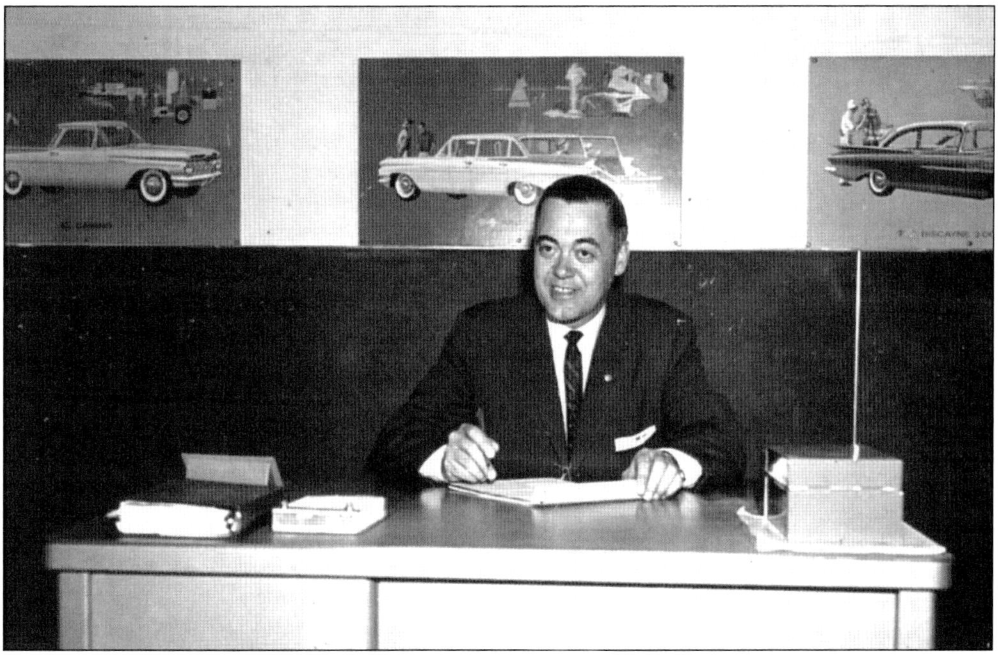

Edward Gatke Chevrolet Sales and Service was at 201–221 East Market Street. It also had a body shop at 113 Chestnut Street. Edward F. Gatke was president, Mason W. Haigh was general manager, and Henry Levy was sales manager. This business started there in 1959. Before that, Purcell Motor Company was at that address from about 1923 until 1958.

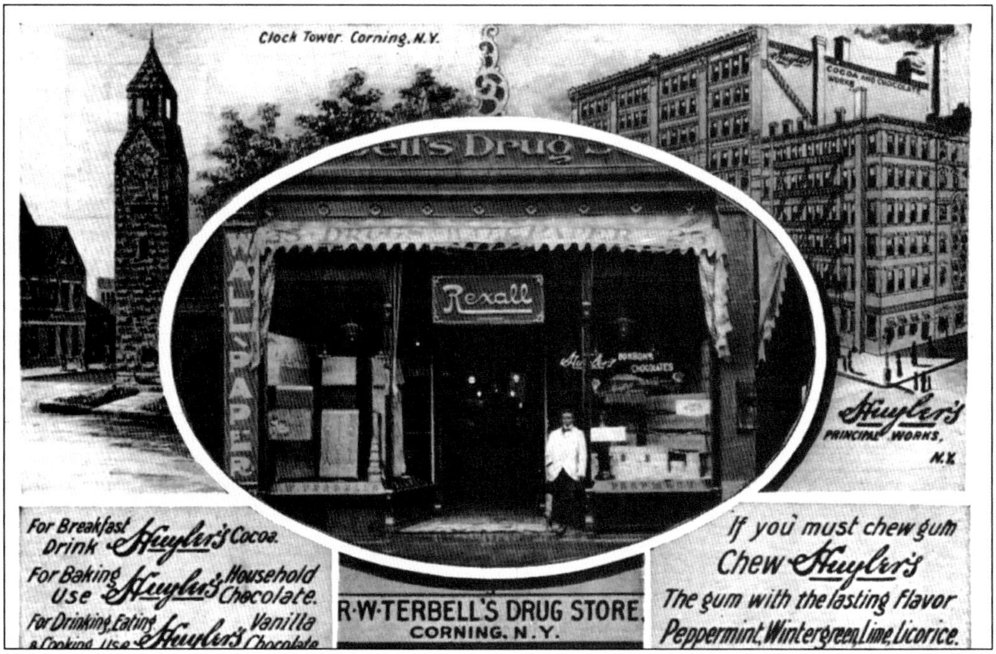

Robert W. Terbell had two drugstores located at 25 East Market Street and 1 East Pulteney Street. Huyler's was a leading chocolate and candy seller about 1910, which co-advertised with store owners such as Terbell. Terbell's store is in the middle, the clock tower is on the left, and on the right is Huyler's production facility. Terbell was considered adventurous because he was one of the first people in Corning to ride a motorcycle, around 1909.

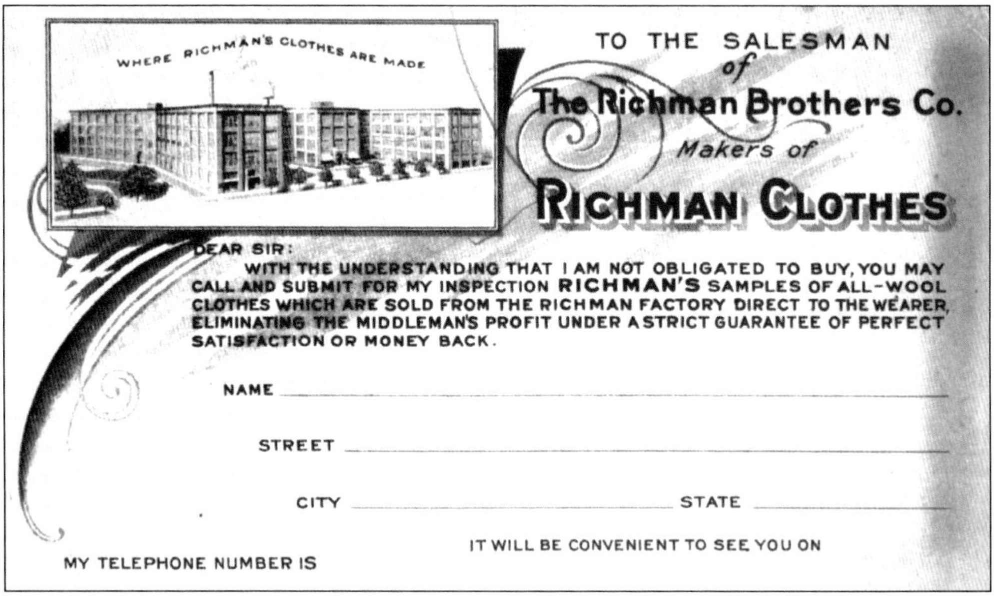

Robert C. Woods lived at 130 Wall Street from about 1921 to 1932. He was a salesman who sold clothes for the Richman Brothers Company, which made and sold men's suites, furnishings, and hats. At one time in the 1950s, it became the largest retail clothing chain in the nation, operating 119 outlets. On the other side of this private mailing card is space for an interested customer to mail information so that the salesman could call on the customer at the right time and place.

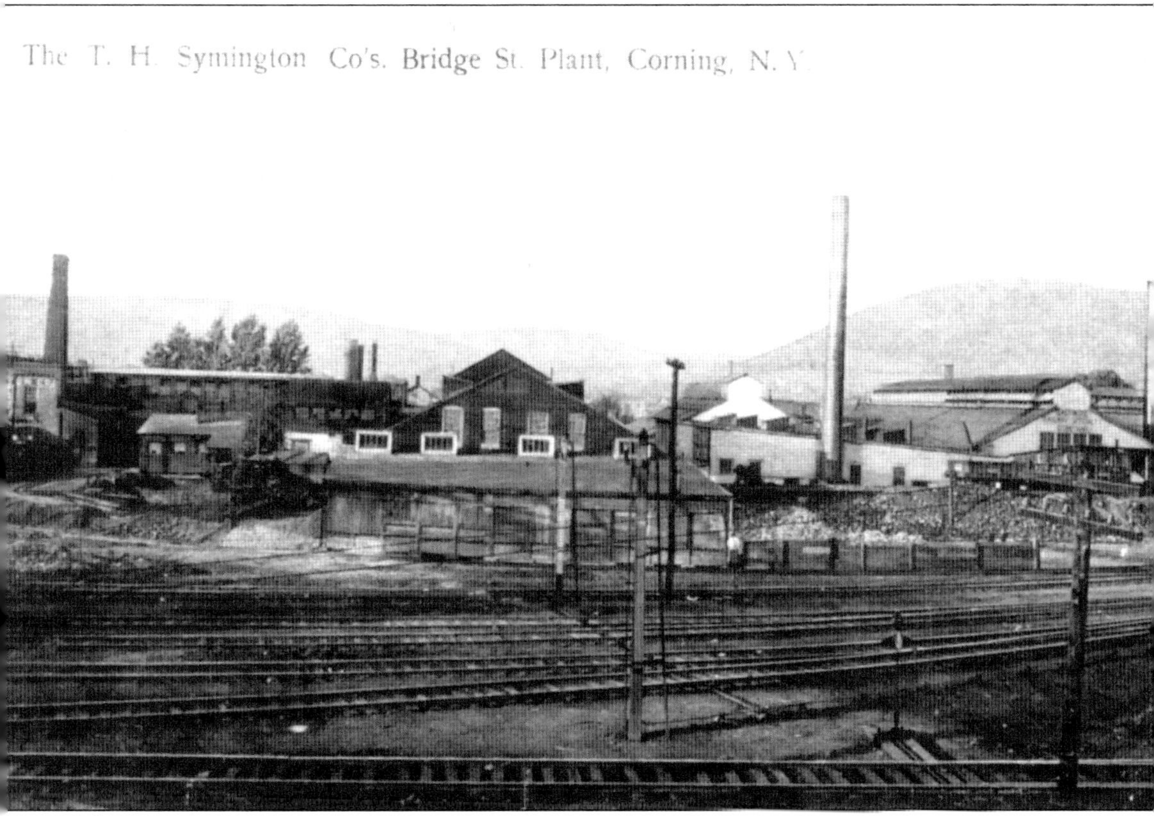

The T. H. Symington Company of Baltimore first came to Corning in 1904. It made railroad car boxes and brake shoes. It first started with one shop on Market Street in the building where the Corning Stove Works used to be. Orders for their products grew, with the need for two facilities. This shows the Bridge Street plant.

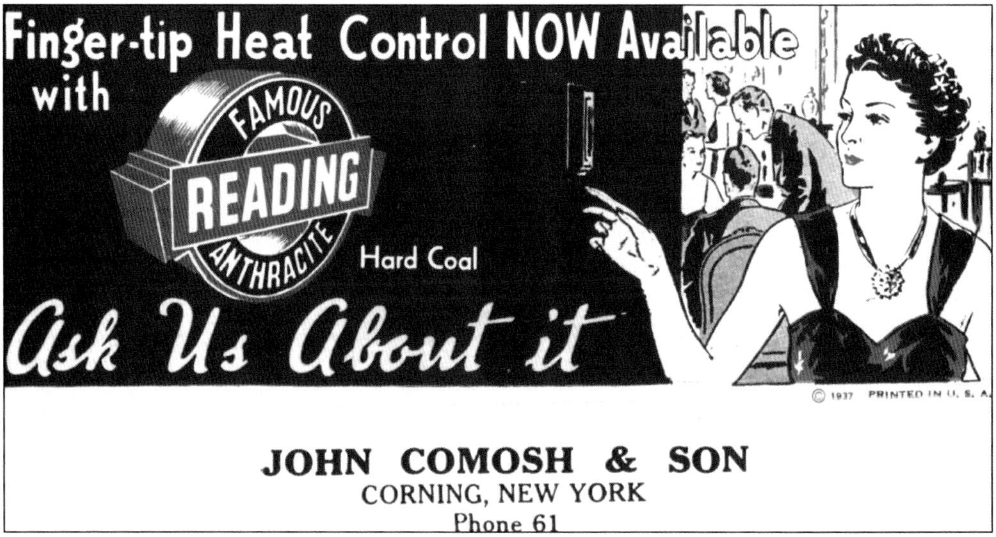

The Comosh family had a long history of dealing coal. At the time of this blotter in the 1930s, they were located on the corner of State and Waters Streets, where they dealt in hard and soft coal and Portland cement. This 1937 blotter advertises the new, modern convenience of a thermostat to control coal heating.

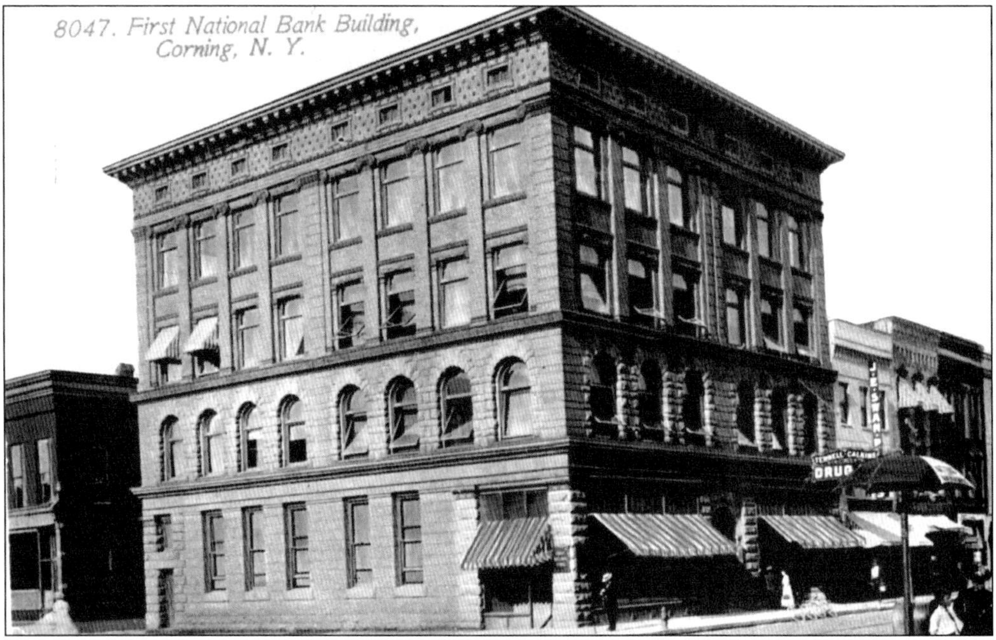

The First National Bank and Trust Company of Corning was granted a charter by the federal government on April 3, 1882. The bank opened in May of that year. When first organized, the bank was in what was then called the Drake block.

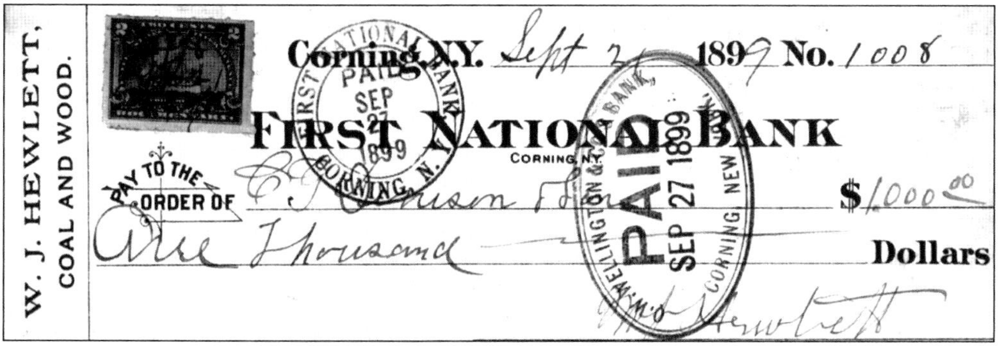

Pictured is a check from the First National Bank. It is from the account of William J. Hewlett, who was from England and had a coal and wood business. It is payable to the C. G. Denison and Son Company.

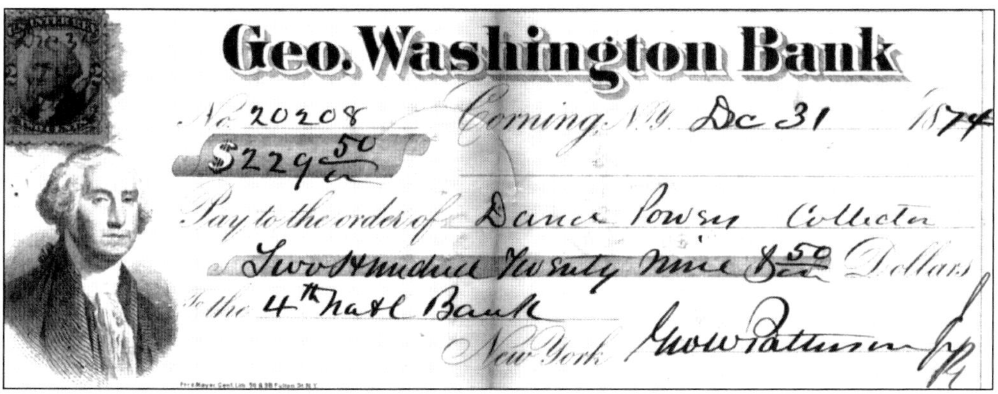

Here is a check from the George Washington Bank. It is signed by George W. Patterson, who was the bank founder. Patterson later went to prison for bilking depositors in this bank.

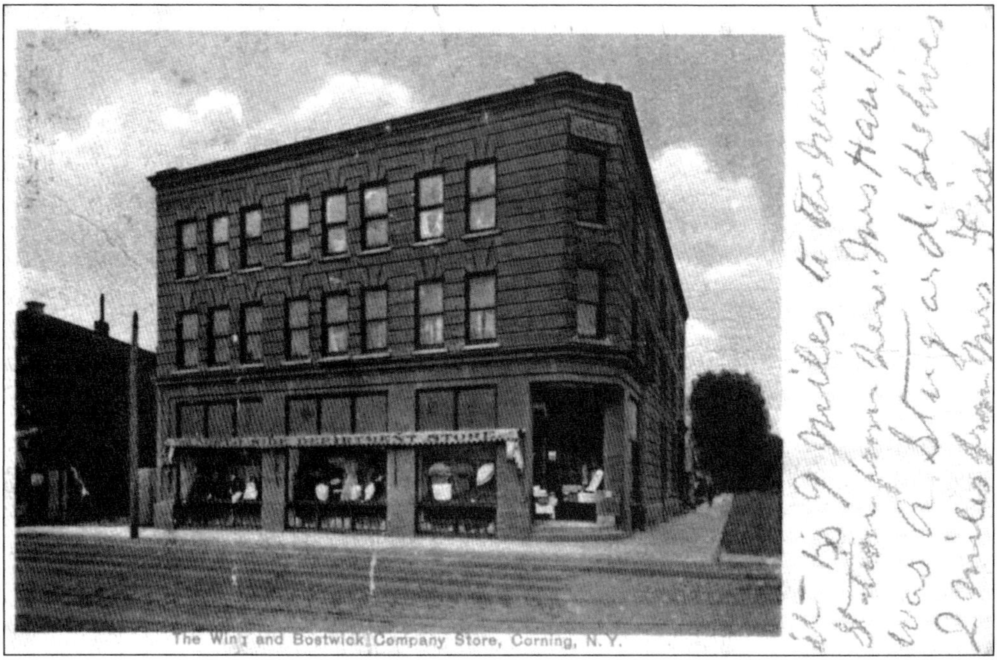

The Wing and Bostwick Company store was on the corner of Wall and Pulteney Streets. It was owned and operated by two Corning businessmen, Charles Burleigh Wing and Elias D. Bostwick. The store hosted a large number of goods throughout its three stories. Clothing, shoes, and rubber items could be found on the first floor. On the second floor there was a large grocery department. The business had an elevator that took customers up to the third floor, which was the furniture department.

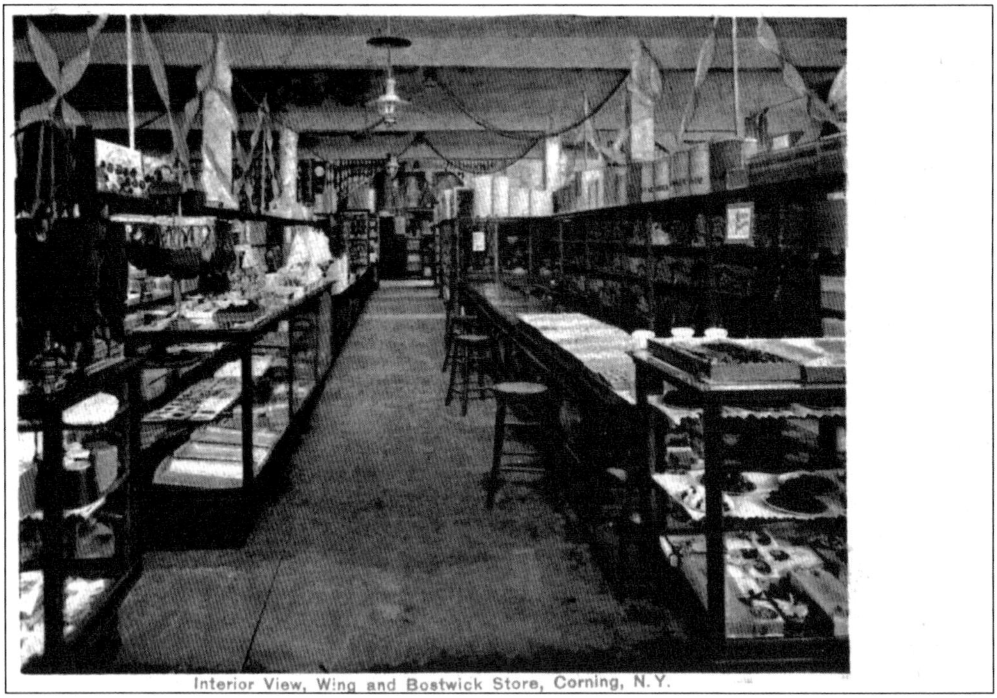

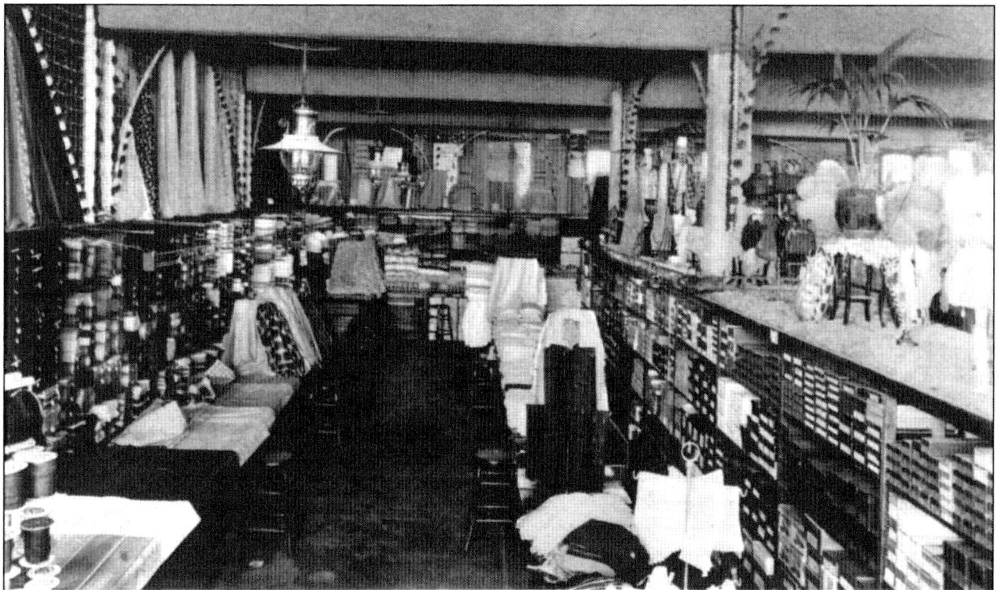

199 Dry Goods Department, of the Wing & Bostwick Co., Corning, N. Y.

These two postcards show the dry goods department and the notions department at the Wing and Bostwick Company. This large store broke up departments on different floors to make shopping more convenient for people.

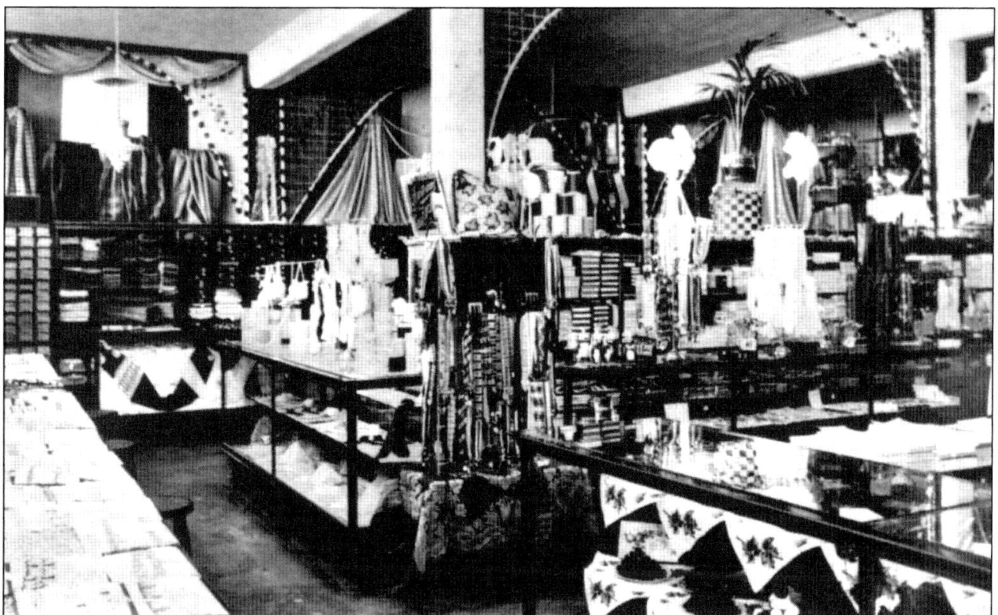

200 Notions Department, of the Wing & Bostwick Co., Corning, N. Y.

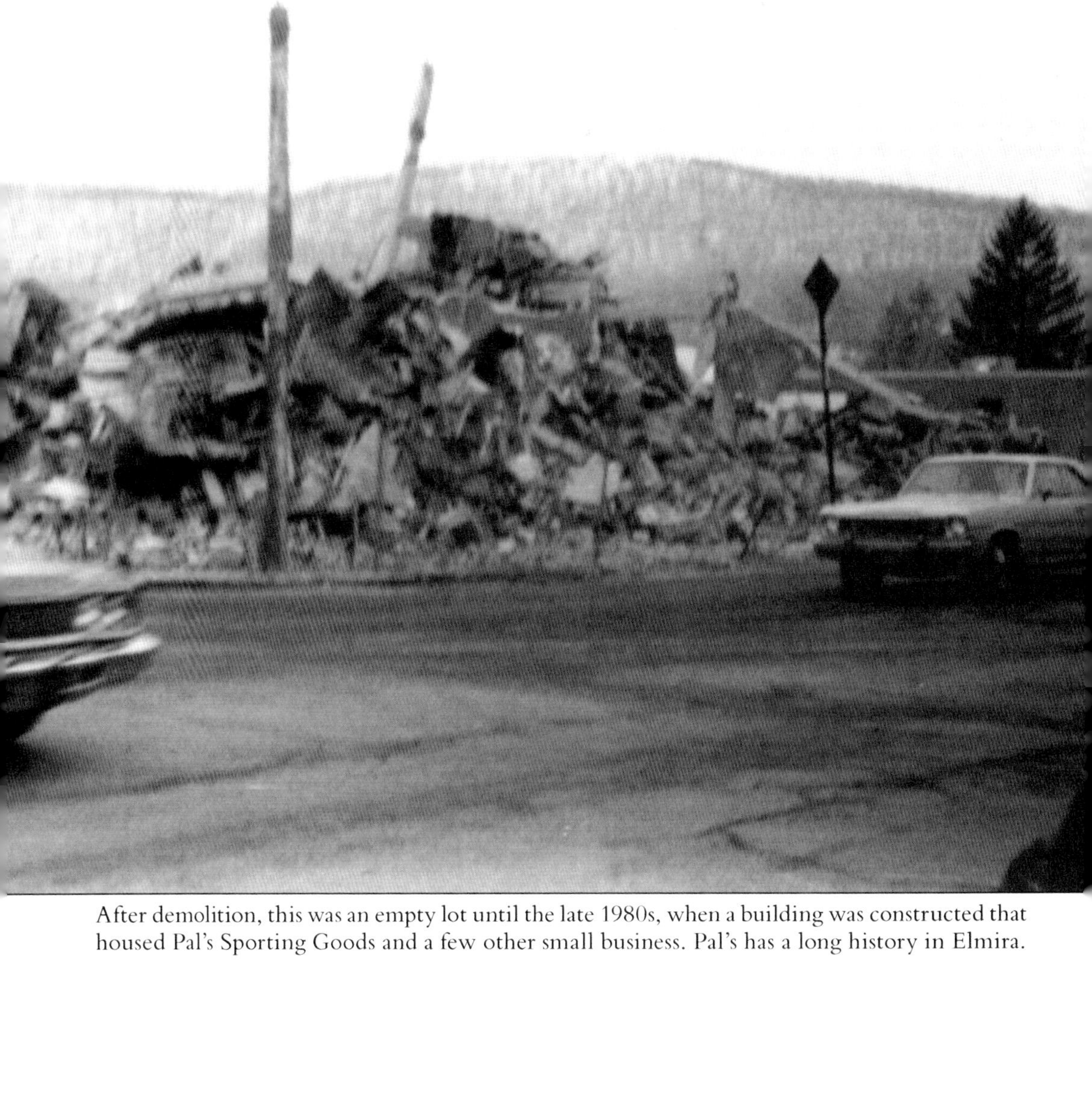

After demolition, this was an empty lot until the late 1980s, when a building was constructed that housed Pal's Sporting Goods and a few other small business. Pal's has a long history in Elmira.

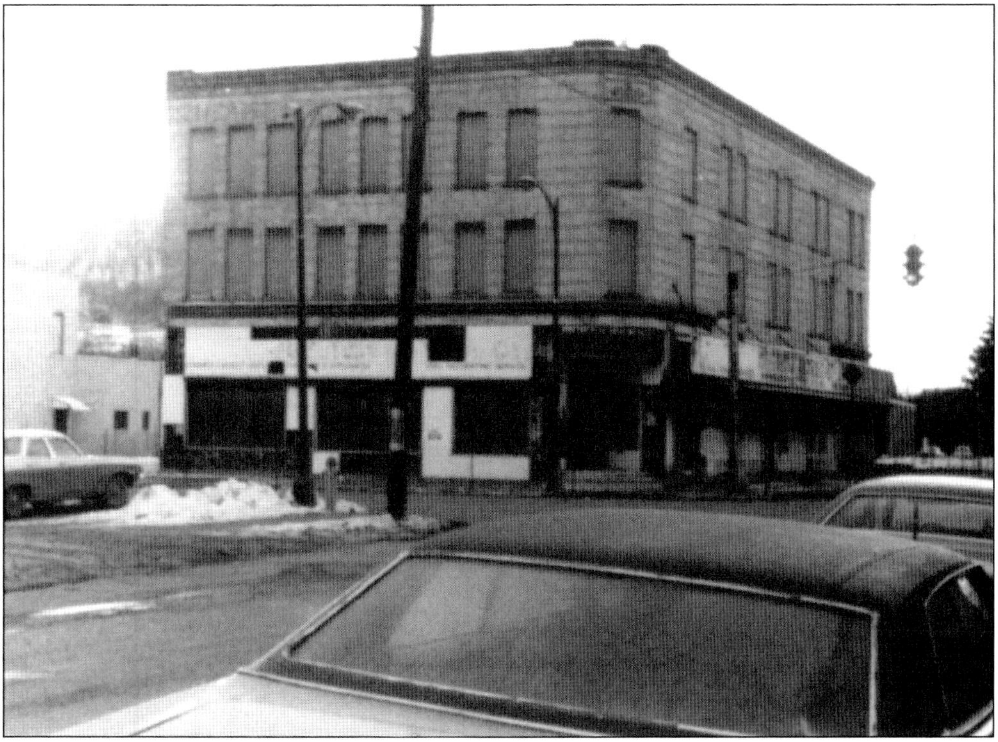

This building, which houses the bar T.O.P., was constructed in 1890. T.O.P., which stands for "That Other Place," opened about 1970. Many different businesses have been there since. Signs for Adsit Boller Hardware (1908–1914) and Boller Brothers Hardware (1914–1941) can still be seen on the front of this building in faded white paint. On the Bridge Street side, a sign for Atwood pool hall, cigars, and tobacco is barely visible in faded paint.

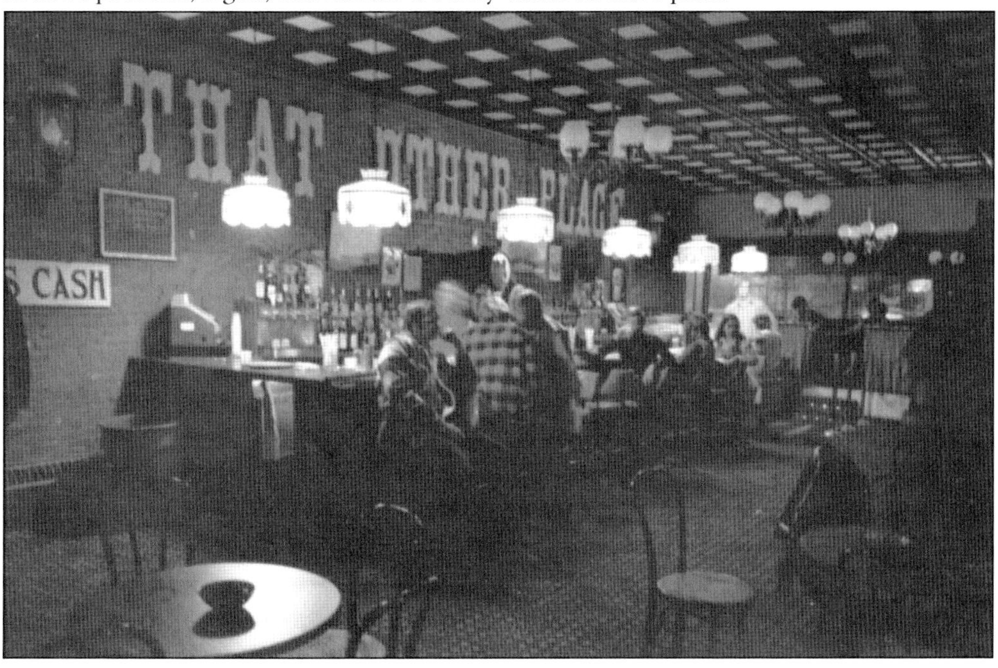

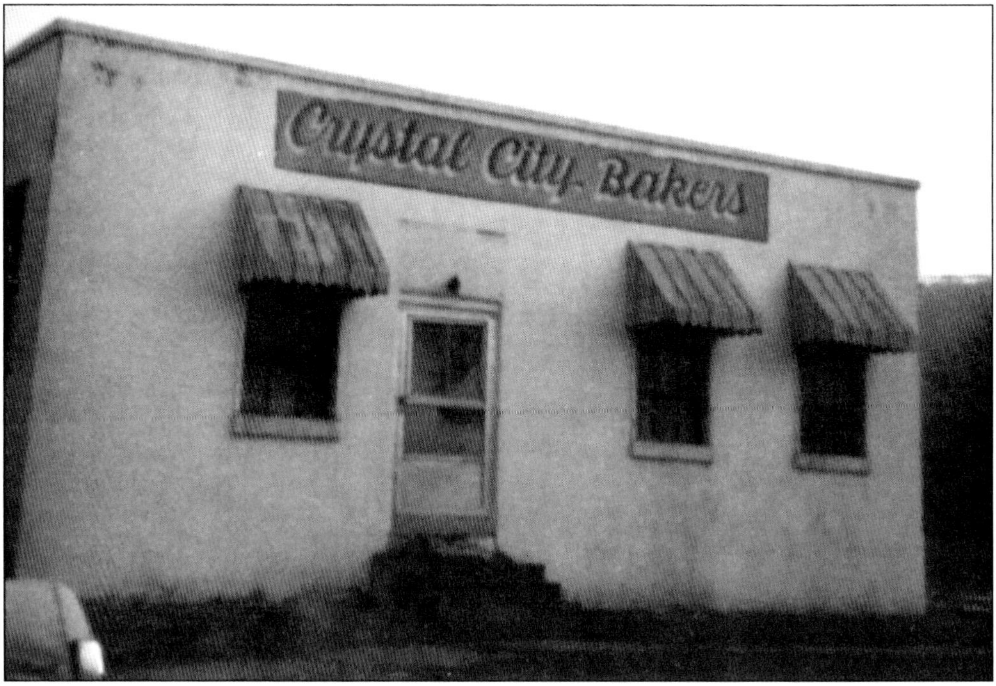

This was the beginning site for Crystal City Bakery. It was located at 55–57 East William Street and was founded in the early 1940s by Vincent D' Ortenzio. The bakery remained open at this location until it moved to its present location. This 1977 photograph shows the emptied building before it was demolished.

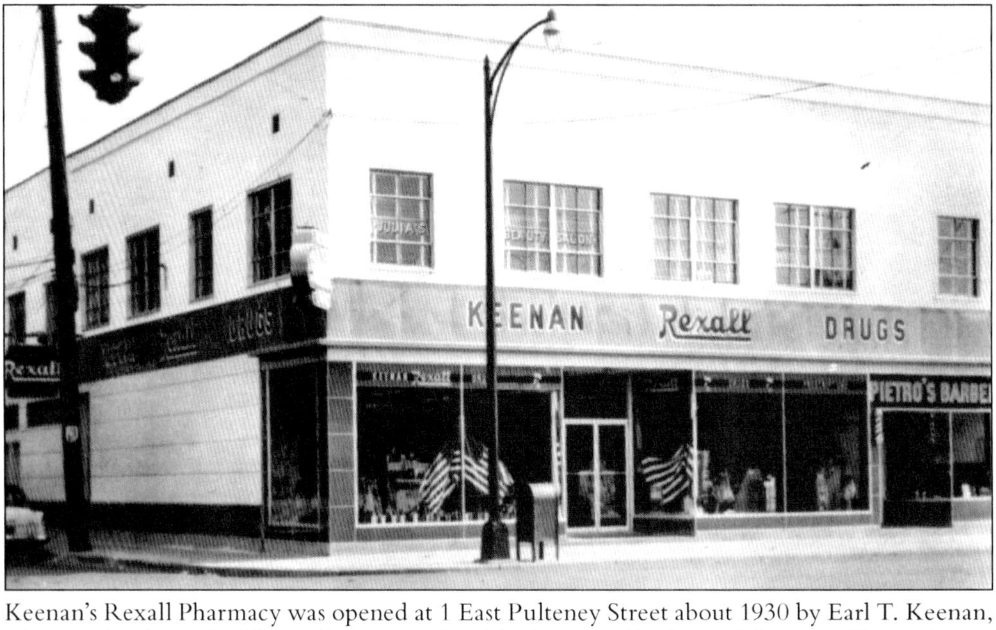

Keenan's Rexall Pharmacy was opened at 1 East Pulteney Street about 1930 by Earl T. Keenan, who previously worked down the street at Lamb's pharmacy for about eight years. Keenan's next owners were Rudy Carlson and William Miles. Later it went under the name Maloney's, from 1978 to 1984. Next door at 5 East Pulteney Street is Pietro's Barbershop. This was run by John J. Pietro from about 1955 until 1969.

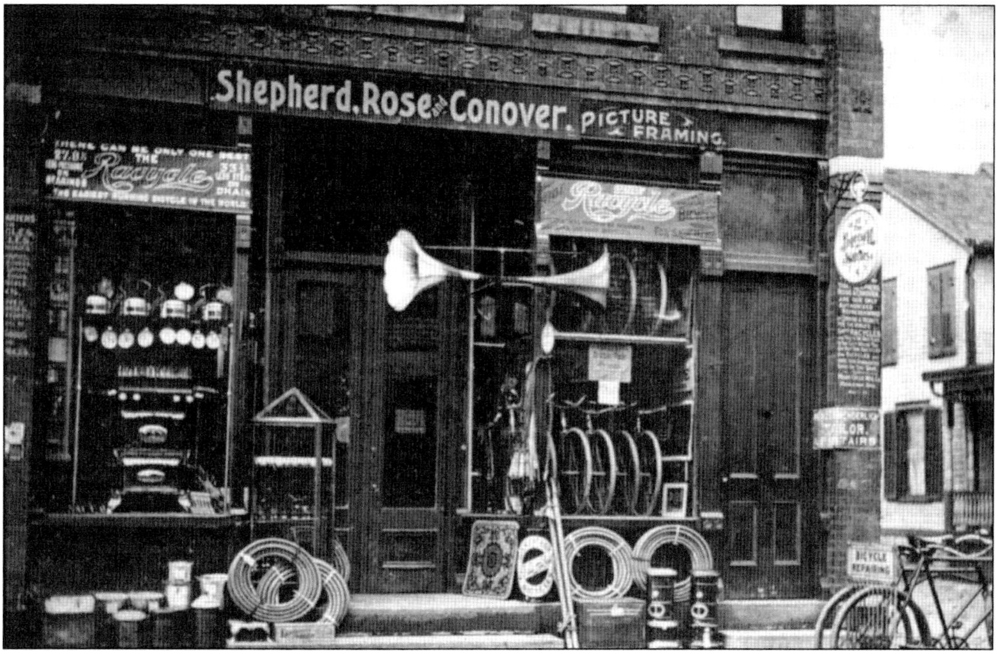

This building was constructed in 1900. This business started out as Shepherd, Rose, and Conover. The photograph for this postcard was taken about 1908. The Great Atlantic and Pacific Tea Company was located there from about 1917 to 1930. The North Side Floral shop started in 1947 and is still in business.

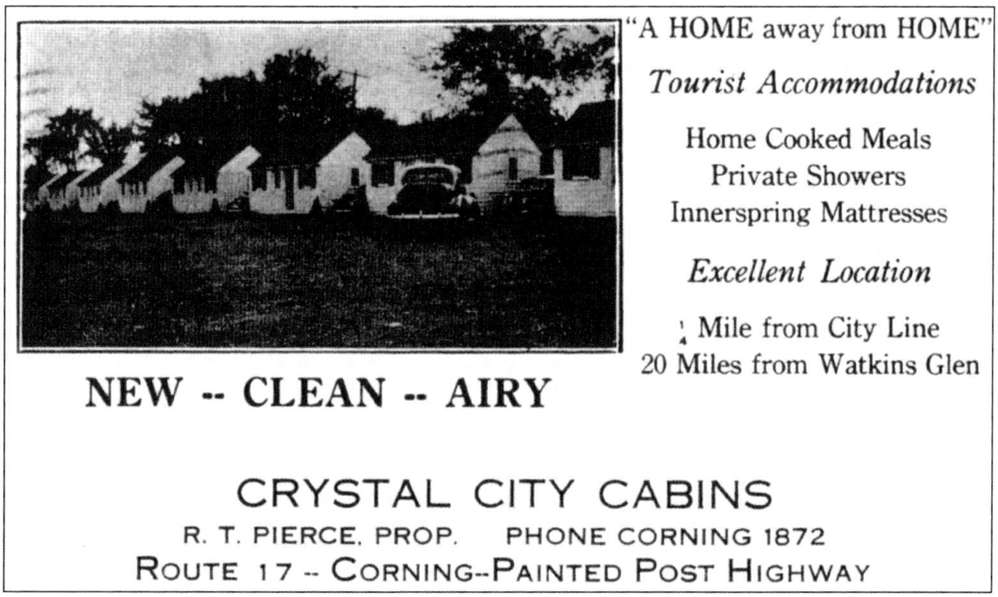

This is an advertising postcard for Crystal City Cabins. (Courtesy of Diane Gardner.)

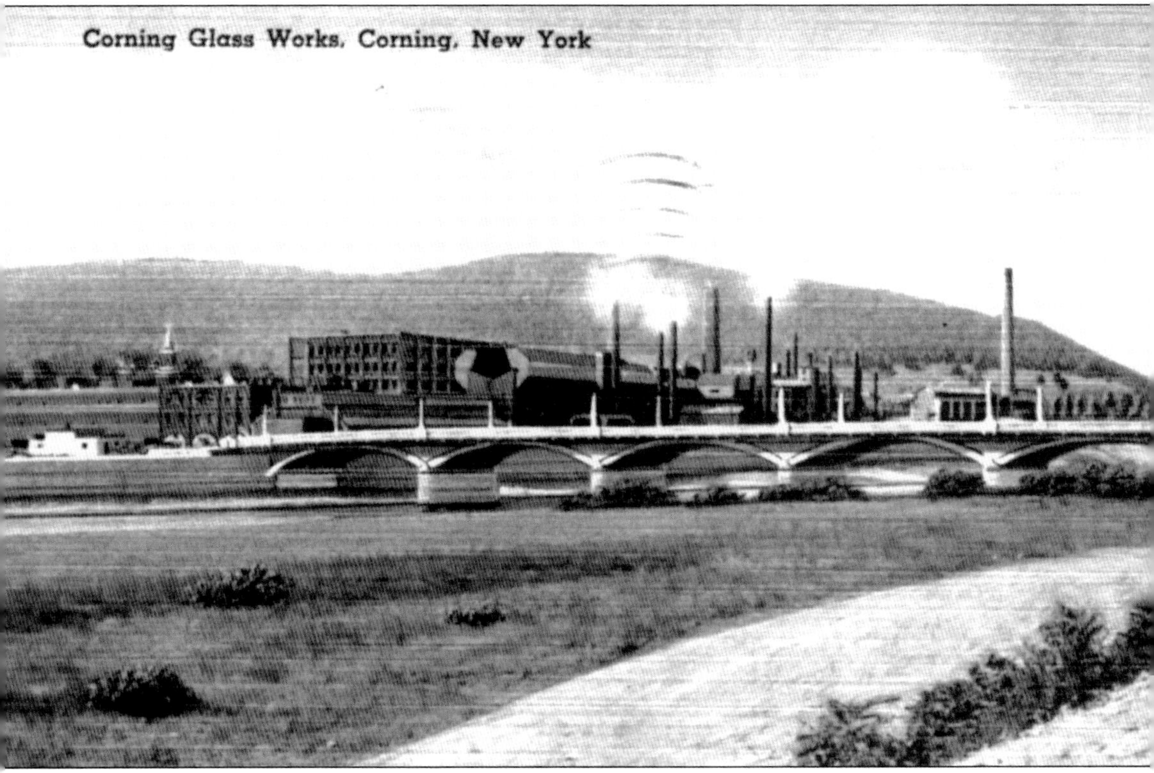

This is a view of Corning Glass Works from around 1909.

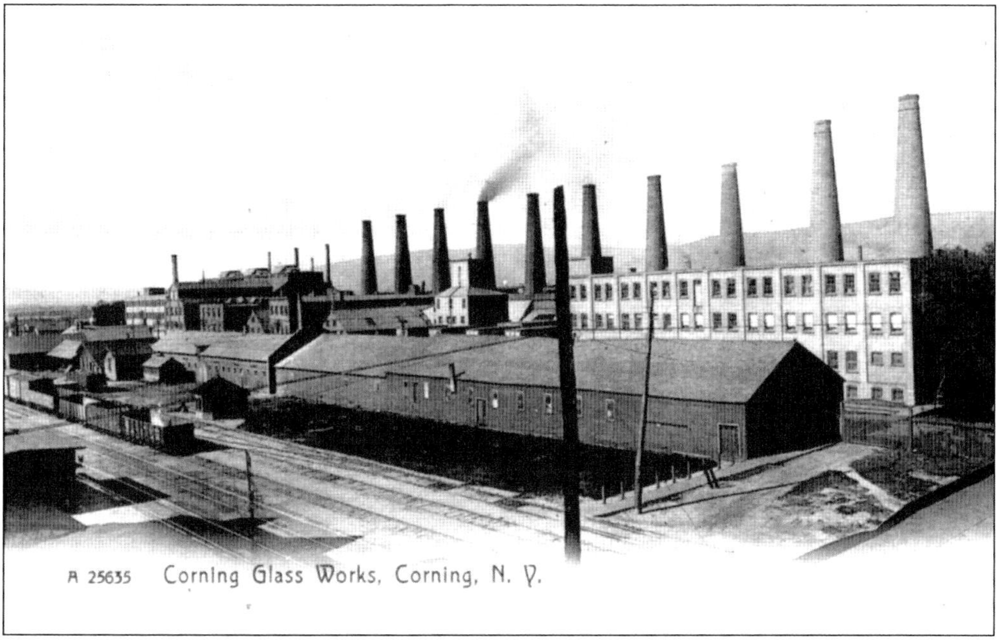

At the time of this 1906 postcard, the Corning Glass Works was using 10 furnaces for the production of glass.

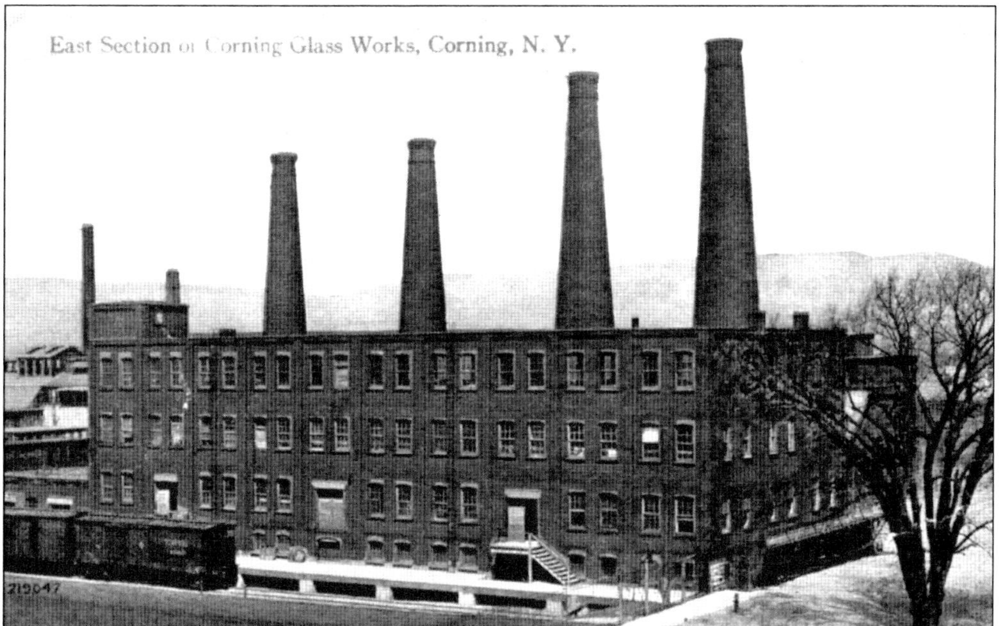

Here is a close-up view of one of the Corning Glass Works brick buildings that have since been torn down and replaced with structures that house the Corning Incorporated world headquarters.

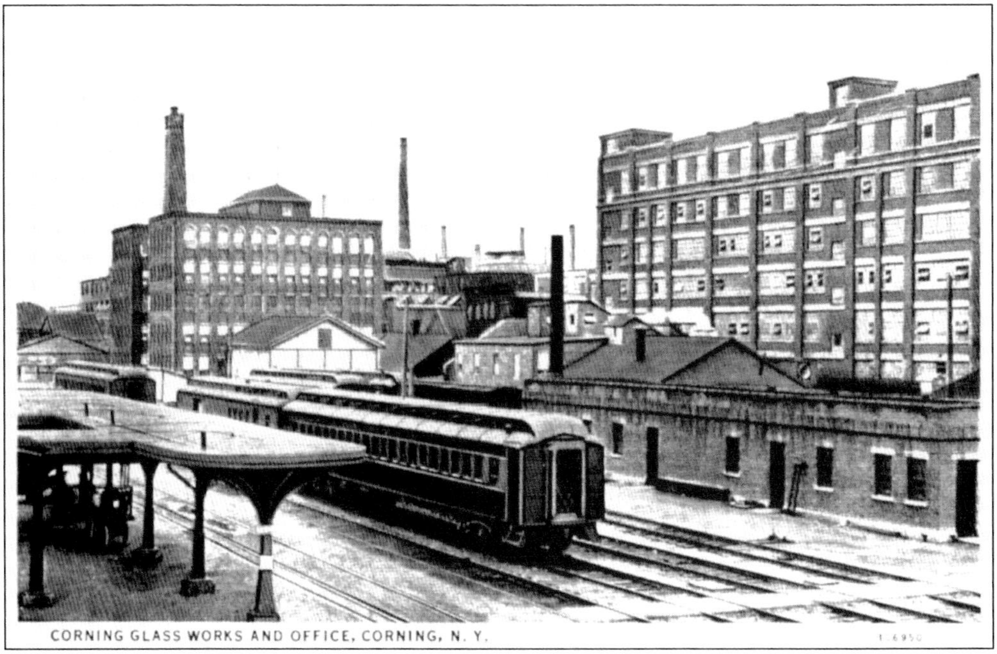

This postcard shows two views of the Corning Glass Works. The glass works and other companies made so much glass in Corning that it came to be known as the crystal city.

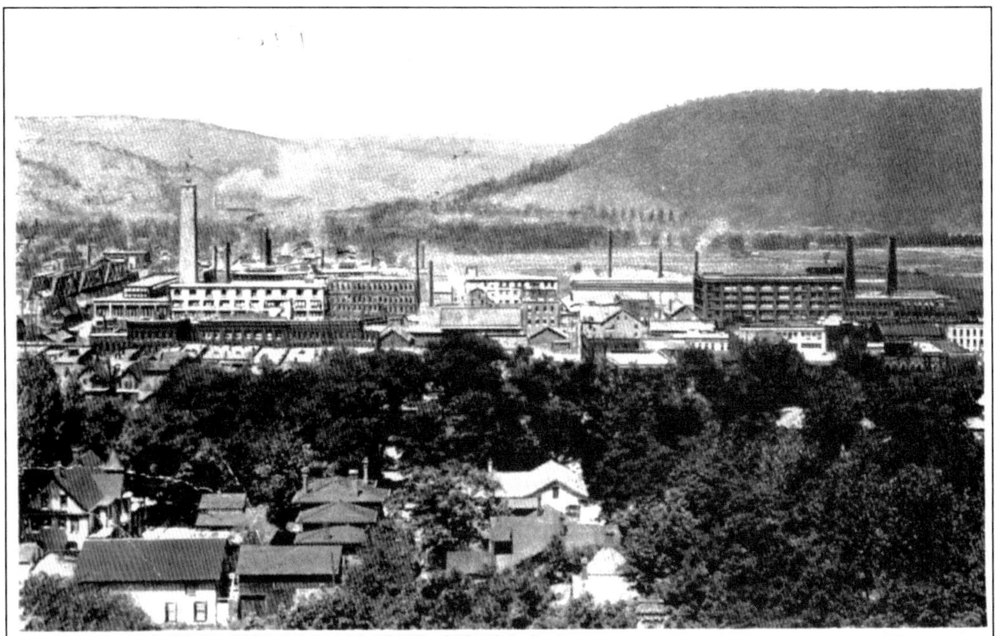

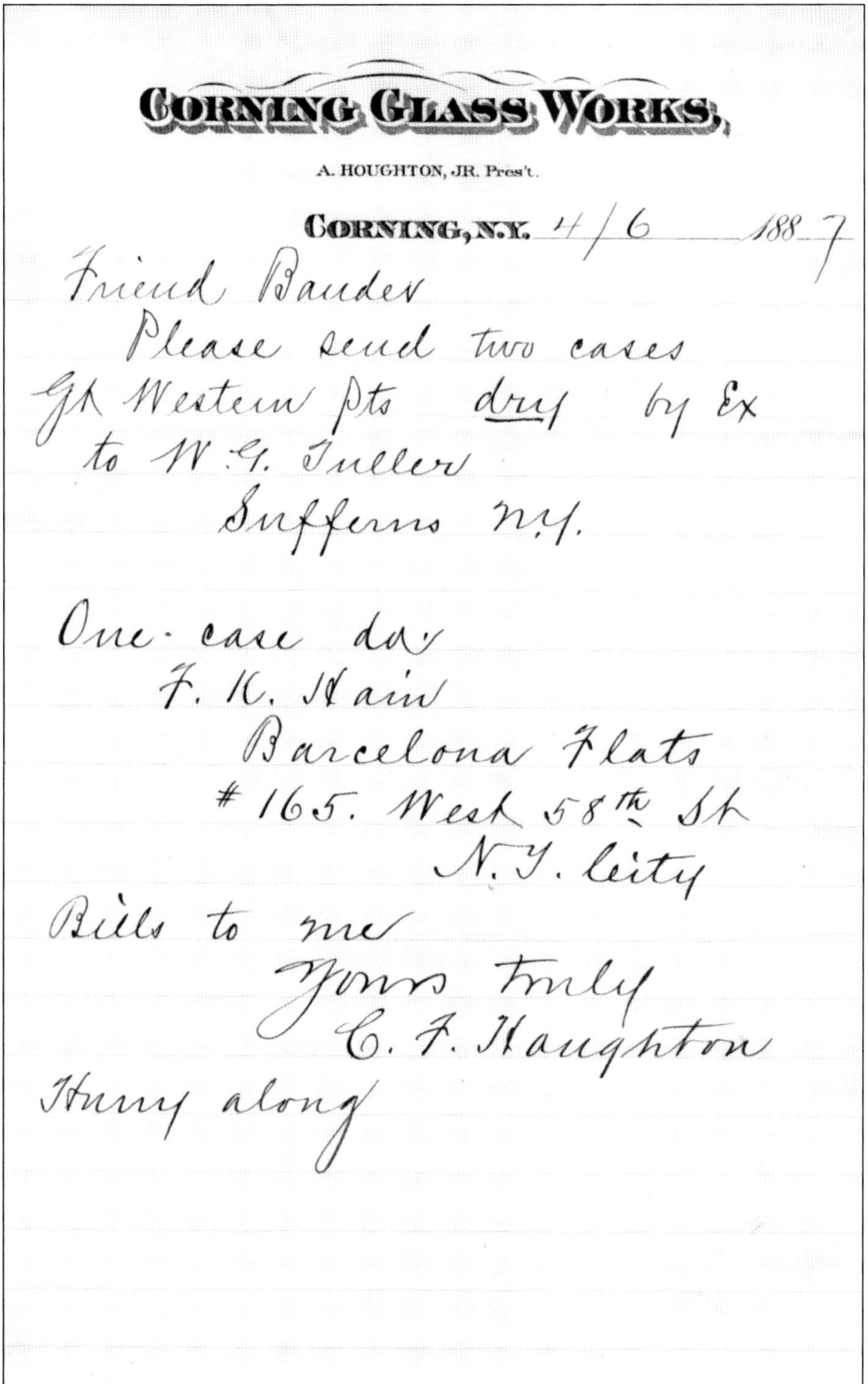
CORNING GLASS WORKS,

A. HOUGHTON, JR. Pres't.

CORNING, N.Y. 4/6 1887

Friend Bauder

Please send two cases
Gt Western Pts dry by Ex
to W. G. Fuller
Sufferns N.Y.

One case do
F. K. Hain
Barcelona Flats
#165. West 58th St
N.Y. City

Bills to me

Yours truly
C. F. Houghton

Hurry along

On this business letterhead from Corning Glass Works, a Houghton family member places an order for wine.

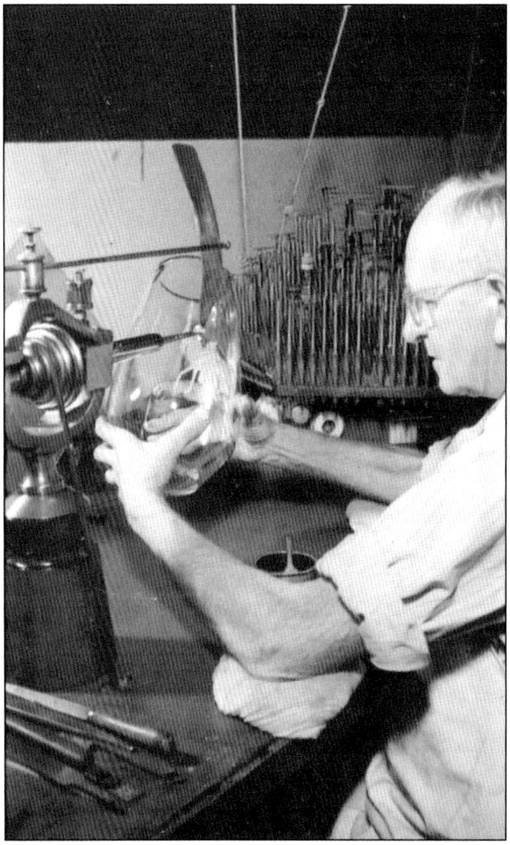

Joseph Libisch was a master at copper wheel glass engraving. This postcard shows him in 1947 making Steuben glass in the Corning glass center. In 1911, he came to New York, and within a week, he was working for H. P. Sinclaire in Corning. He was very involved with glass until he retired in 1956 at age 70.

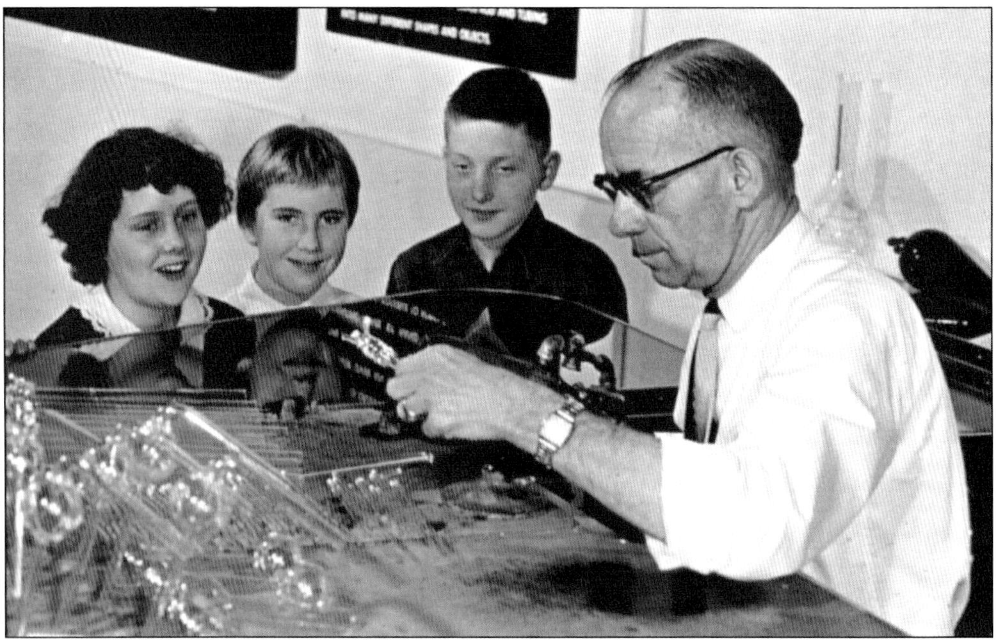

This is Pat Keeler. He put on a show in the glass center in the 1950s and 1960s. He heated glass tubes and bent them into lab ware and miniature glass animals.

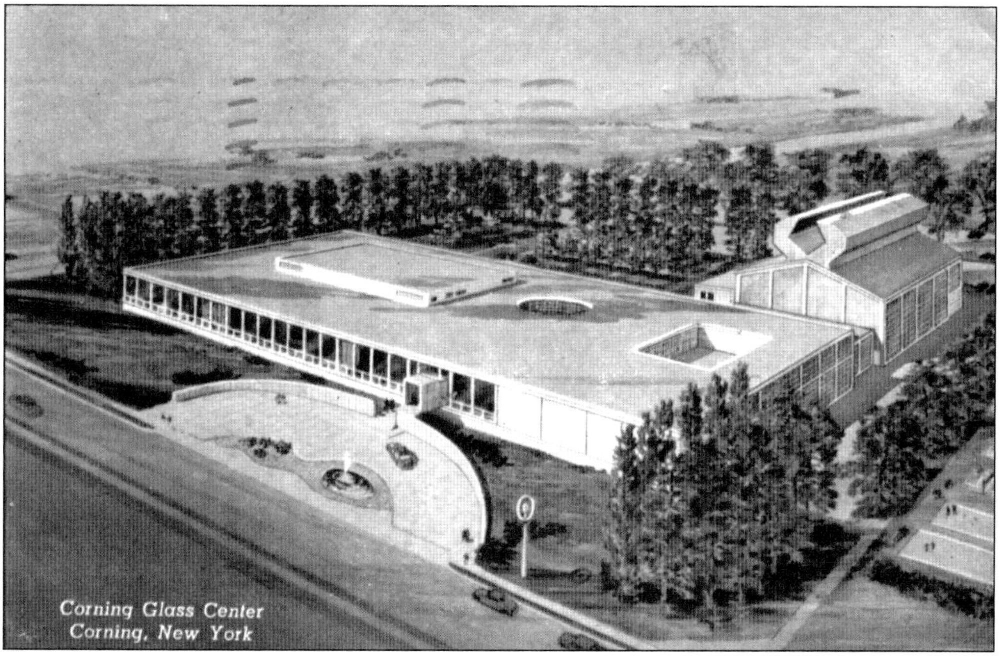

This postcard was mailed in 1951. The overhead view shows how the old street went in front of the glass center.

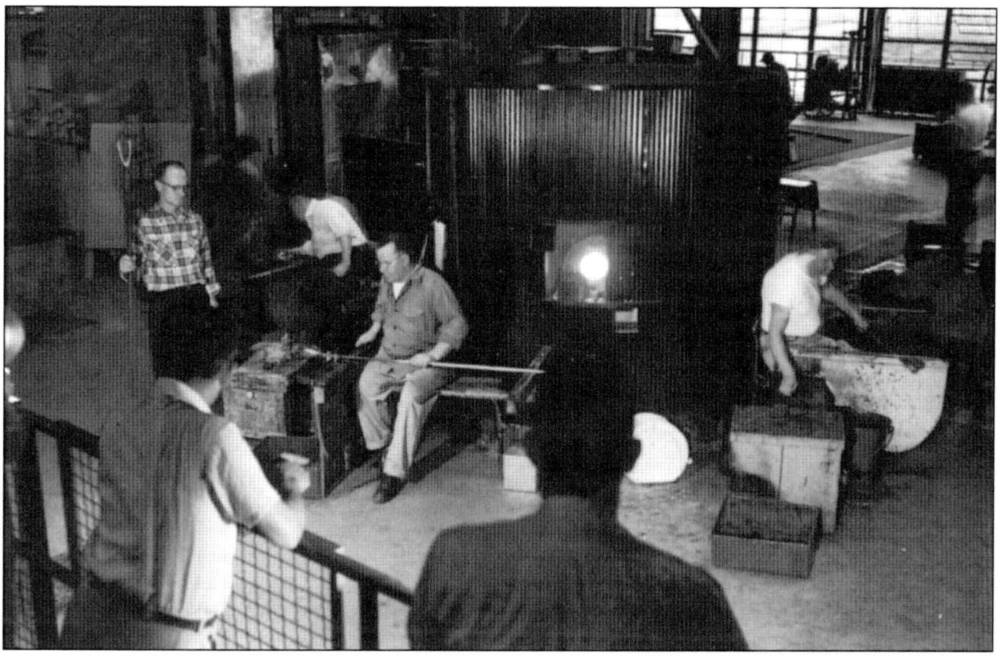

This was called the Steuben factory in the glass center. It shows master glass blowers making the artistic Steuben Crystal. People still visit today to watch the craftsmen.

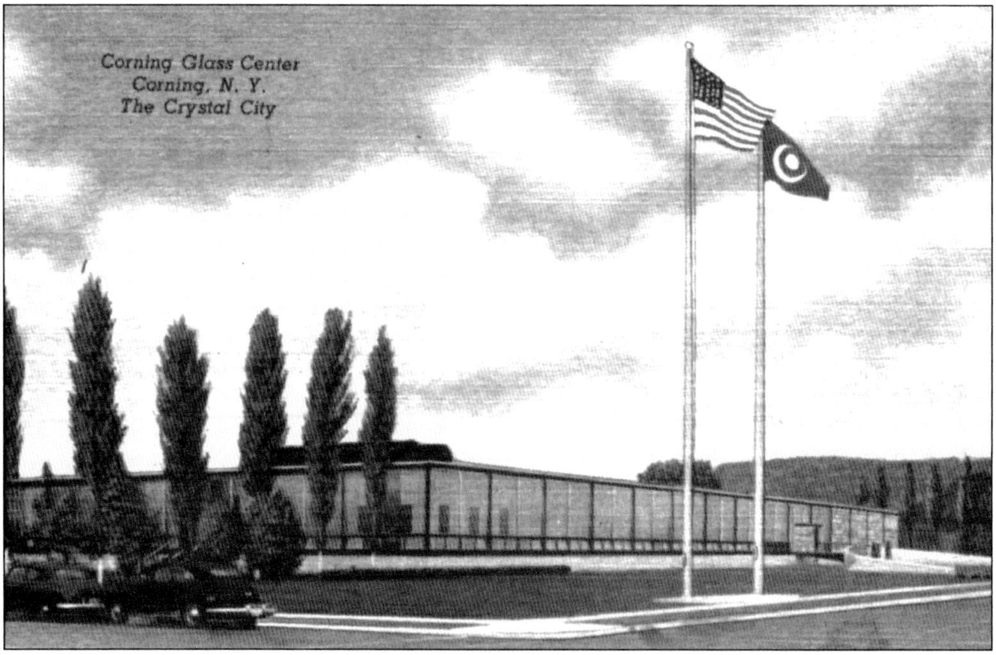

Sullivan Park was named after Eugene C. Sullivan, who lived from 1872 to 1962. He was called the dean of American glass research. He was the first full-time scientist of Corning Glass Works and was responsible for the development of heat-resistant glass. He trademarked Pyrex and was an inventor who held many patents.

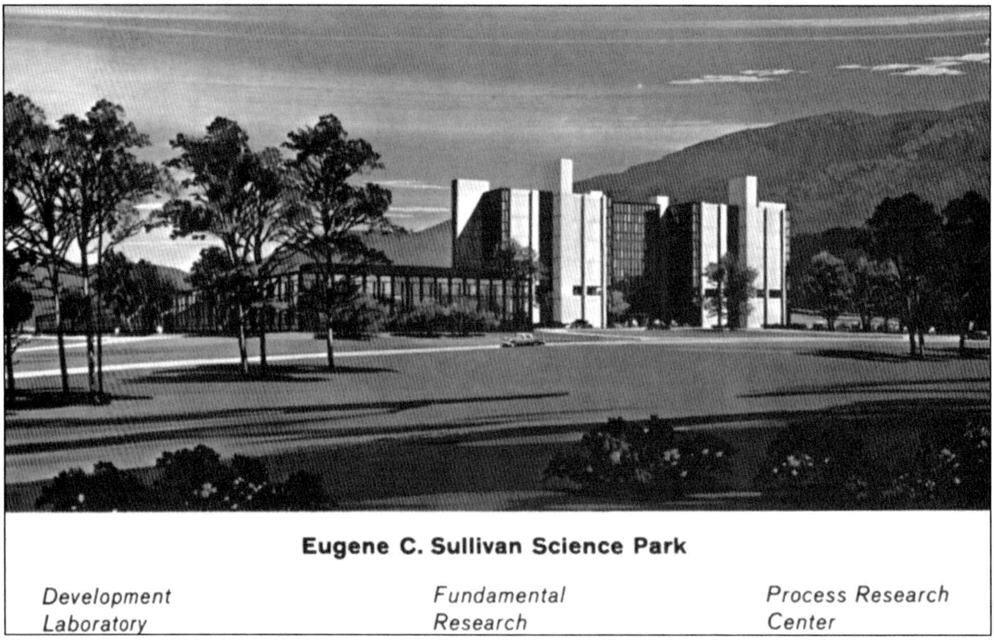

Eugene C. Sullivan Science Park

Development Laboratory — *Fundamental Research* — *Process Research Center*

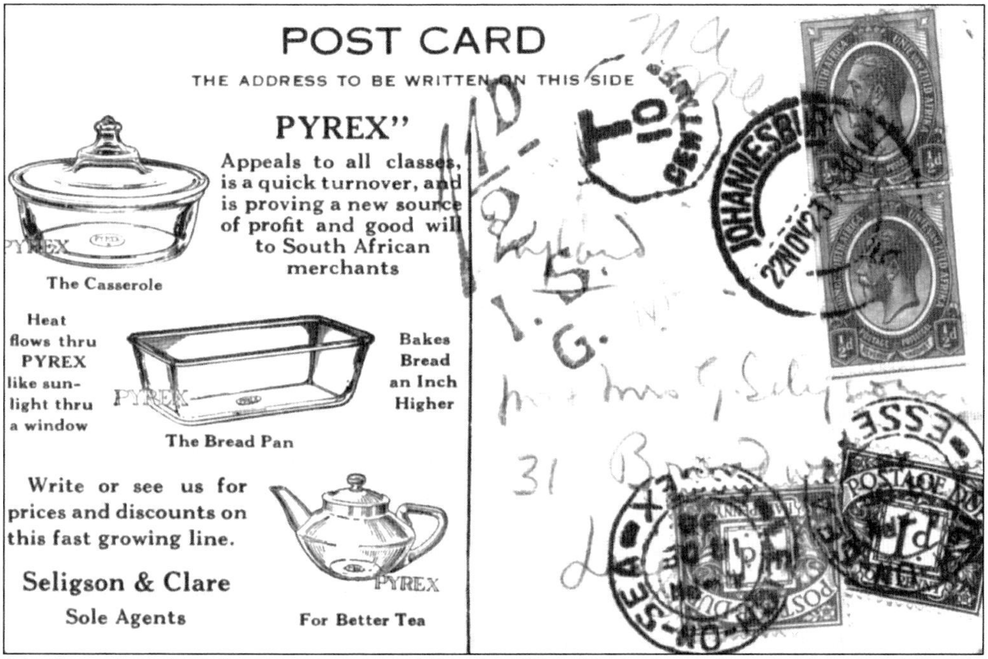

The Pyrex brand of glassware was one of Corning Glass Works best sellers. In the second decade of the 20th century, the notion of baking in glass was a whole new concept to the public. Corning was working on a plan. In 1915, a wondrous new line of "glass dishes for baking" appeared in the nation's hardware, department, and china stores. Pyrex later became the famous name that it is now.

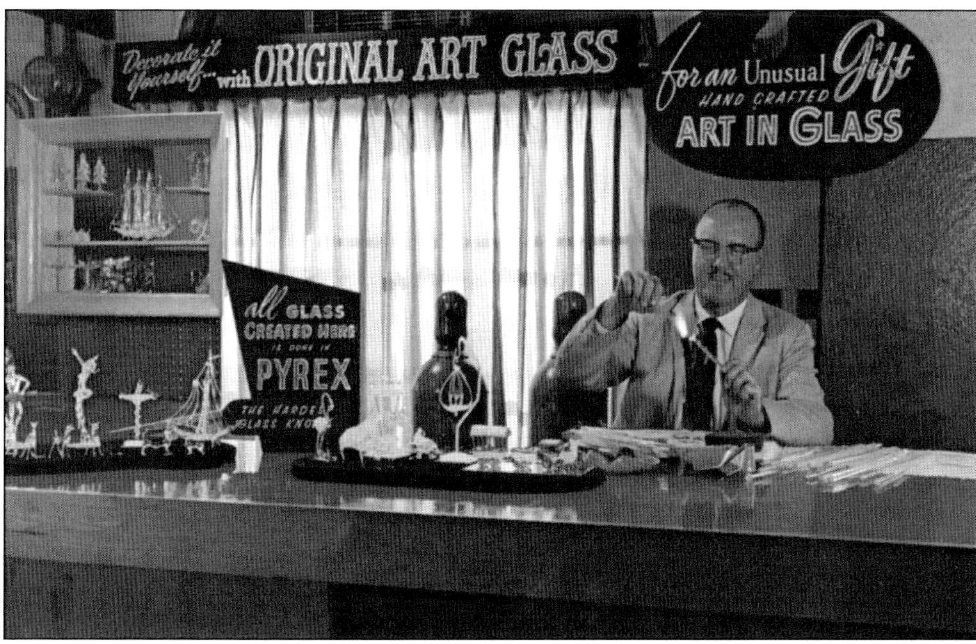

This is an advertising postcard for W. A. Triggs. He made objects of art out of Corning Glass Works Pyrex. The back of this mid-1950s postcard advertises that he makes "glass ships, bird cages ballerinas, merry go rounds and hundreds other creations."

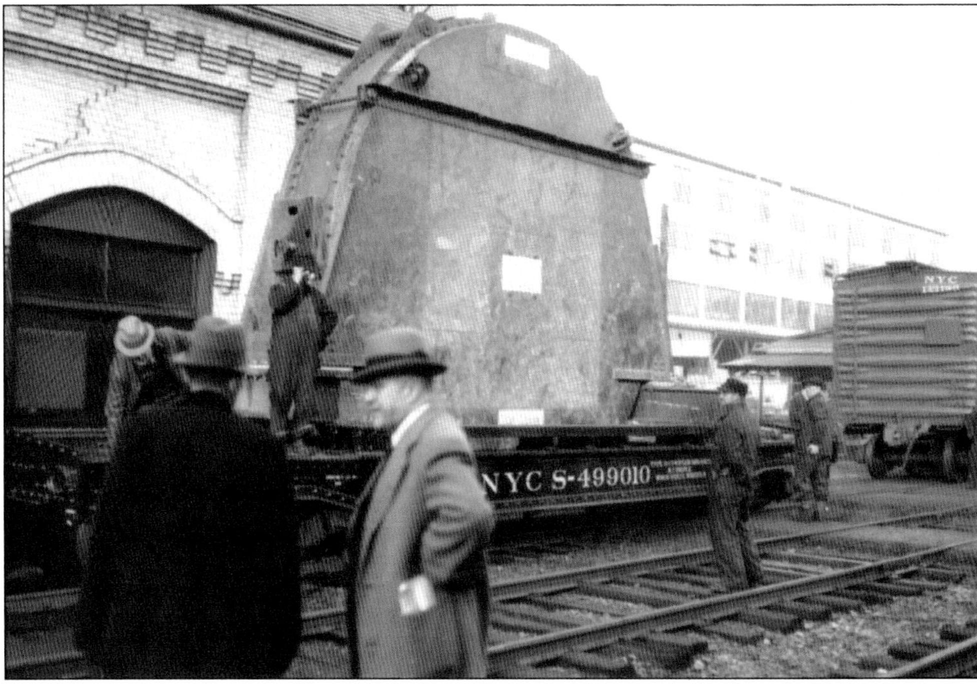

This photograph shows a disk being loaded onto the train that took it to be displayed at Pine Street Square on August 2, 1939. It was the first 200-inch Pyrex disk made for the Palomar telescope. It cracked and has been on display since 1939. The second disk is in the Palomar telescope, which is still in use.

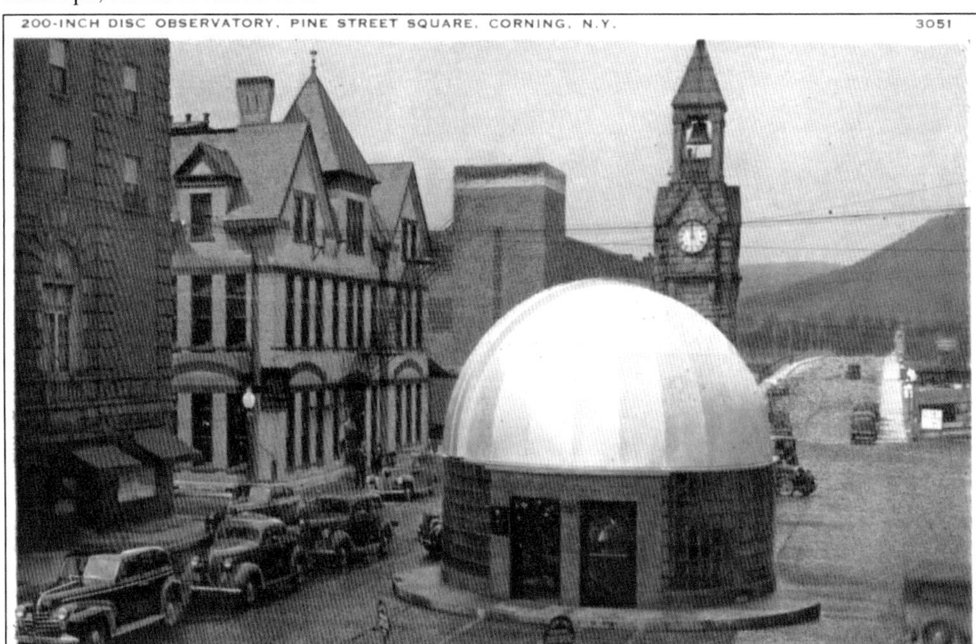

This postcard was mailed in 1943 to Pvt. Richard Peer of Company D, 35th Infantry Regiment, Platoon 3, at Camp Croft. Peer went on to fight in Europe and later was editor at the *Corning Evening Leader* and a local historian.

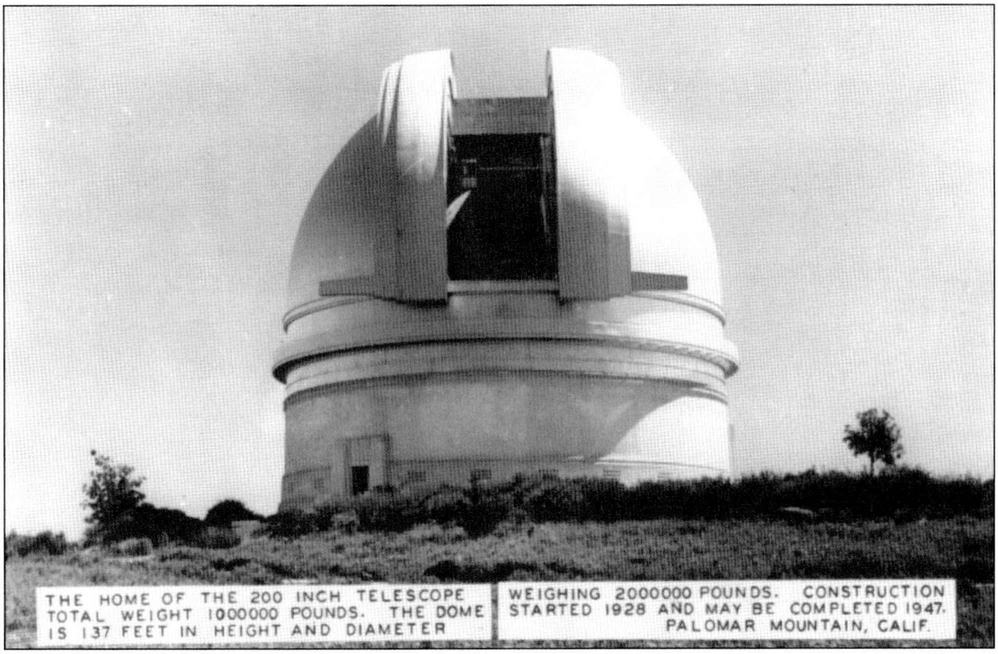

In Southern California, construction of a building to hold a telescope began in the 1930s but was delayed because of World War II. The building was finished on November 18, 1947. Corning's 200-inch disk finally made its way there that year and was in use in 1949. Mount Palomar is at 5,600 feet in San Diego County, California.

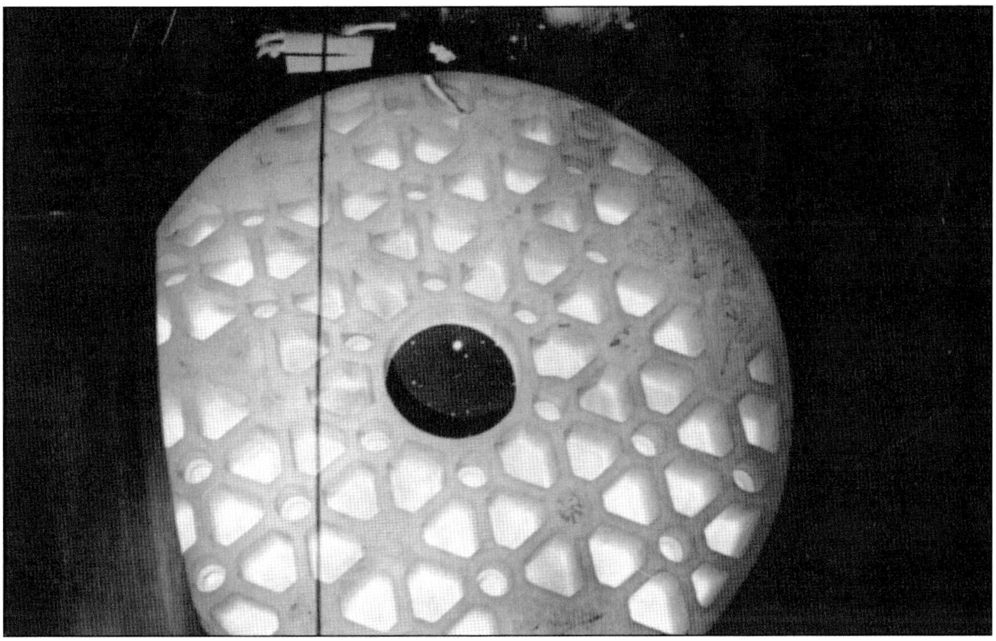

The first attempt to make the telescope disk failed when it cracked. This early try has been in the glass center since the 1950s. Today the facility is known as the Corning Museum of Glass.

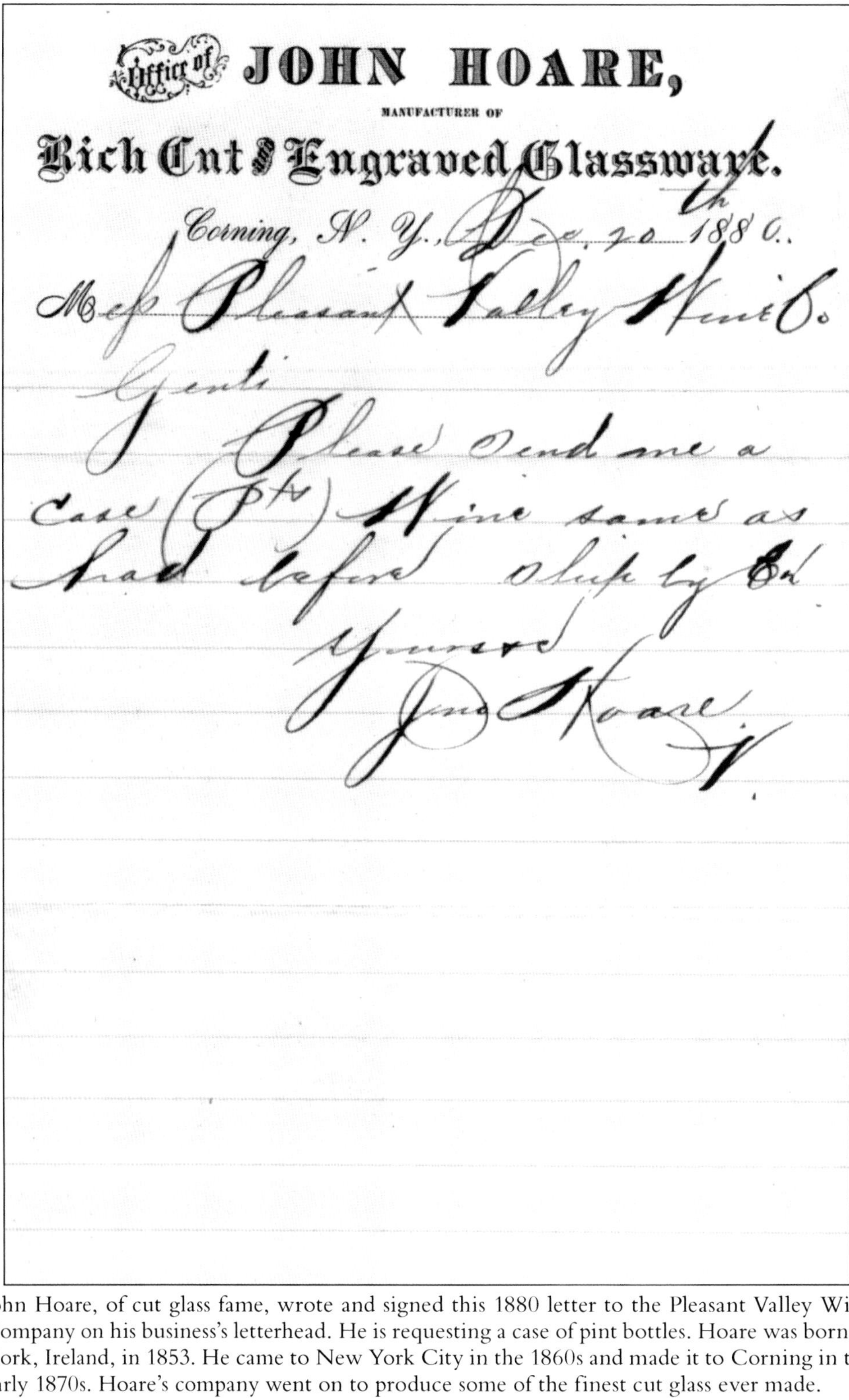
Office of JOHN HOARE,

MANUFACTURER OF

Rich Cut & Engraved Glassware.

Corning, N. Y., Dec. 20th 1880.

Mess Pleasant Valley Wine Co.

Gents

Please send me a case (Pts) Wine same as had before ship by Ex

Yours

Jno Hoare

John Hoare, of cut glass fame, wrote and signed this 1880 letter to the Pleasant Valley Wine Company on his business's letterhead. He is requesting a case of pint bottles. Hoare was born in Cork, Ireland, in 1853. He came to New York City in the 1860s and made it to Corning in the early 1870s. Hoare's company went on to produce some of the finest cut glass ever made.

Four

Market Street and around Town

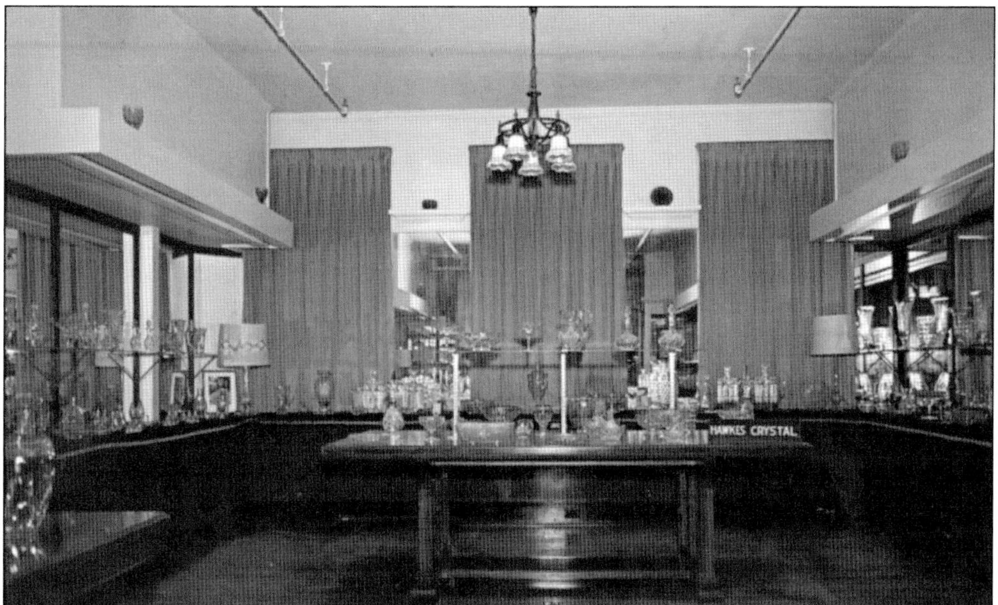

Thomas Gibbons Hawkes was born in 1846. He studied civil engineering for two years at Queens College in Cork, Ireland. In 1863, he left school and went to New York. He ended up in Corning working for Hoare. About 1880, he started his own business and in 1882 was granted his first patent in design. This 1960s postcard shows the interior of the Hawkes Company, which stayed open until the 1960s at 75–77 West Market Street.

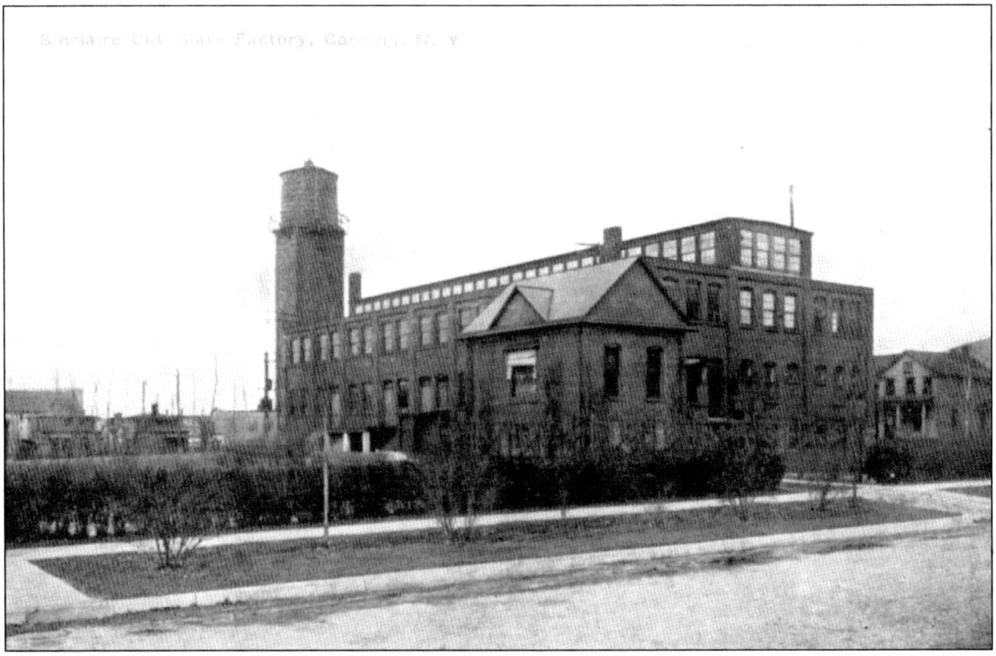

Harry (H. P.) Sinclaire was born in New York City in 1864. He moved with his family to Corning in 1868. He and his brother William went to Rochester Business University. Sinclaire went to work for Thomas Gibbons Hawkes in 1883 and learned everything about the cut glass business. Sinclaire and Company was located in a two-story brick building facing Cohocton Street on the northeast corner of Erie Avenue.

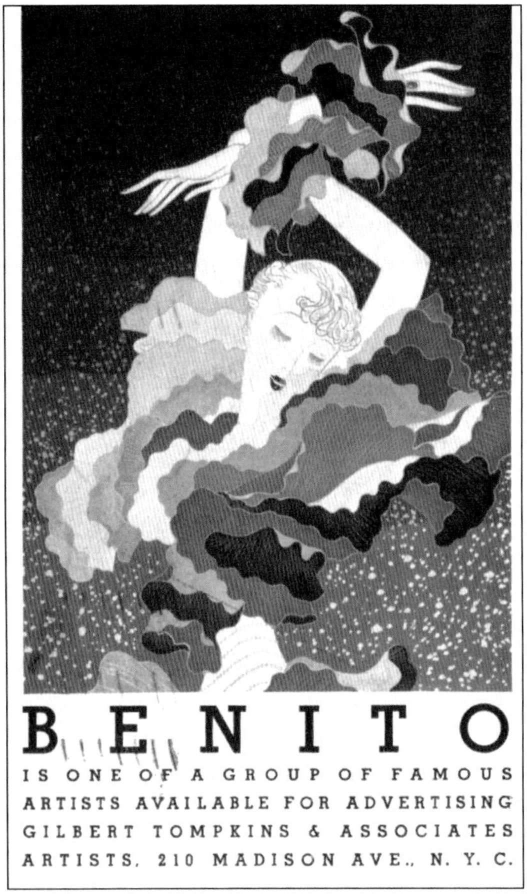

Edouard Garcia Benito (1892–1981) mailed this postcard to Fredrick Carder in 1934. Benito was a Spanish-born painter, engraver, and fashion illustrator. In the 1920s and early 1930s, he did the artwork for several covers of *Vogue* and *Vanity Fair* magazines, as well as some advertising posters.

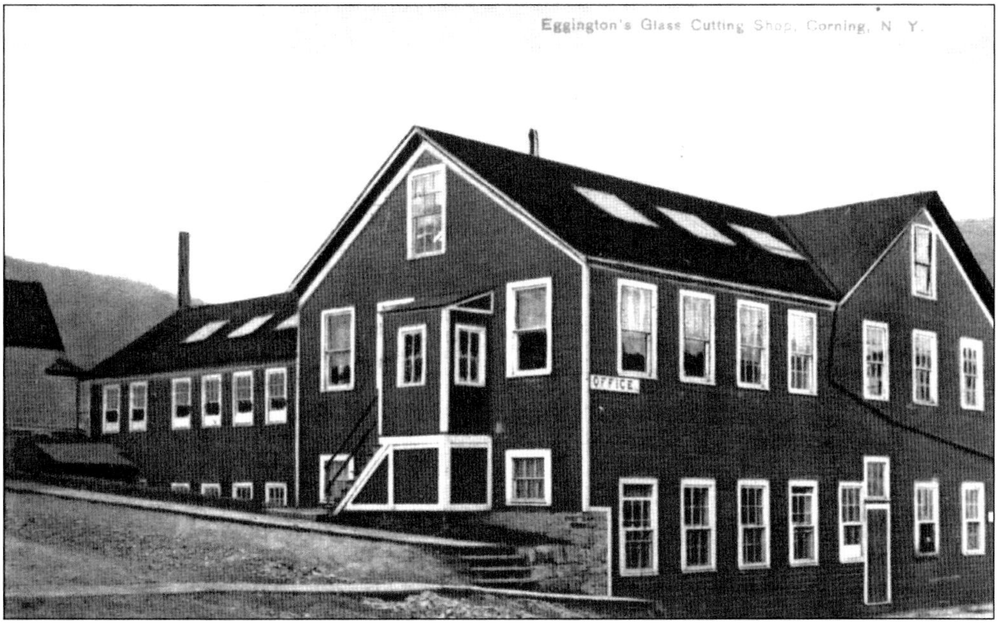

Oliver F. Eggington was born in 1822 in Birmingham, England. Before 1865, he worked as a cutter for Thomas Webb and Son. About 1873, he and his sons Joseph, age 20, and Walter, age 17, came to Corning. Eggington had a factory that opened in 1896 on Fifth Street. By 1898, business was doing great, and he employed 52 skilled hands. The business did well for many years, but by 1910, it started to falter. By February 1918, it was bankrupt.

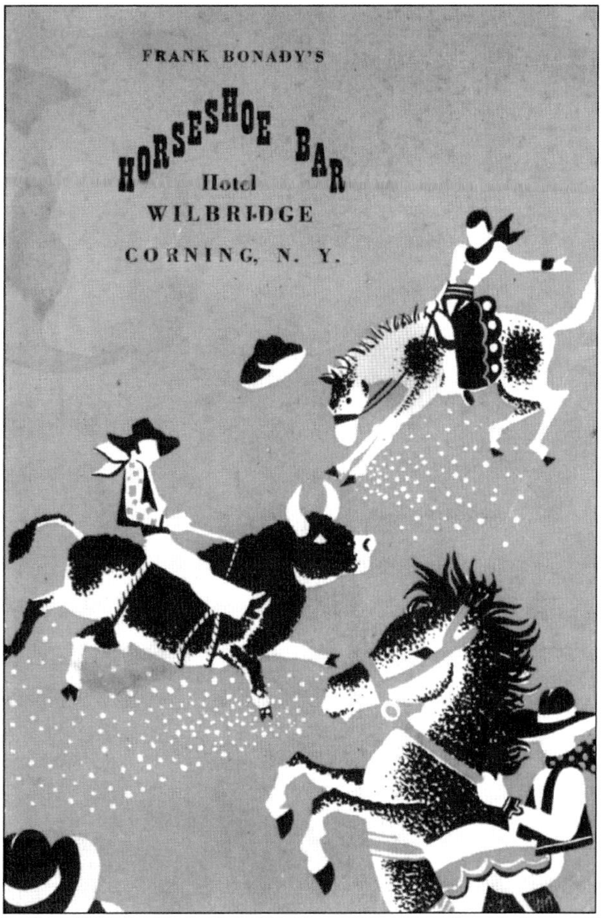

The Hotel Wilbride was on Bridge Street in the 1940s and 1950s. This is a menu from the restaurant and bar. Owner Frank Bonady also owned a fruit stand at another location.

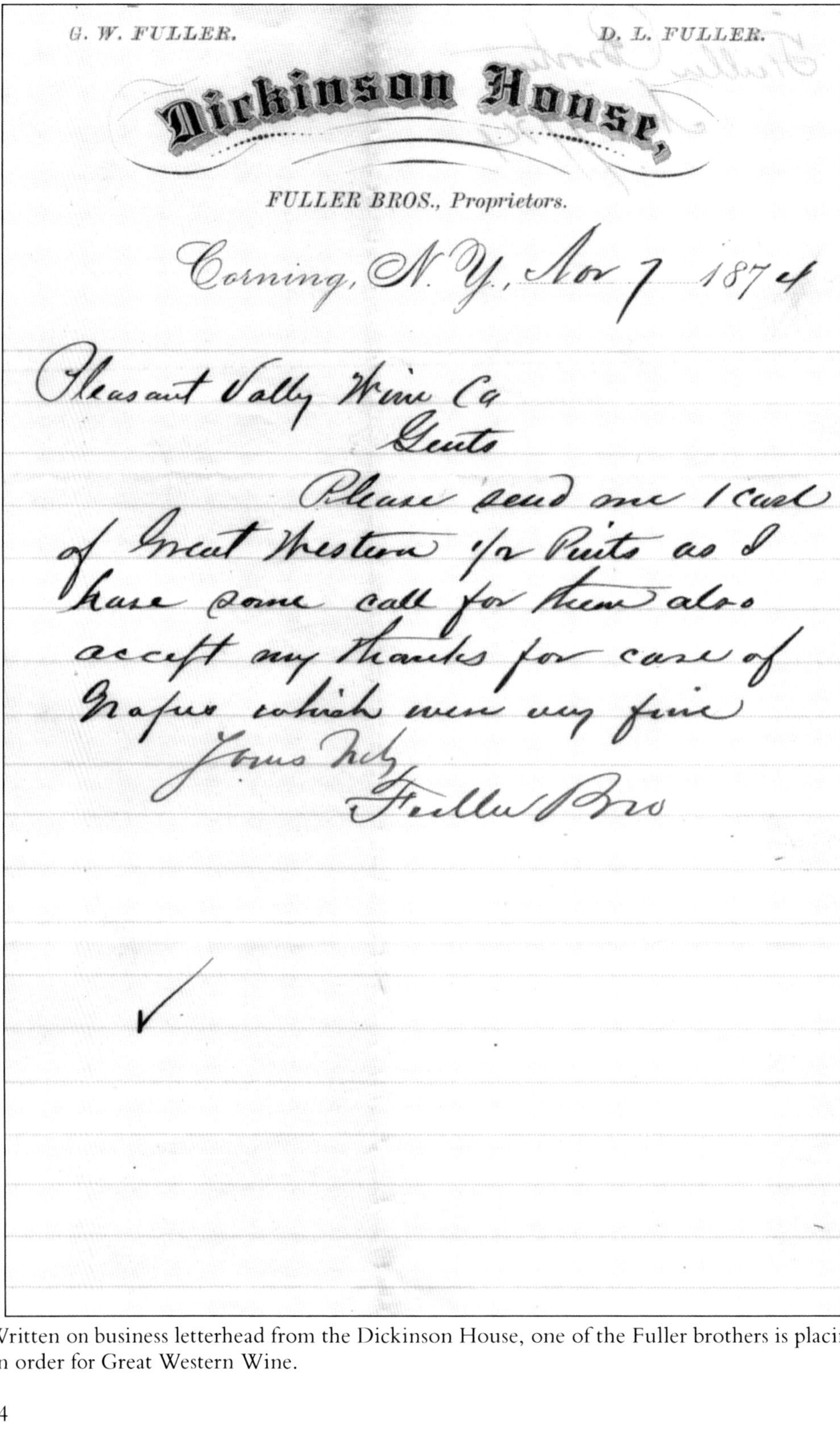
G. W. FULLER. D. L. FULLER.

Dickinson House,

FULLER BROS., Proprietors.

Corning, N.Y., Nov 7 1874

Pleasant Valley Wine Co

Gents

Please send me 1 case of Great Western 1/2 Pints as I have some call for them also accept my thanks for case of Grapes which were very fine

Yours Truly

Fuller Bros

Written on business letterhead from the Dickinson House, one of the Fuller brothers is placing an order for Great Western Wine.

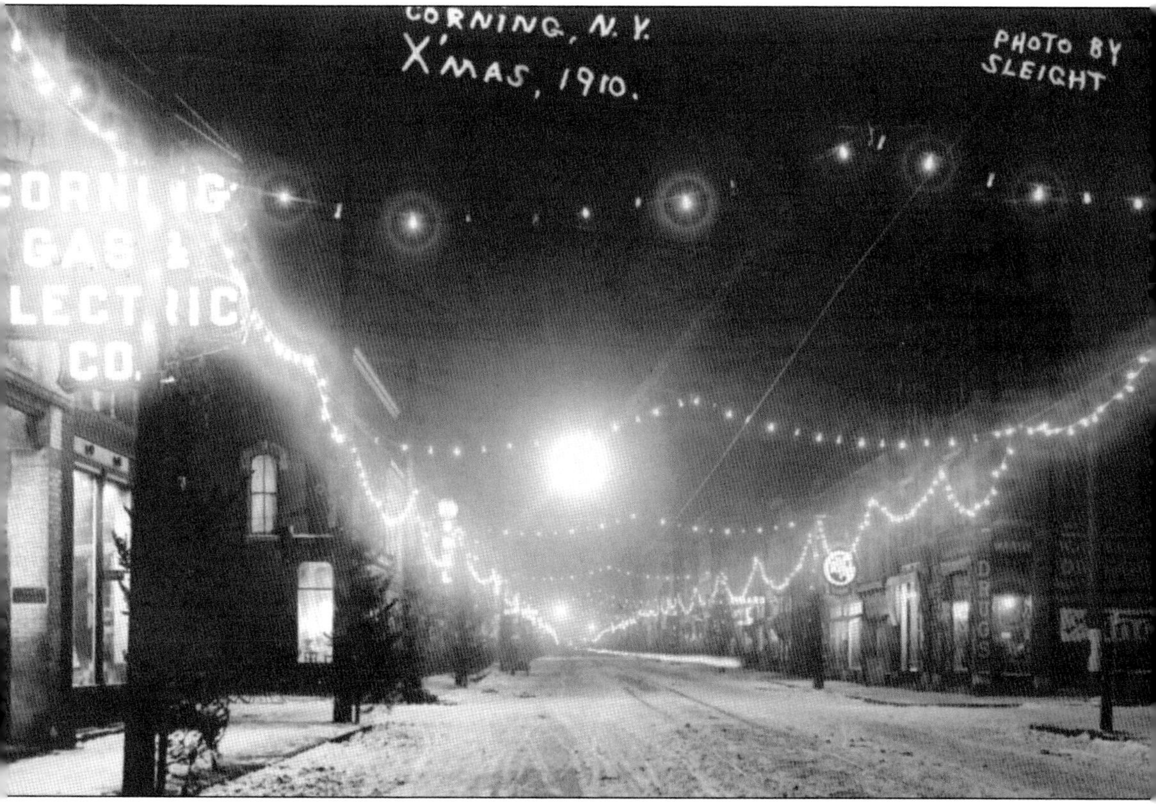

A photographer named Sleight left his name on this 1910 real photo postcard, which shows Market Street at Christmas. Corning Gas and Electric Company was at 54 East Market Street, and all these lights electrified Market Street. On the right side of the photograph is the drugstore of William Judson Marsh. The round sign a little farther down was for Carroll's Grill Room. (Courtesy of Diane Gardner.)

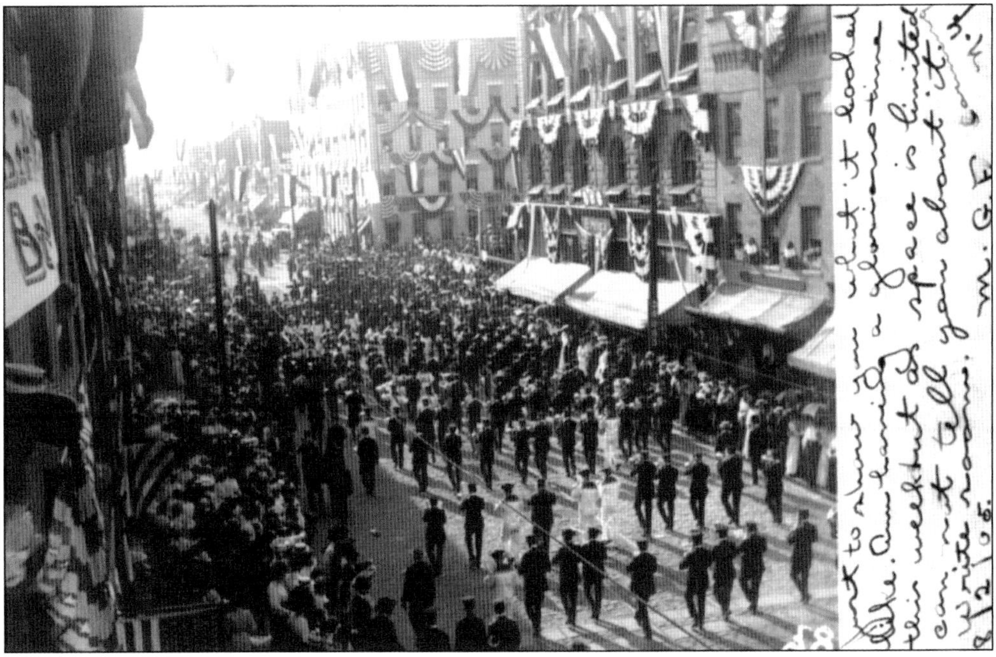

This is a parade on Market Street looking west. It was mailed on August 12, 1905. In the center of the photograph is the Dickinson House. Look at the flag on the lower left of the picture. It has 45 stars, which were on the flag from 1896, when Utah became a state, to 1908, when Oklahoma became the 46th state.

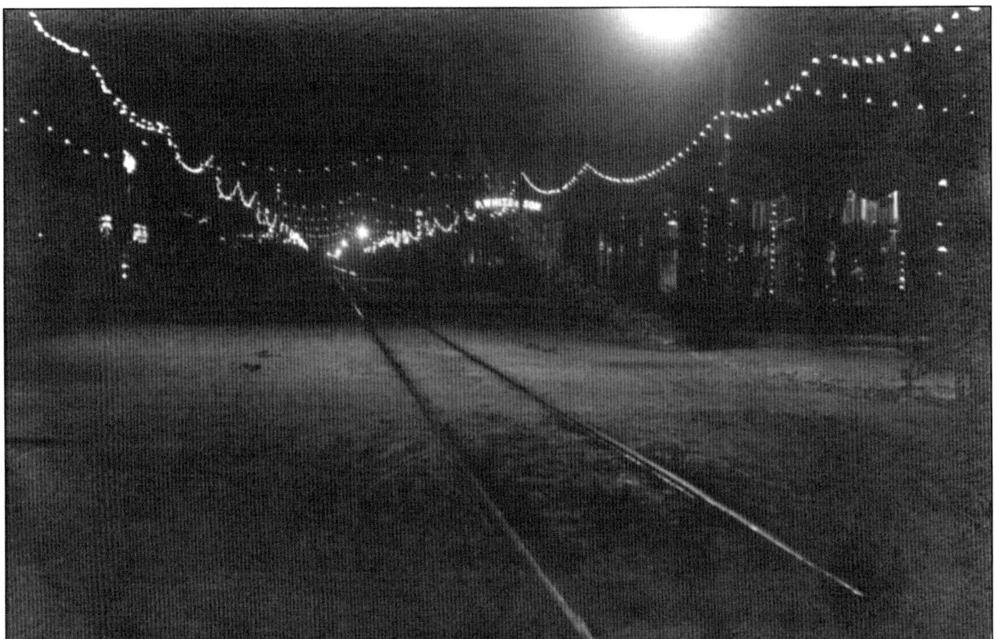

This postcard was mailed on Christmas Eve in 1910. On the right side of the street, a sign from P. White and Son can be seen. In the message from the sender are Christmas greetings.

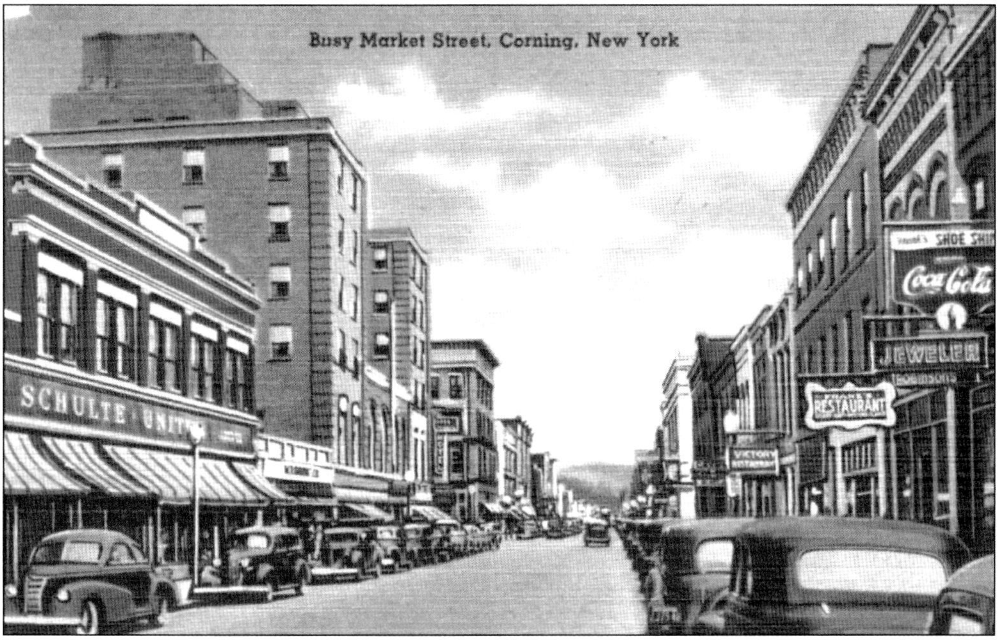

This view is from the 1940s. On the left side of the street is Schulte United, which advertised itself as Corning's Super Value Store. On the right side of the street above the Coca-Cola sign is a sign for Frank Avagliano, who shined shoes. Other businesses were Robinson Jewelers', Franz's Restaurant, and the Victory Restaurant.

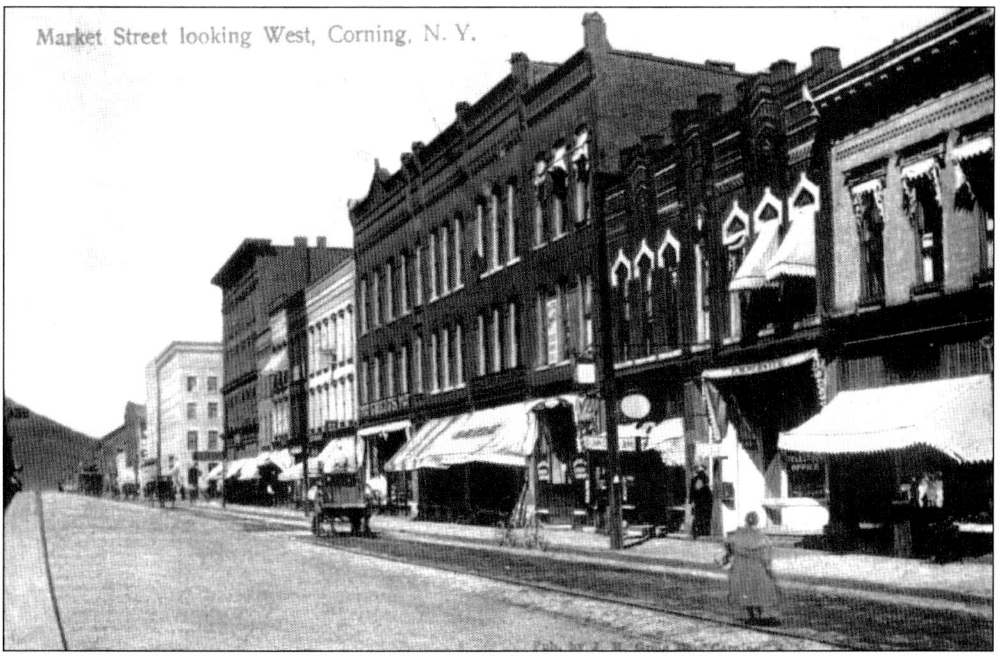

This postcard was mailed in 1912. The four-story-high Dickinson House can be seen down the road. The building with two white awnings is 33 East First Street.

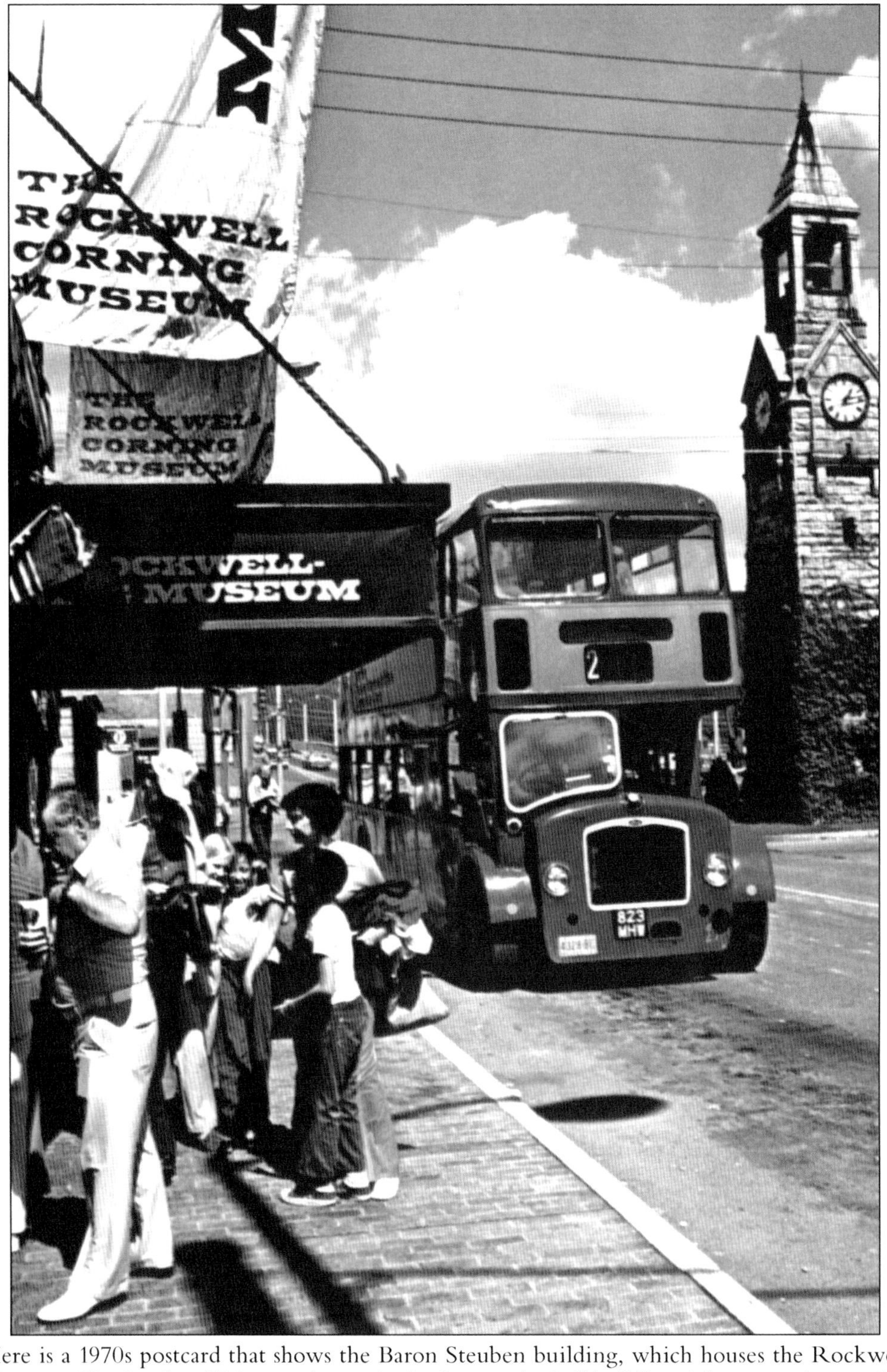

Here is a 1970s postcard that shows the Baron Steuben building, which houses the Rockwell Museum. The Rockwell Museum is now in the former city hall building. It has a very interesting collection of historic items and art. Here the old Pine Street bridge keeps going, meaning the other bridge was not built yet.

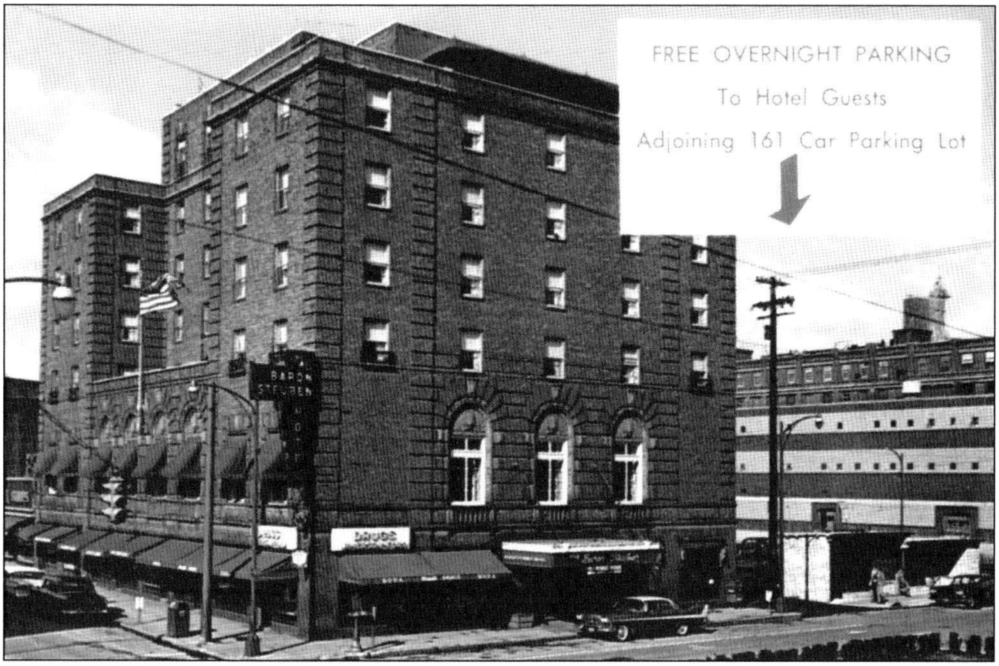

The Baron Steuben Hotel was one of the area's finest hotels from the 1930s to the mid-1970s, when it closed. It had 100 rooms, air-conditioning, a coffee shop, a lounge bar, and a dining room called the Emerald Room. A 1950 advertisement lists rates at $3 for singles and $5 for doubles.

GOVERNOR DEWEY

GUEST OF HONOR

At the Dinner Given to Members of the Republican County Committee of Steuben County

Baron Steuben Hotel, Corning, N. Y.

Friday, Nov. 16, 1945, 6:45 p. m.

Complimentary . . . Admit One

Your acceptance MUST be sent to Chairman Geo. A. King, Corning, N. Y., NOT LATER than Nov. 14

The Baron Steuben Hotel had many interesting visitors. This is an invitation card for when Gov. Thomas E. Dewey visited Corning in 1945. Dewey gained national attention as a prosecutor into the investigation of organized crime. Dewey later became a three-term New York State governor from 1943 to 1954.

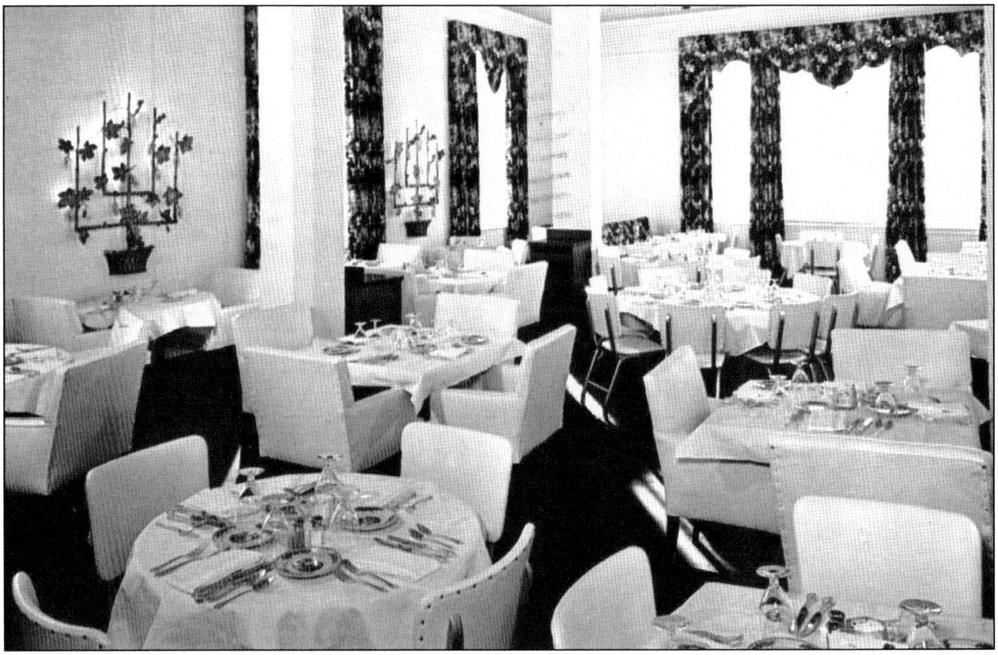

The Baron Steuben Hotel had rooms with air-conditioning, television, and free overnight parking. The vintner's room featured fine wines from nearby Finger Lakes wineries.

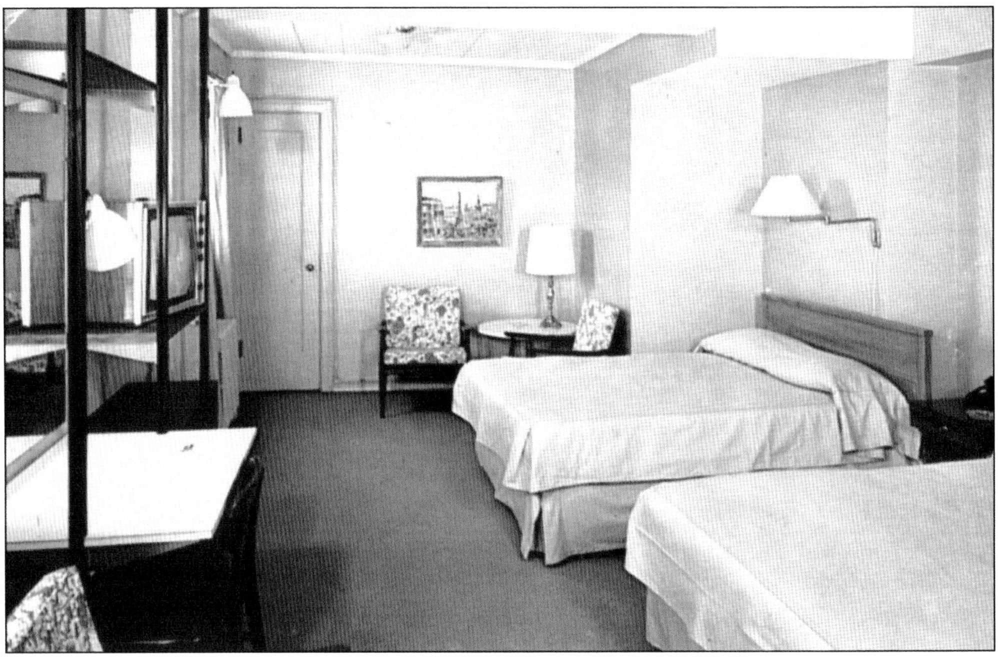

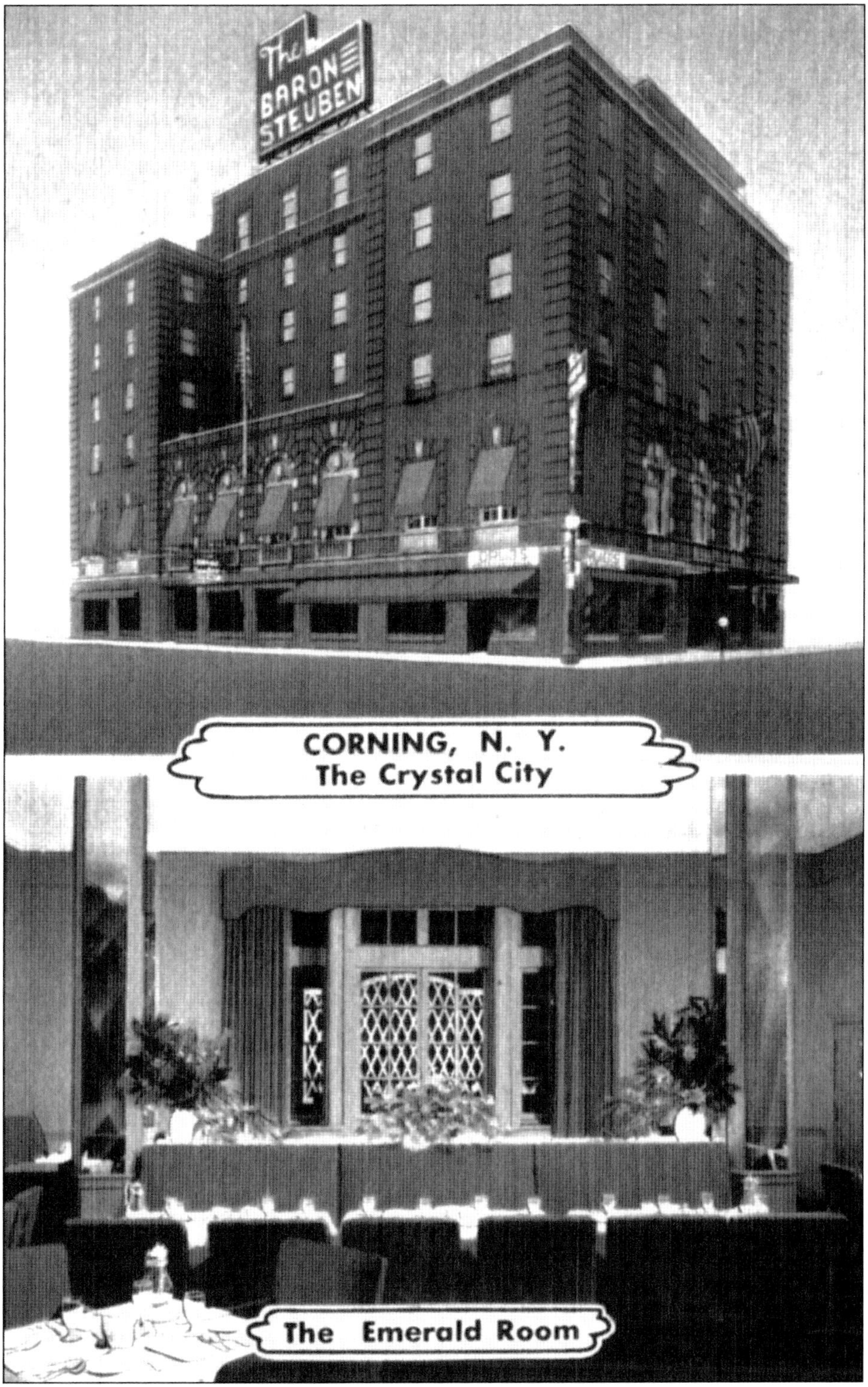

This 1950s multi-view postcard shows the exterior and interior of the Baron Steuben Hotel. It was mailed in 1951 and in the message the sender talks about visiting the glass center.

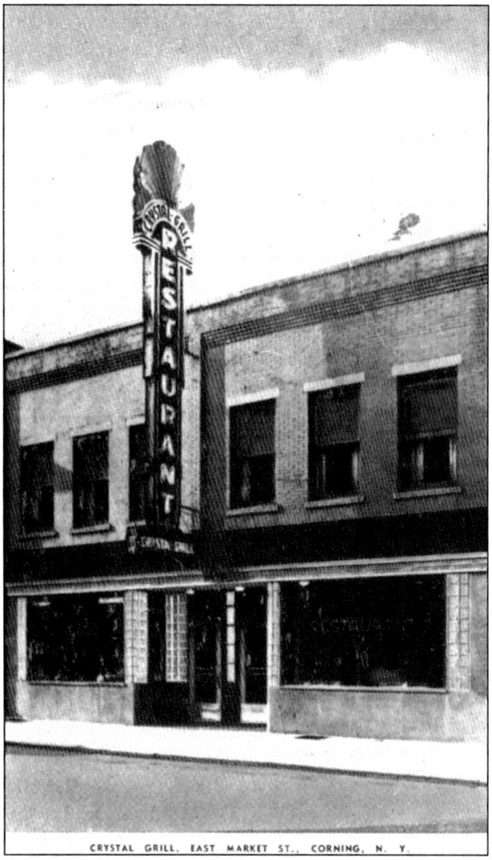

The Crystal Grill was at 63–65 East Market Street. The establishment went through several owners over the years, including Percy W. Ross and Fred Carpenter (1936), Lula Ross (1947), Marion Coughery (1952), and Milton Ebersale (1953). In the early 1900s, Corning had many restaurants for a city of its size. The 1936 Corning city directory lists 62 restaurants. The postcard was mailed in 1942 to radio station WENY, which is still on the air. During the week of December 12, 1937, customers who spent 25¢ or more got a ticket (below) for a chance to win a $5 prize. This ticket was good for eight chances.

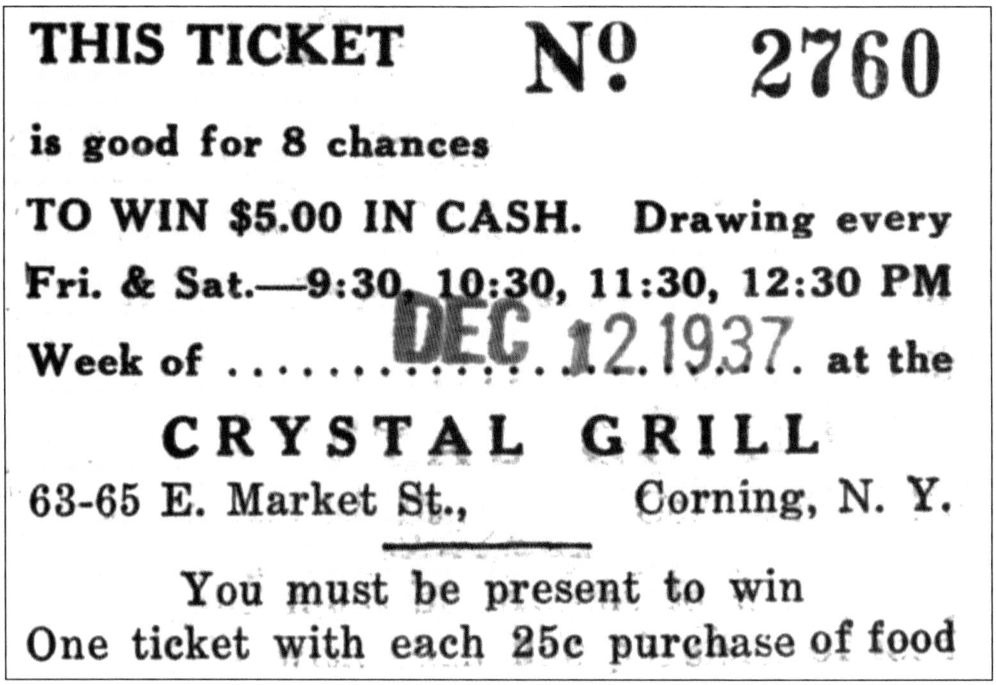

THIS TICKET **Nº 2760**

is good for 8 chances

TO WIN $5.00 IN CASH. Drawing every

Fri. & Sat.—9:30, 10:30, 11:30, 12:30 PM

Week of ....DEC 12.1937. **at the**

CRYSTAL GRILL

63-65 E. Market St., Corning, N. Y.

You must be present to win

One ticket with each 25c purchase of food

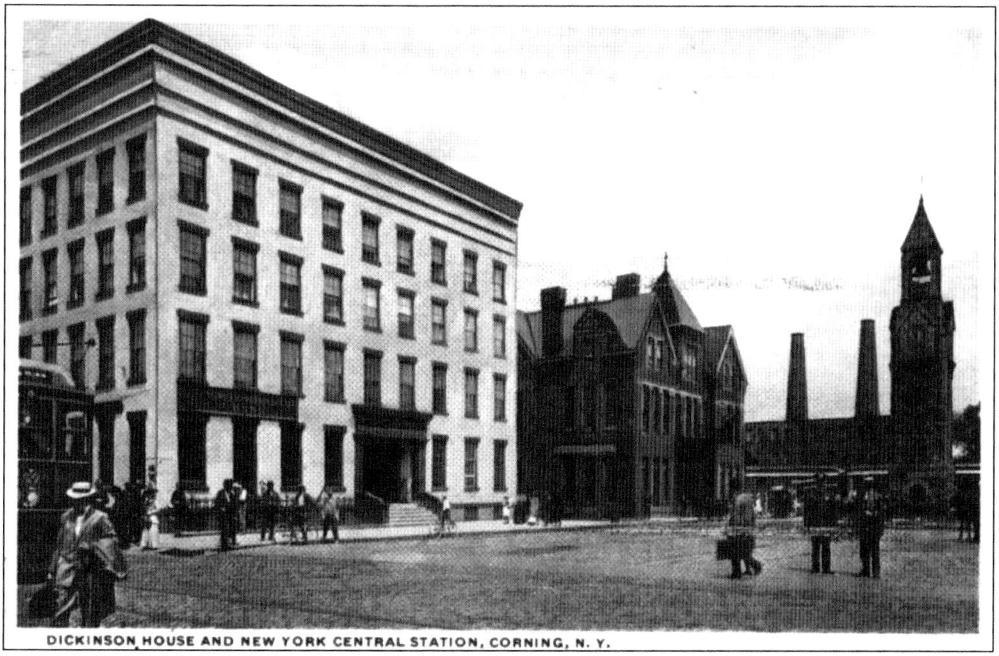

The Dickinson House was at the sight where the Baron Steuben Hotel later stood. The building was constructed by Andrew B. Dickinson and Col. H. W. Bostwick. Standing tall at four stories high, the Dickinson House opened in 1851. In 1865, George W. Fuller became proprietor of the hotel. In 1904, extensive improvements were made.

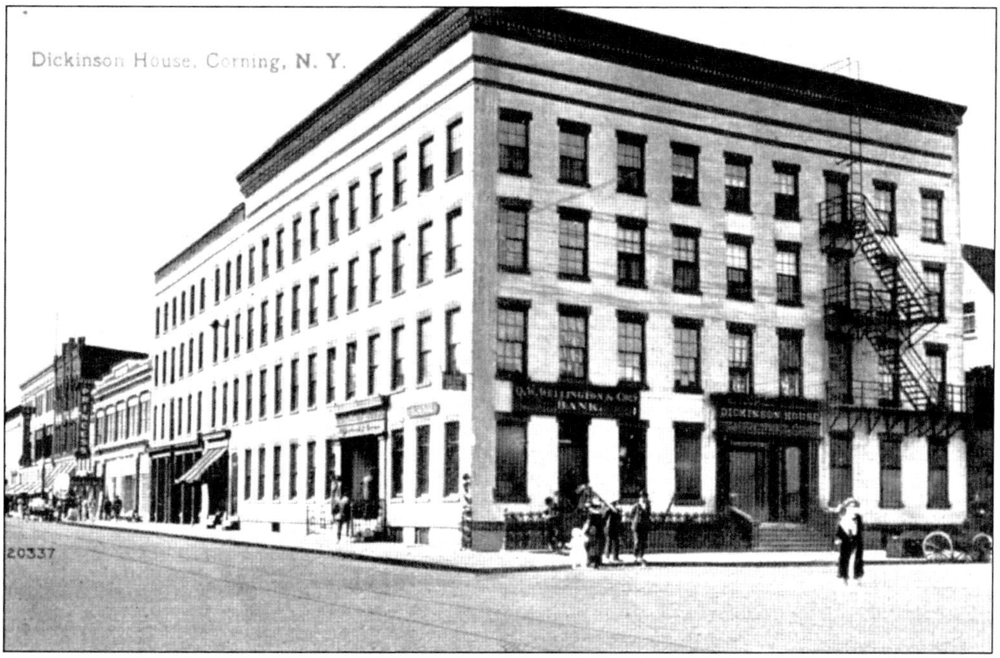

This postcard shows where the Dickinson House was located near Pine Street Square. It was close to the railroad station too.

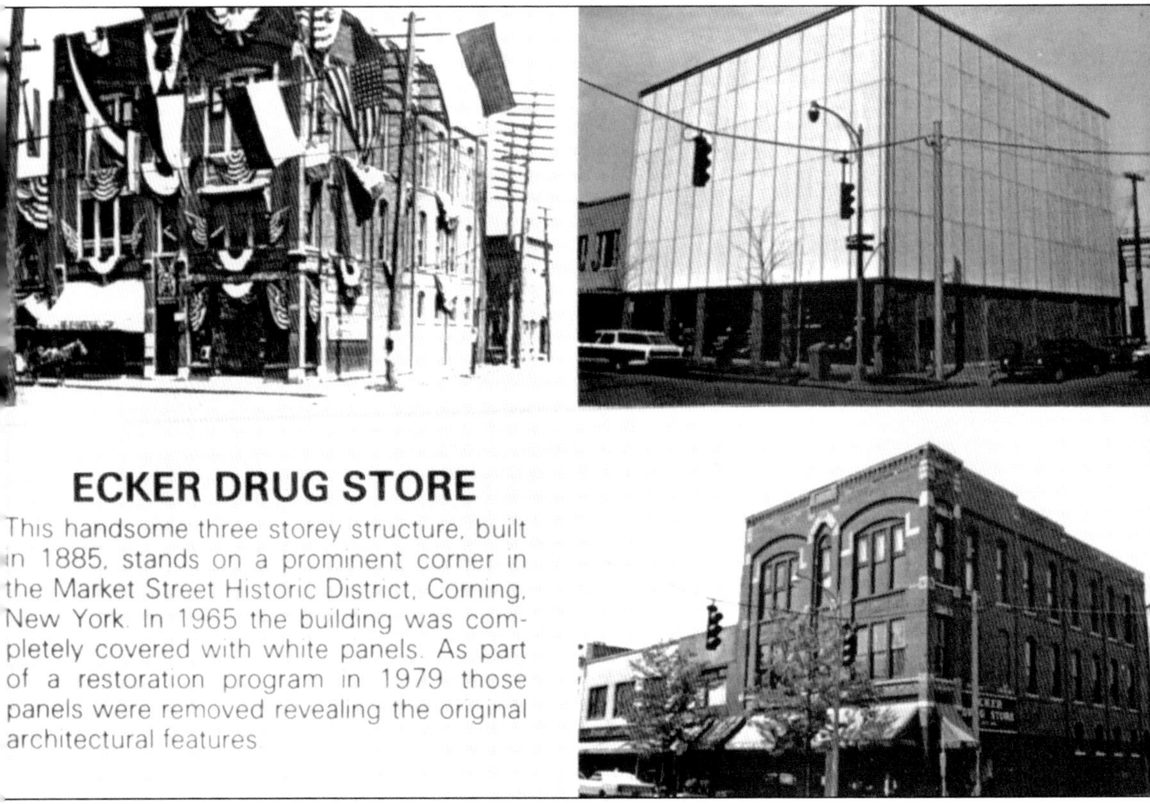

The Ecker Drugstore was the longest resident of this building, which was constructed in 1885. It was started, owned, and operated by Harry B. Ecker in the second decade of the 20th century. A store with the name Ecker's was here until the 1990s. This 1980s postcard shows three different views of the building. Its architect, E. B Gregory from Elmira, left his name in a stone near the corner. Today an office supply store is on the bottom floor.

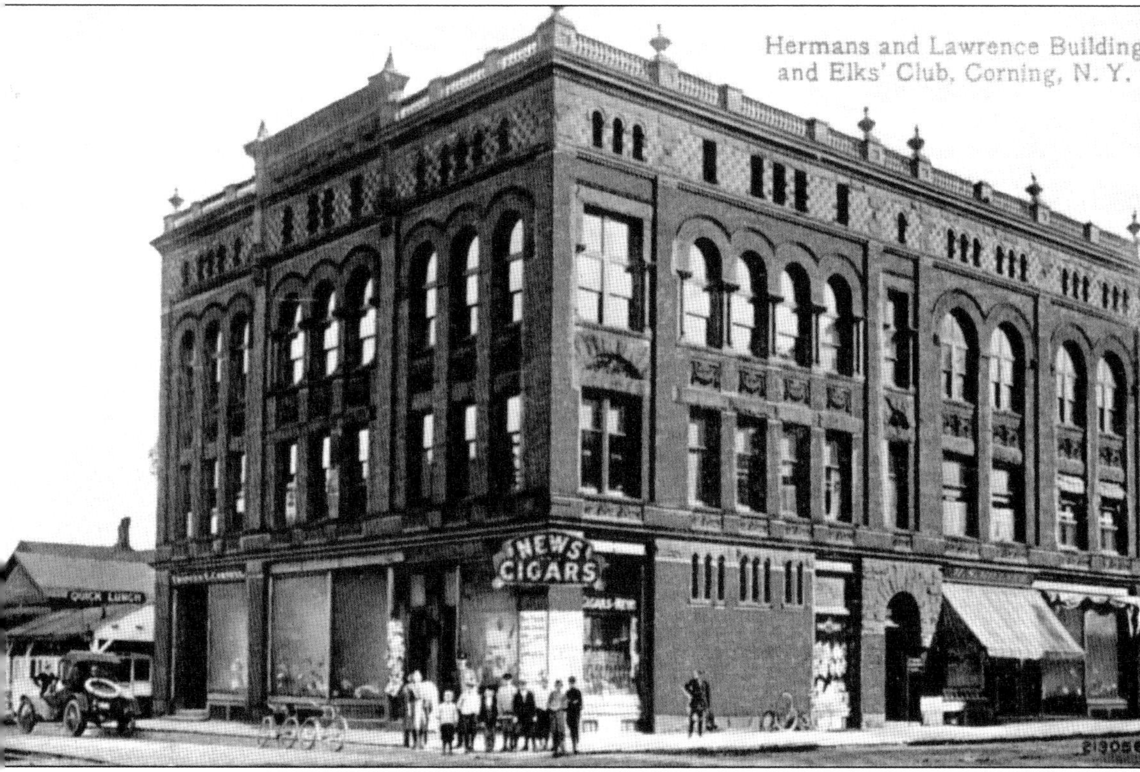

This building was named after H. C. Heermans and Thomas Lawrence. They were civil engineers who did things like run the Corning Water Works. The Elks club was in this building until 1916. The upstairs was used as office space by doctors, lawyers, insurance firms, and other businesses.

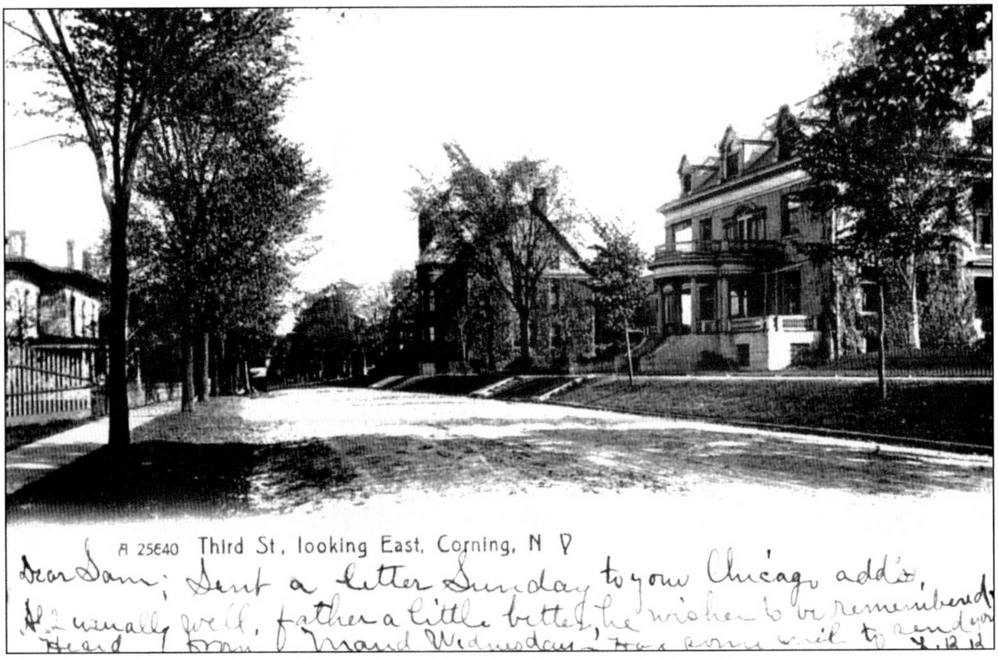

Here are two views of Third Street. The College Center of the Finger Lakes is now in the building on the right, which was once home to Arthur A. Houghton Jr. Looking east, the house of H. P. Sinclaire can be seen. The houses across the street are where Corning Free Academy is now.

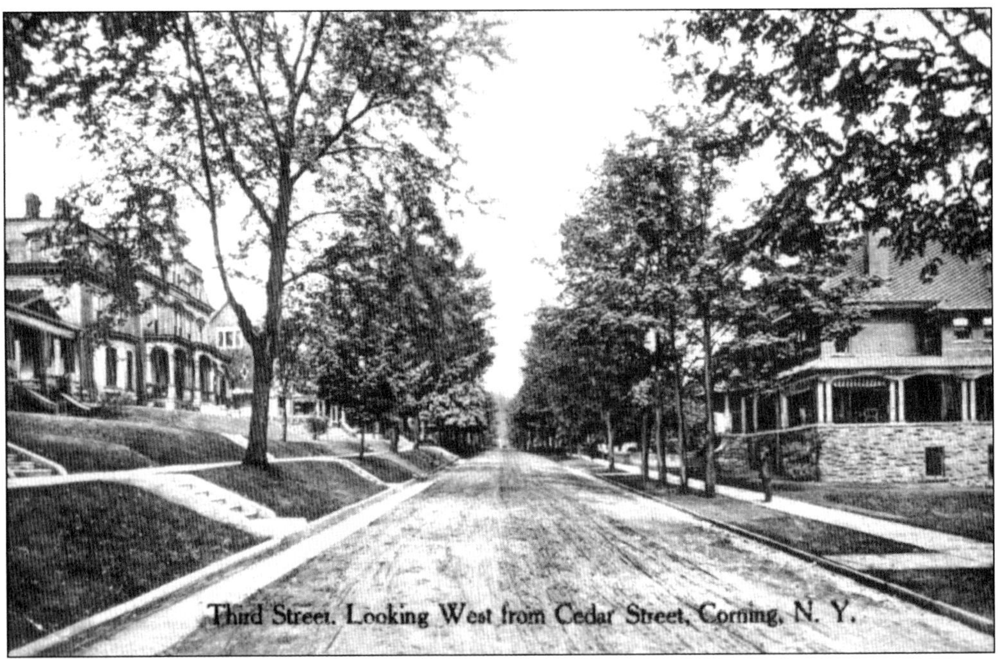

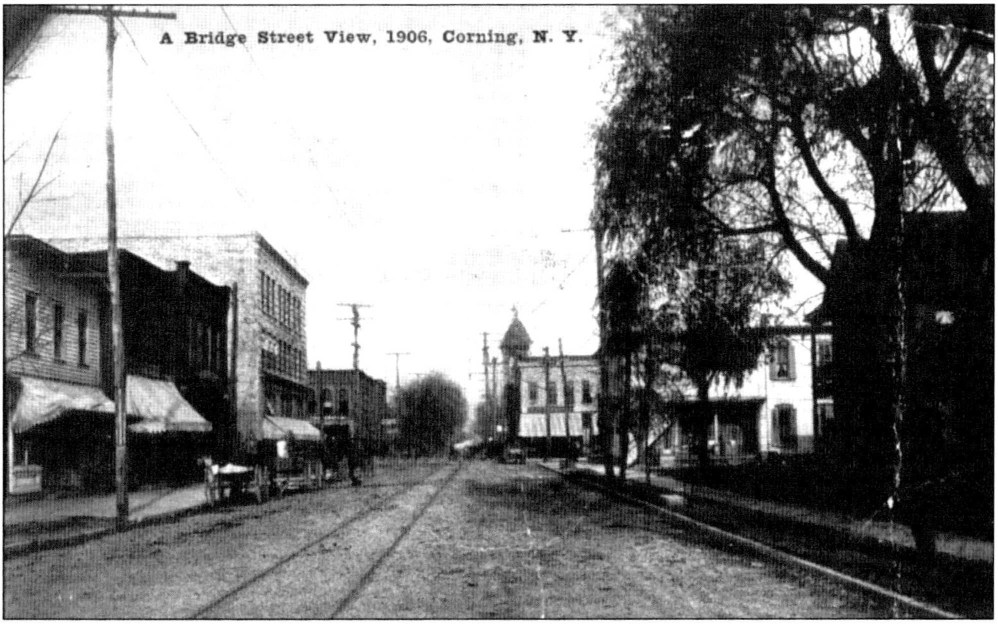

The First Congregational Church can be seen on the right side of Bridge Street. Terbells's drugstore is in front of that. On the left side of Bridge Street on the corner is the building that became the T.O.P. bar. Before that is the Wing and Bostwick Company store building.

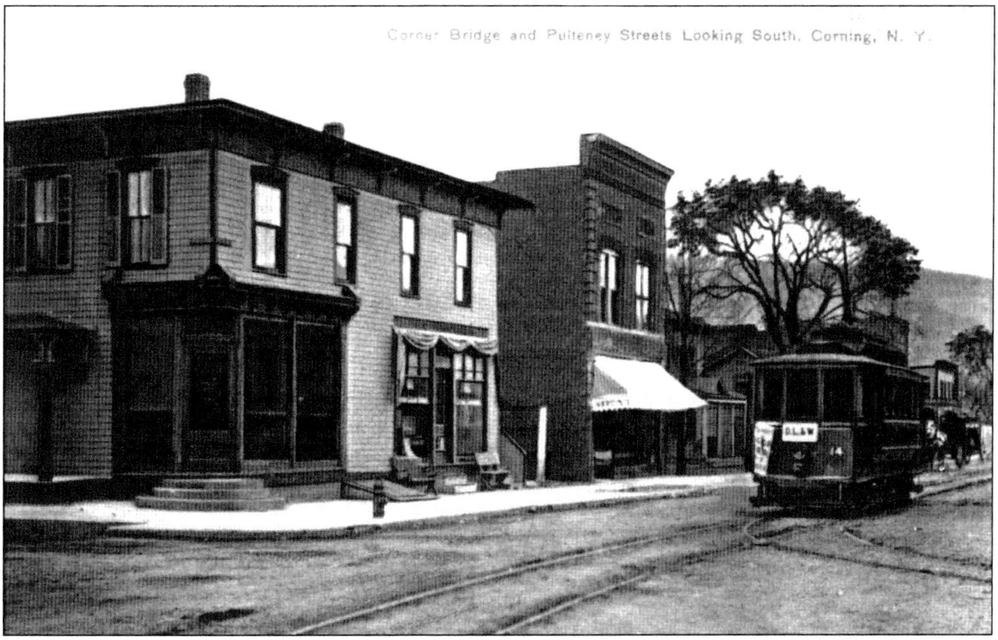

The corner building at 96 Bridge Street was the site of a private bank called North Side Banking and probably had three apartments in it. The brick structure next to the corner building was the home of Clarence G. Palmer's meat market at 80 Bridge Street. The word "meat" is barley visible on the edge of the awning. This building is not on the 1906 Bridge Street postcard at the top of the page because it was made a few years after that. These two buildings were torn down in the mid-1940s to make way for an Atlantic gasoline station on the corner.

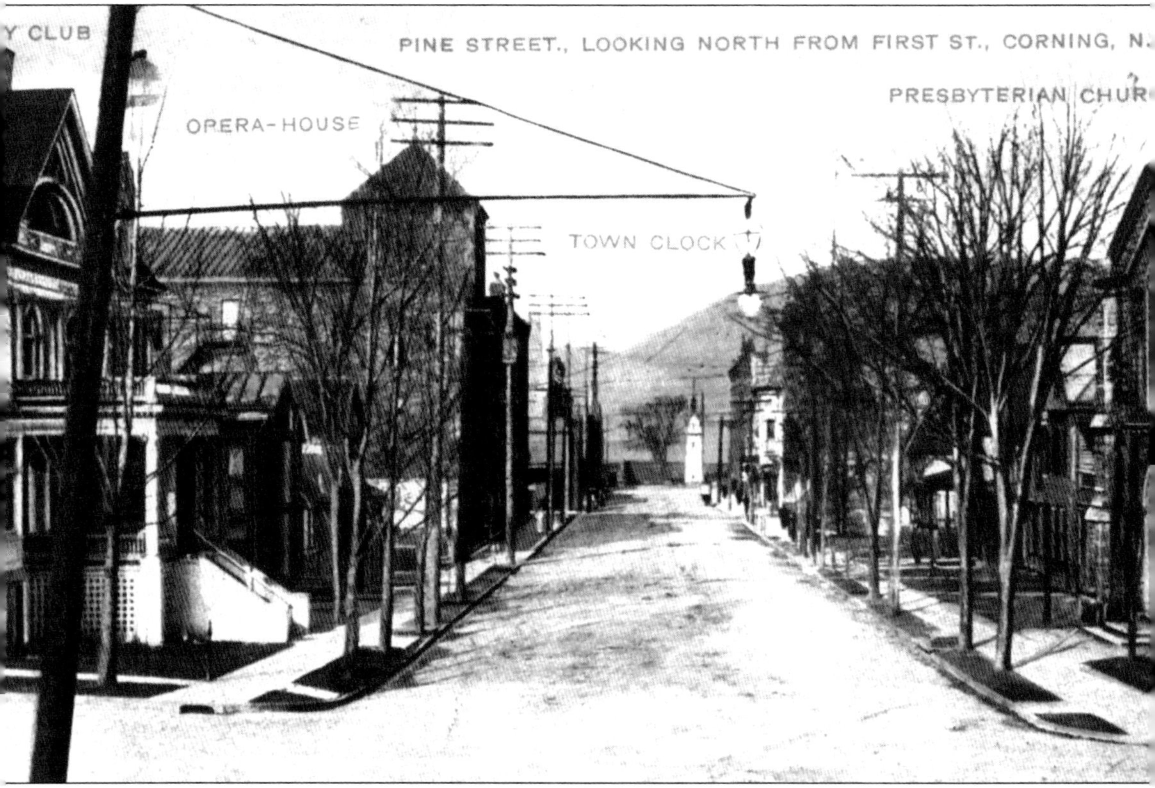

This postcard has landmarks of Corning labeled. It was mailed from the New York and Salamanca Railroad post office. It has the RPO (railroad post office) cancel date of April 20, 1908. RPO cars (also known as mail or postal cars) were equipped and staffed to sort, cancel, and drop off in-town mail. In spots where the cars did not stop, they grabbed mail bags with a special hooked tool that had a long handle as the train went by.

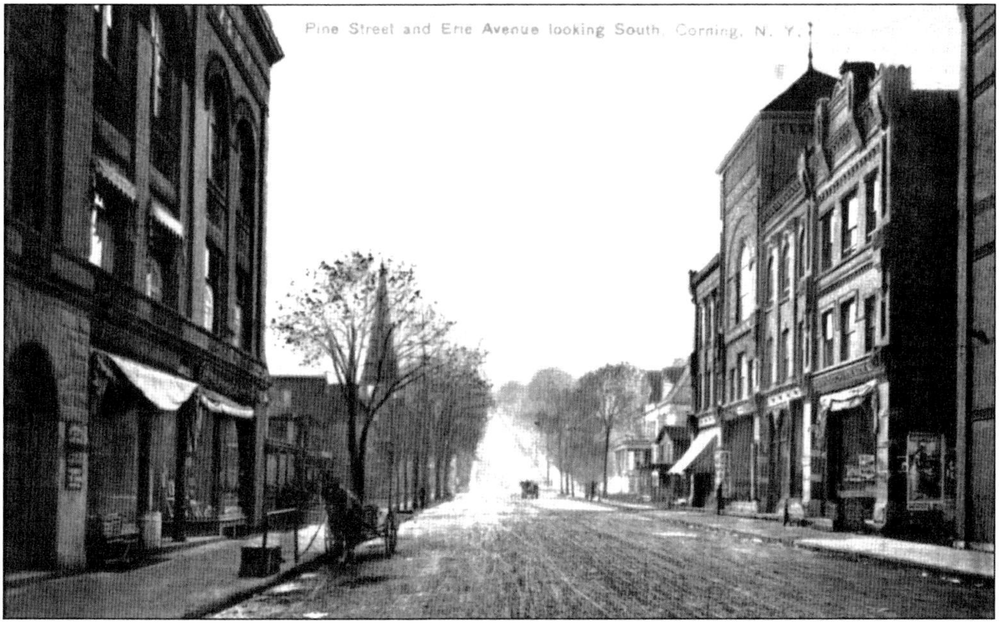

On the right side of the street is the opera house. On the left side, the First Presbyterian Church can be seen in the distance.

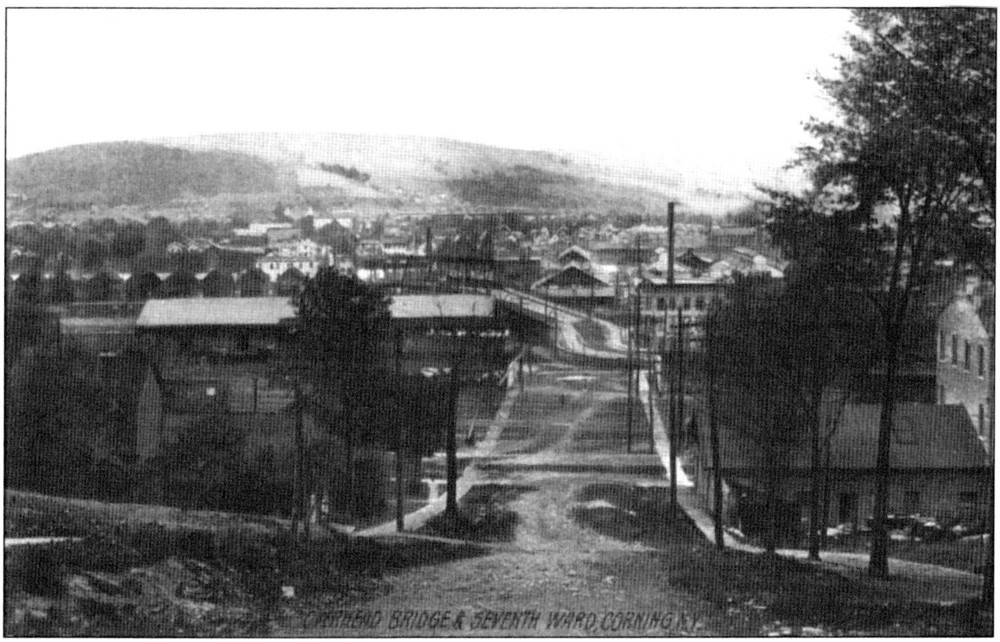

Corning's seventh ward was the part of city lying north of the Chemung River and west of the center of Bridge Street. Corning is still divided into wards. Each ward is represented by an alderman.

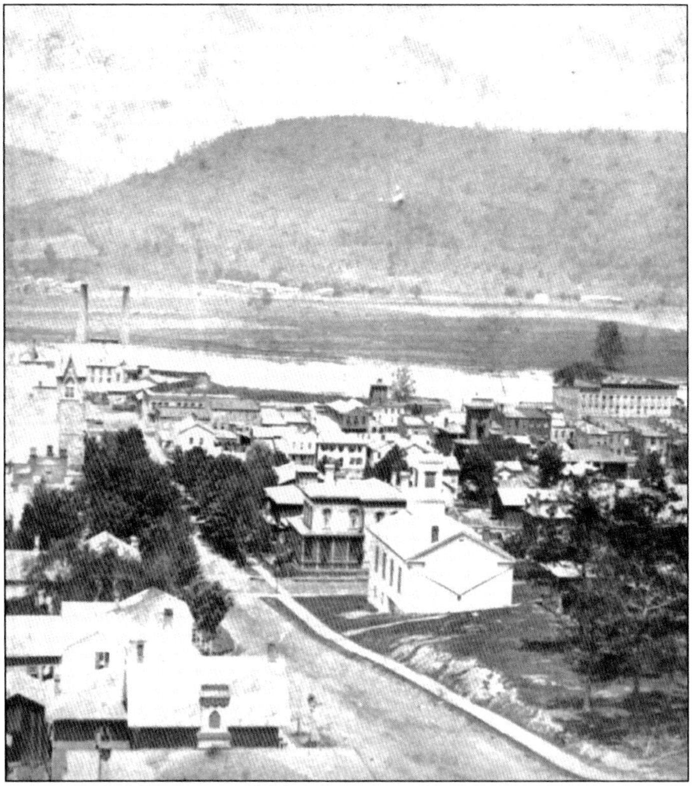

This is a view from a tower at the Corning Free Academy. The picture was taken about 1880. Two smokestacks from the Corning Glass Works can be seen. Each smokestack was part of the furnace system. Later there were more furnaces, as the need for production grew.

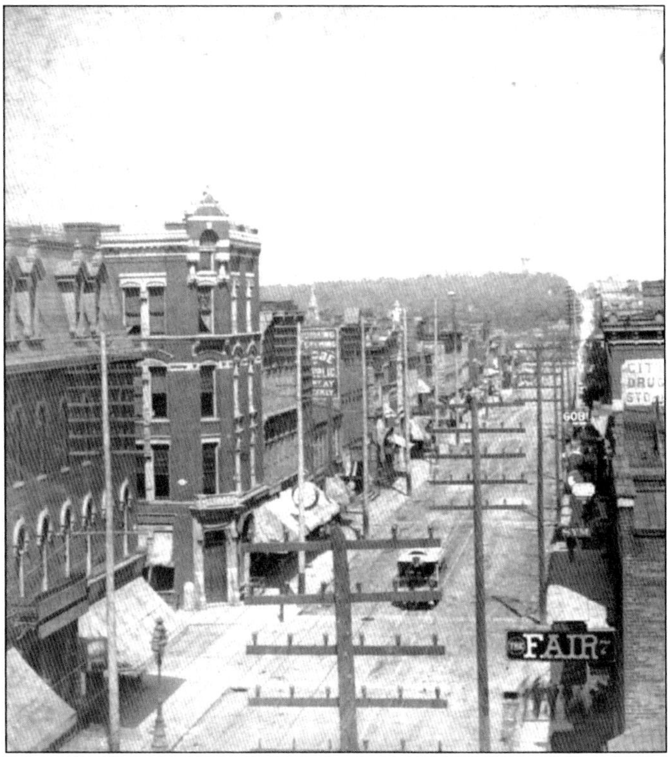

This is a stereo view that shows Corning in the late 1880s. On the right side of the street is a store called the Fair. In an 1890 advertisement, it claimed to be Corning's mammoth department store, having an area of over 8,000 feet.

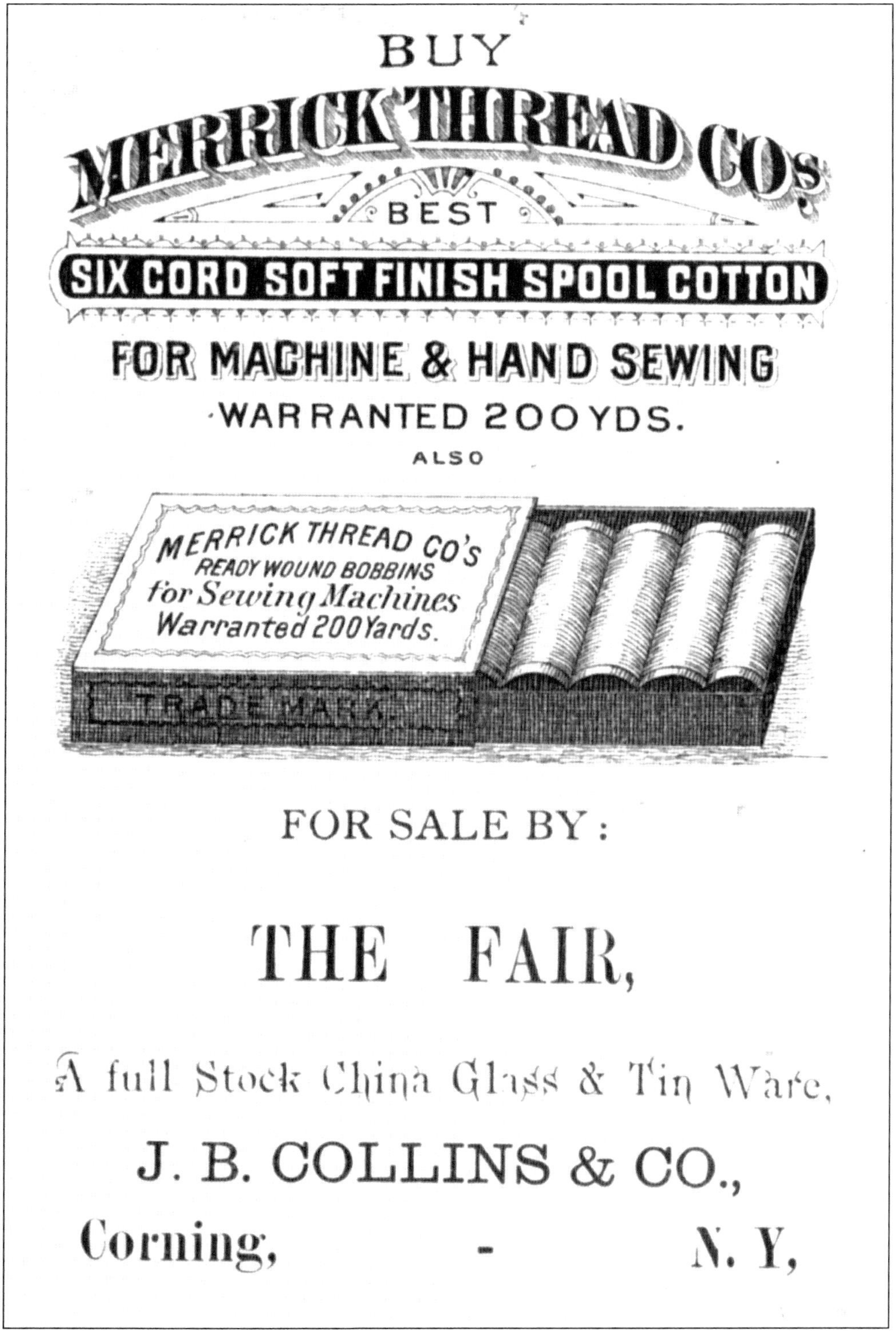

This is an 1880s trade card from J. B. Collins. Thread makers gave these cards to retailers, and they could put their names on them.

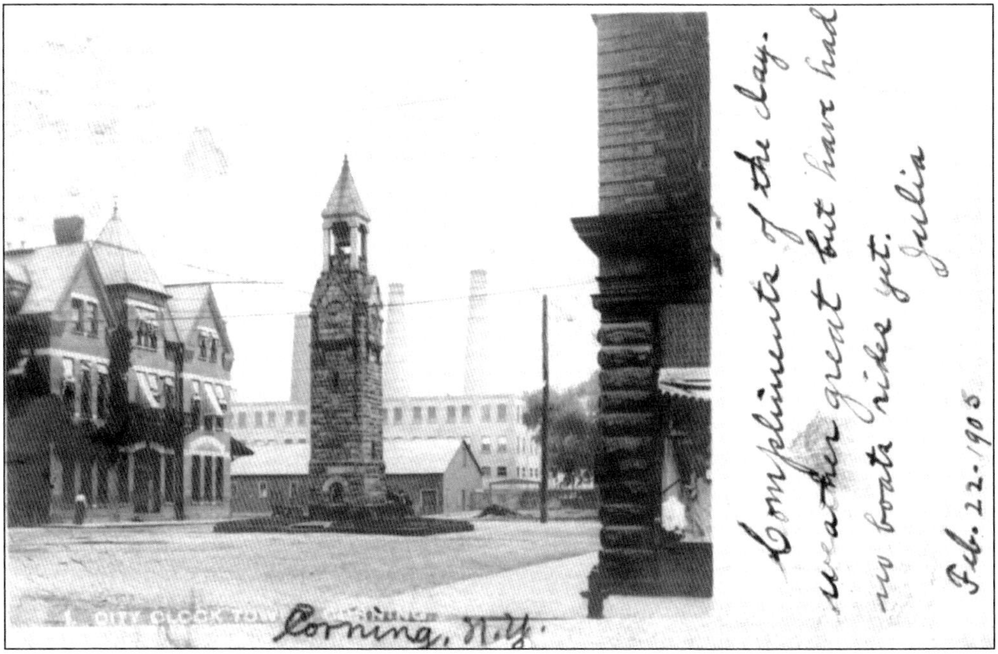

What is now called Centerway Square was once called Pine Street Square. Money was donated by the heirs of Erastus Corning for its construction. The building of this great clock tower was started in 1883 by John Cogan, using native stone. The clock part was made by a great French clock maker named Fessolt. The left side of the postcard is dated February 22, 1905.

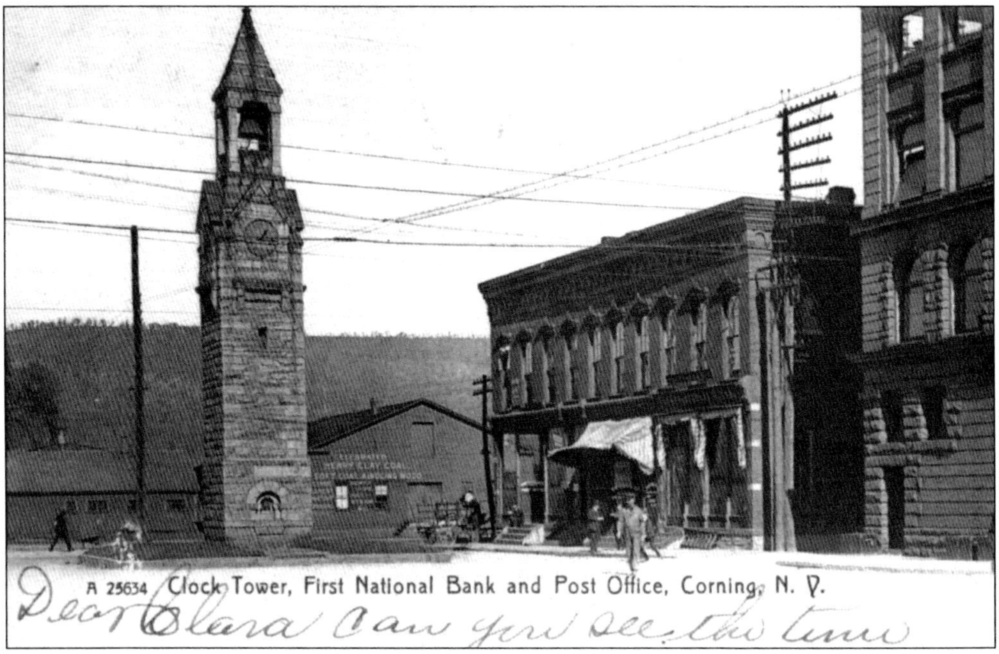

The building to the left of the First National Bank on the corner is the post office. It was at this spot until a new one was opened in 1910. "Henry Clay Coal and Wood" is written on the building toward the river.

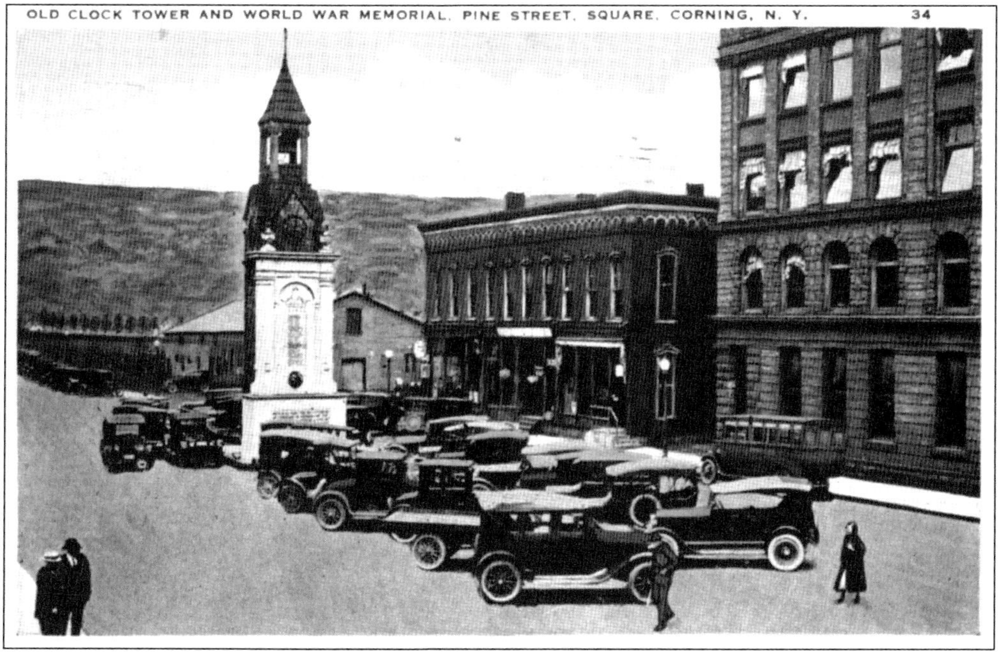

During the 1920s, this memorial honoring those who died in World War I was at Pine Street Square.

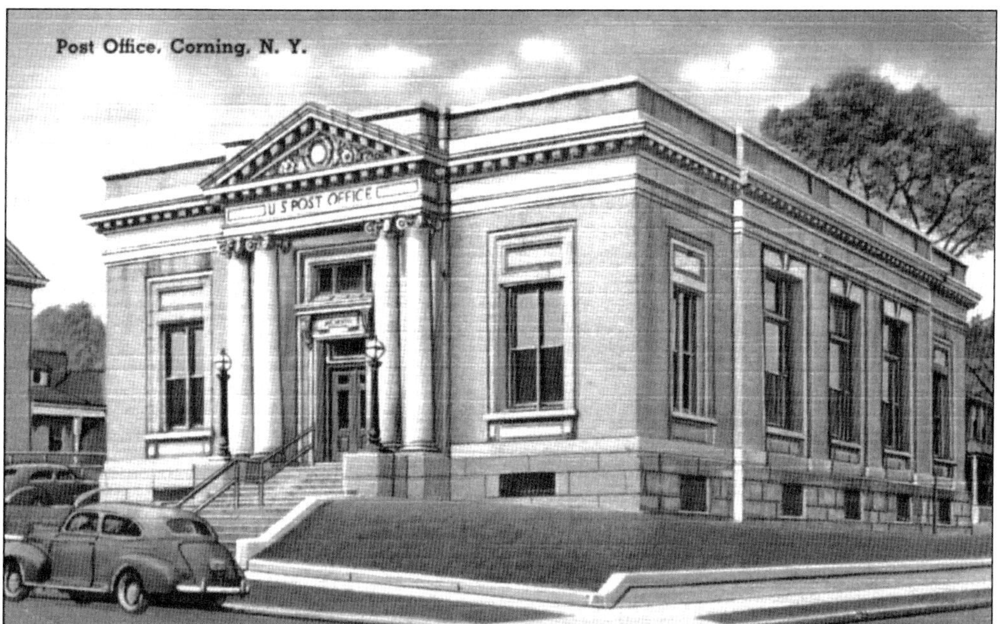

This postcard shows the post office that opened in 1910 and is currently still in use. The inside is ornately made with marble floors, hardwood walls, and brass post office boxes.

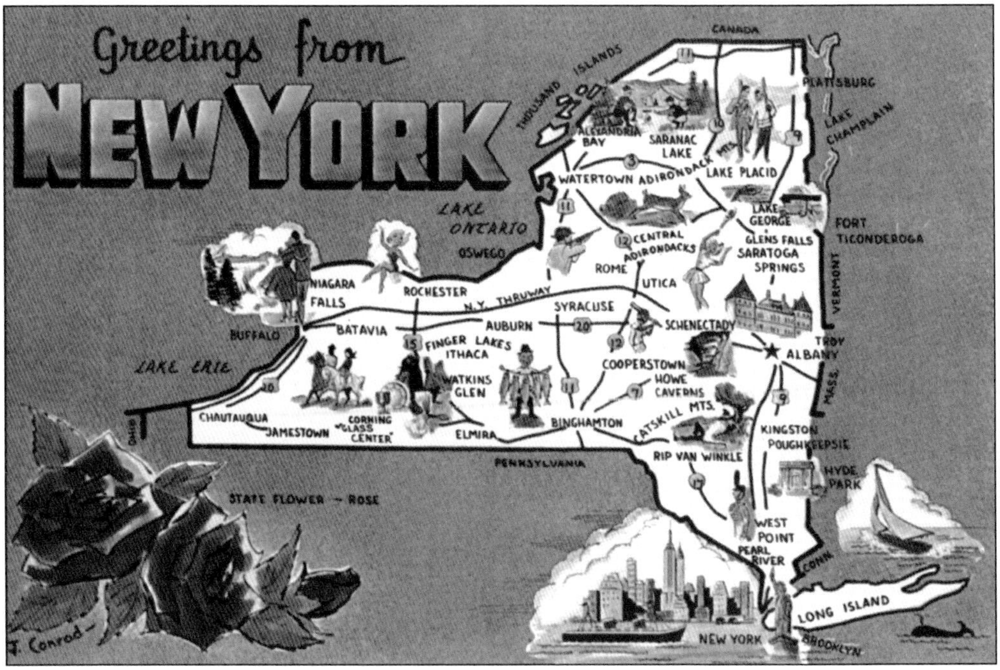

This 1960 postcard shows where Corning is located in New York State. Corning is identified as "glass center."

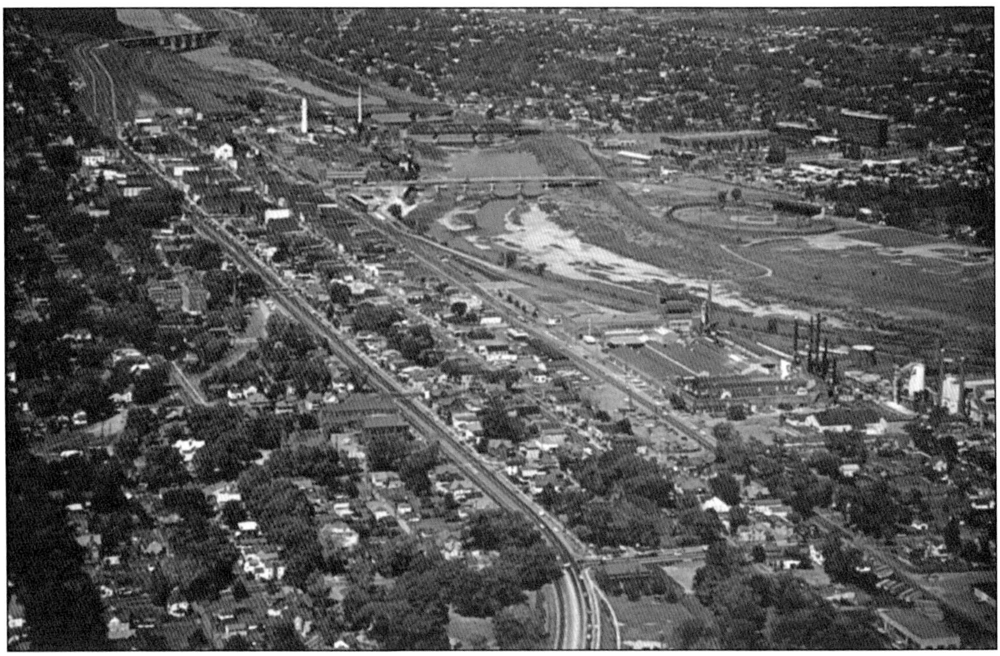

This large aerial view shows much of Corning. On the right side of the postcard is how the war memorial stadium looked before East High School was built next to it. Between the Pine Street bridge and the Bridge Street bridge, there used to be a railroad bridge, which fell in the river during the flood in June 1972.

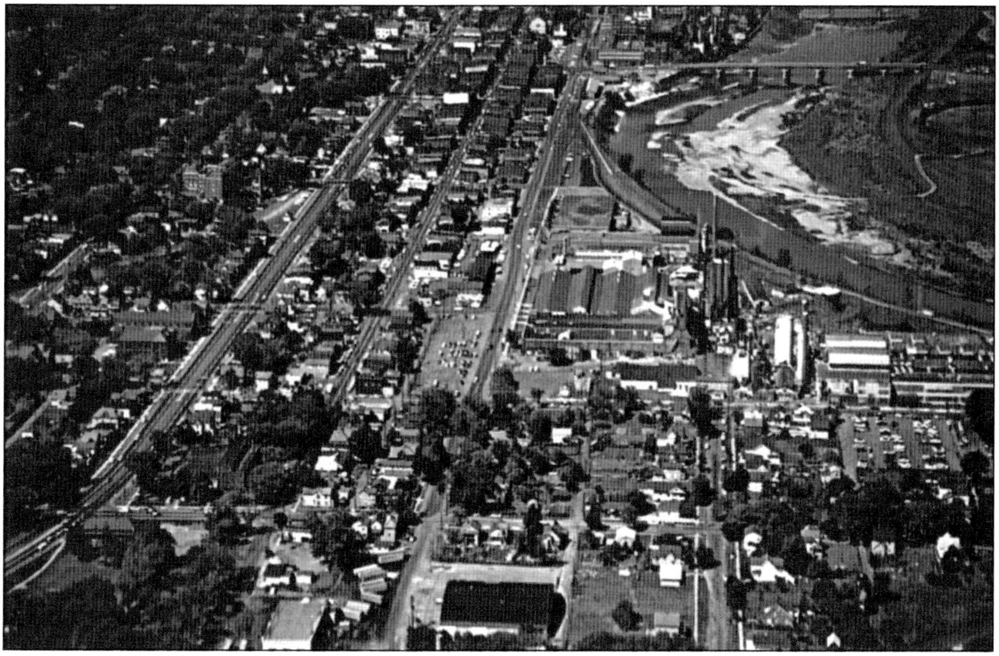

These two postcards show different aerial views of Corning. Above shows Corning's north side from about 1960 or before. Corning Glass Works takes up the center block of the picture. In front of it is the old North Pine Street. The two large buildings were automobile dealerships. The area between the railroad tracks and the Bridge Street bridge was the home to residents that lived on East William, Evelyn, and East River Streets. The postcard below shows Commerce Street on the lower left. A couple of the houses are still there. On the left edge of the postcard is what is now called World of Kitchen, which was formerly the Pressware plant. To the left is the Fallbrook plant, which was torn down a couple years ago.

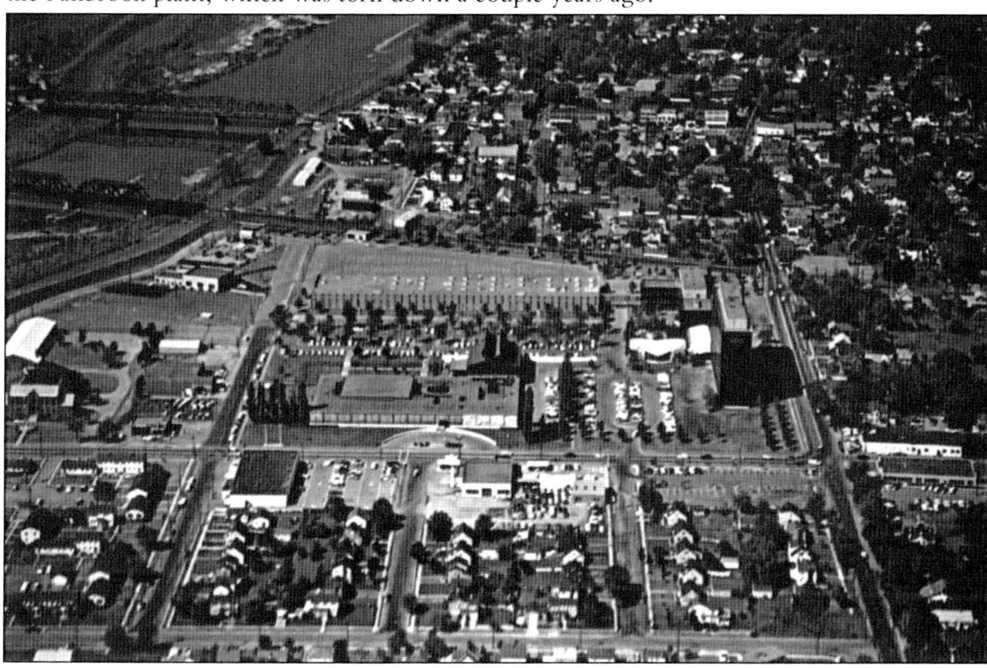

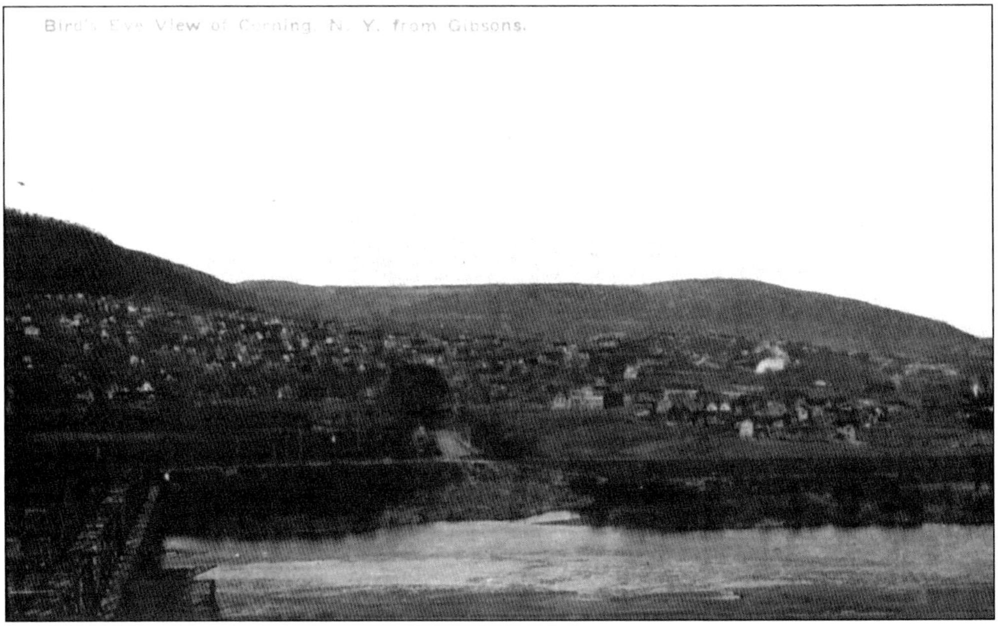

Bird's Eye View of Corning, N. Y. from Gibsons.

Here are two views showing Corning from outside of town. Spenser Hill, one of the highest hills in the Corning area, is where Corning Community College is located.

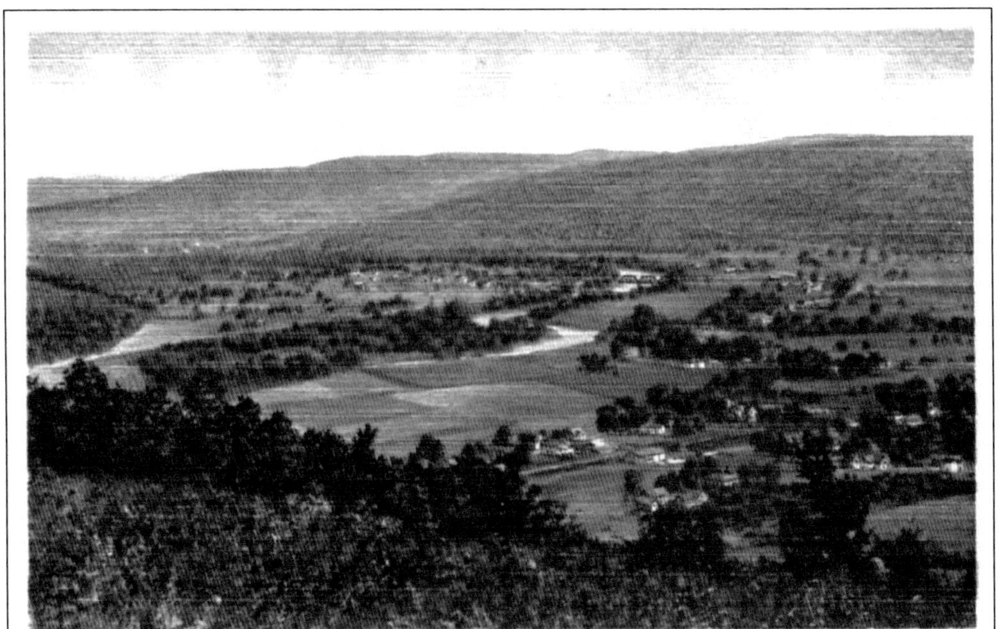

View from Spencer Hill Looking Toward Big Flats, Corning, N. Y. 7A-H2617

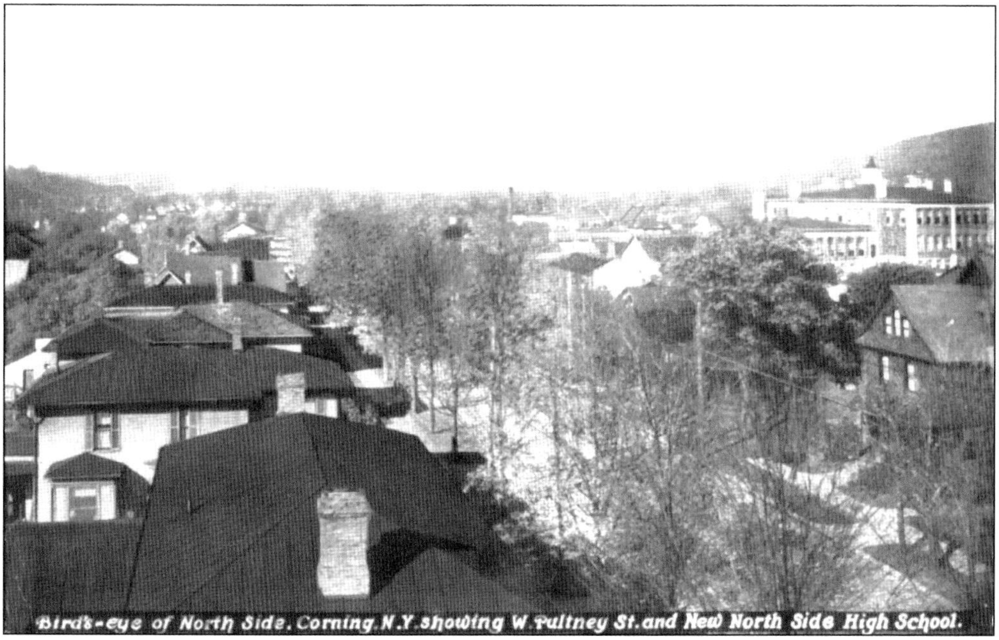

This postcard from 1912 shows Pulteney Street looking west.

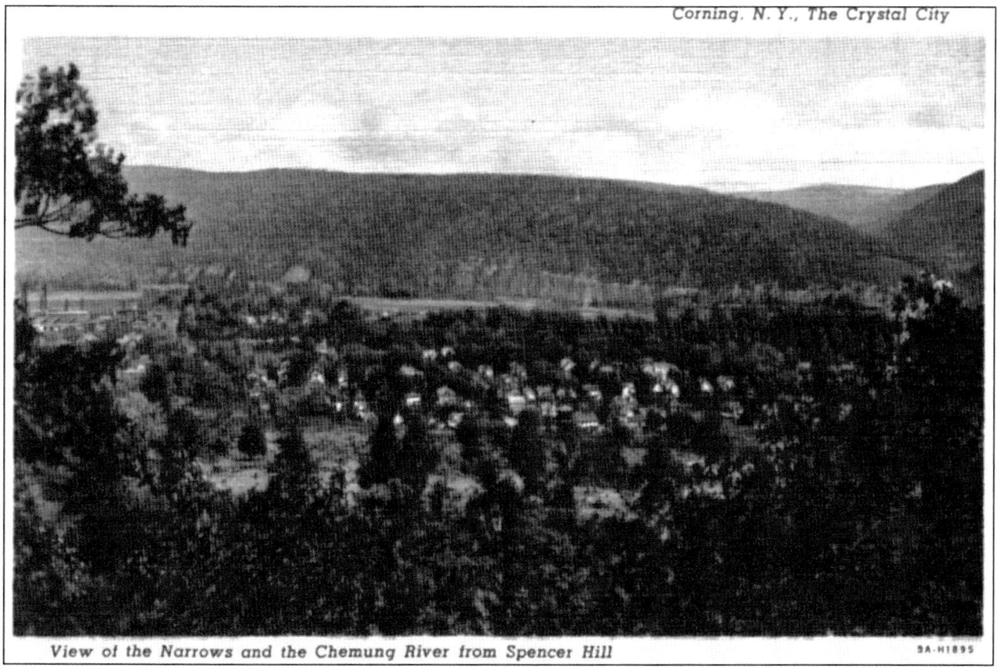

The narrows gets its name from being a narrow strip of land between the hill and the Chemung River.

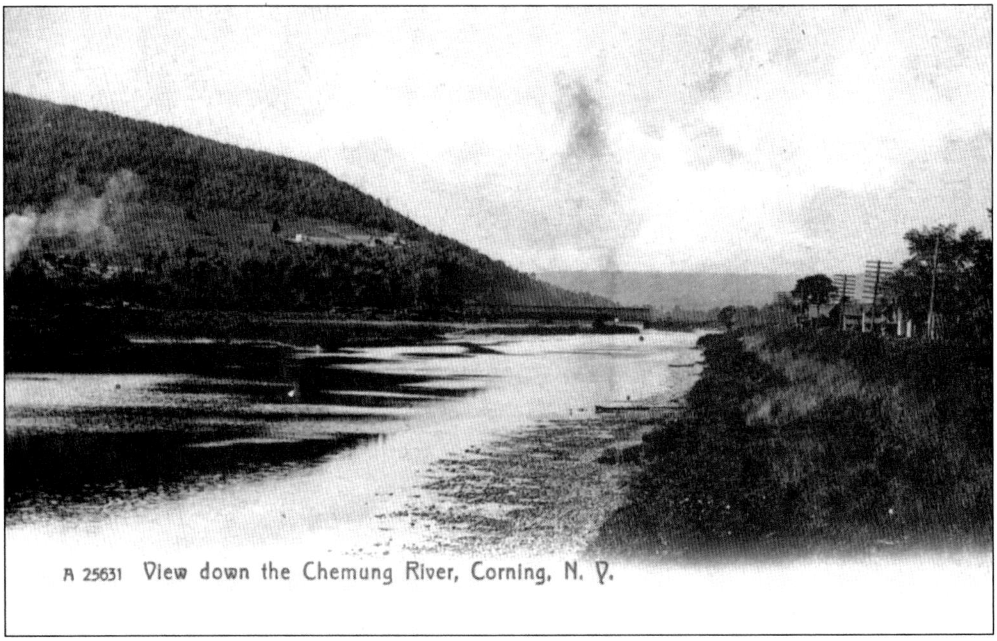

The name of the Chemung River comes from an Iroquois word, meaning "big horn" or "horn-in-the-water." The Chemung River is a tributary of the Susquehanna River. With the construction of the Chemung Canal in 1833 between the Chemung River and the southern end of Seneca Lake and the Erie Canal system, the Chemung River connected Corning to the rest of the world.

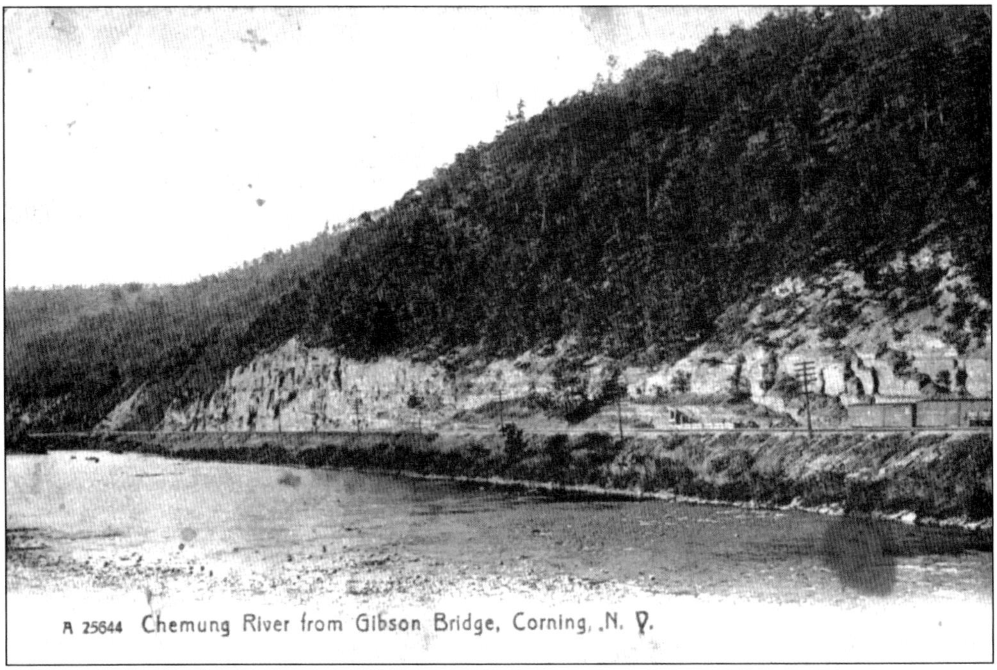

This shows the area that is now part of Interstate 86 along the river. The railroad tracks still parallel the highway in places. Around here, the railroad tracks have probably been in the same spot with the materials being upgraded over the years.

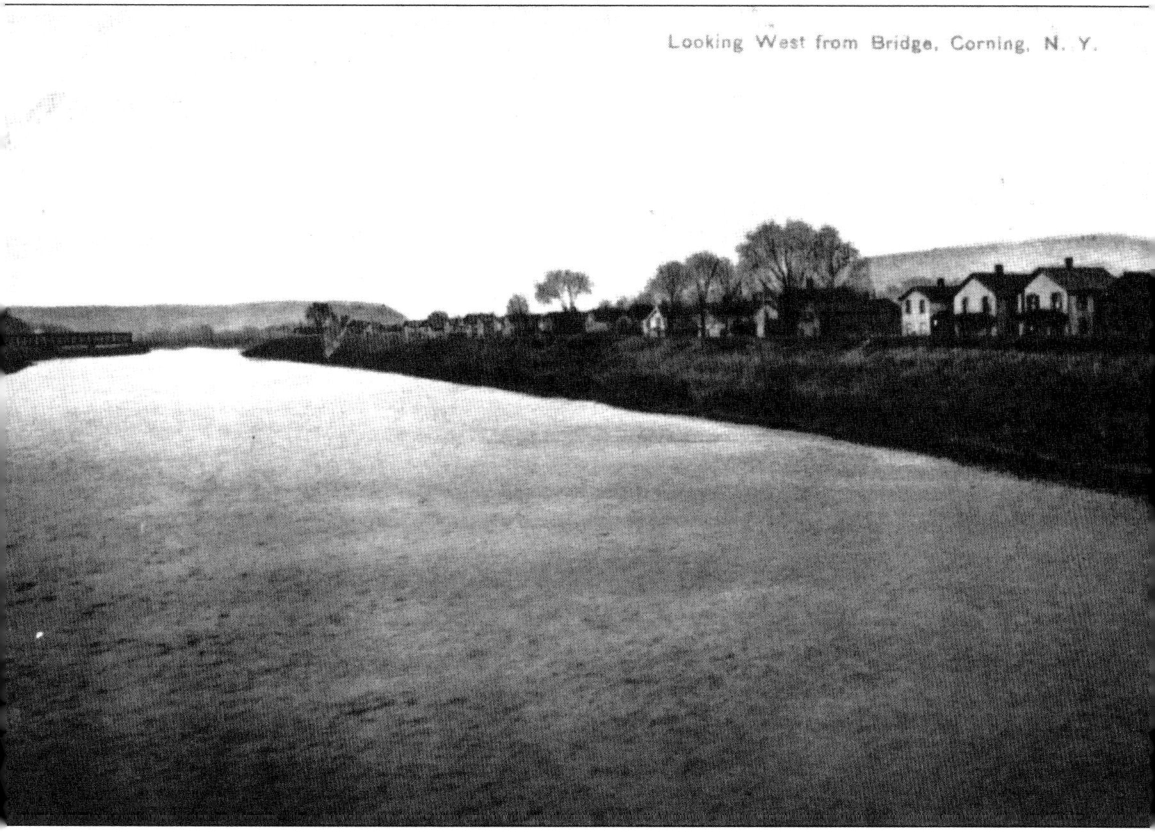

These houses along the west side of the river were all torn down after the flood of 1972. This was about where the area of Hillview Avenue is today.

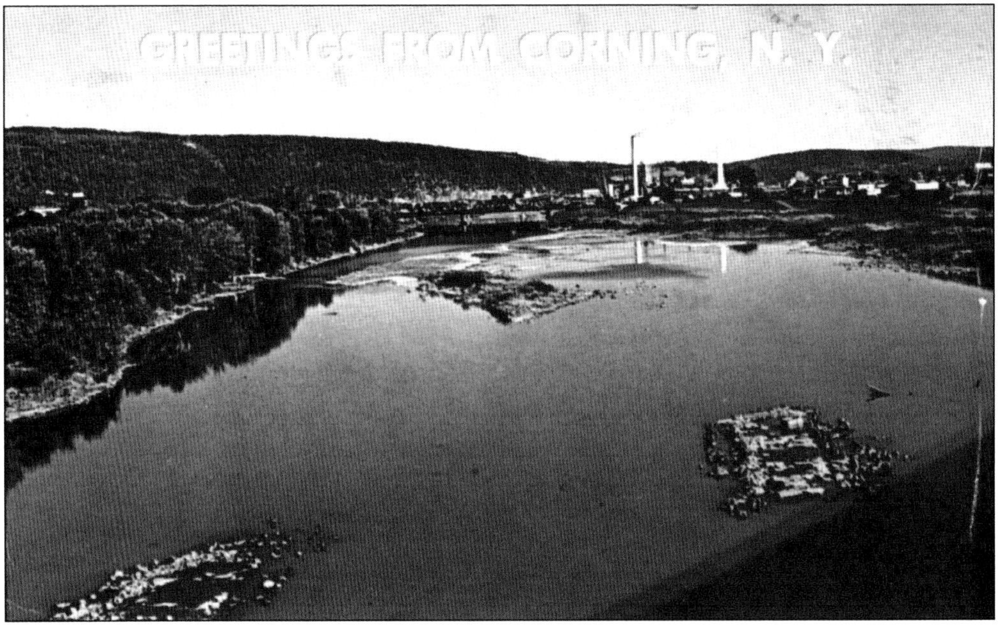

This postcard was mailed in 1964 and shows Corning from the middle of the Chemung River. The Corning Glass Works thermometer glass tower can be seen near the center of the postcard.

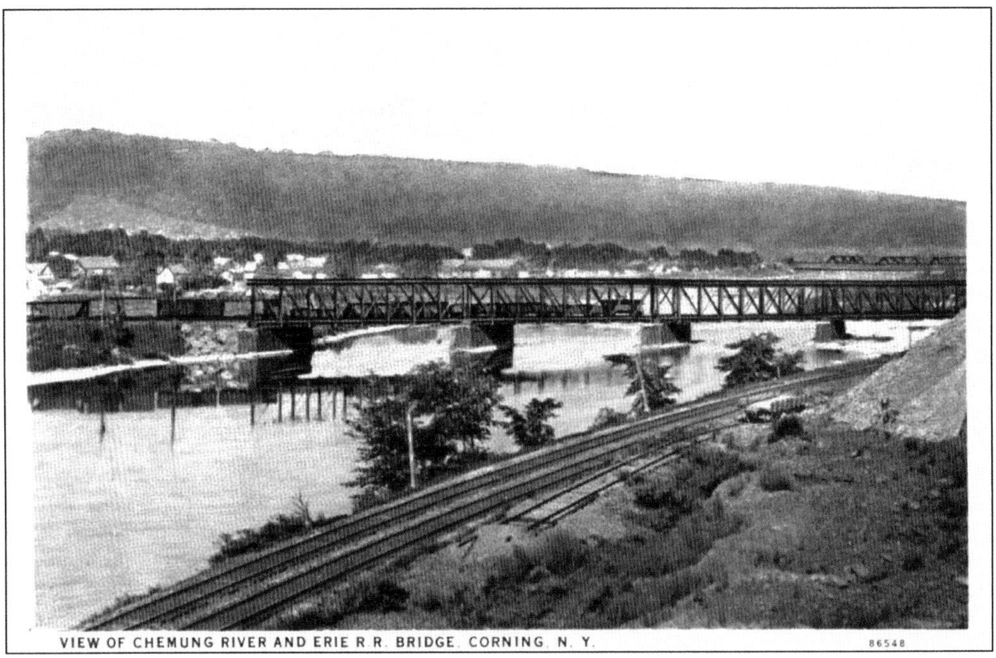

This was the railroad bridge that connected tracks on the north and south sides of the river. It was between the Bridge Street bridge and the Pine Street bridge before it fell in the river during the flood of 1972.

Five

People and Organizations

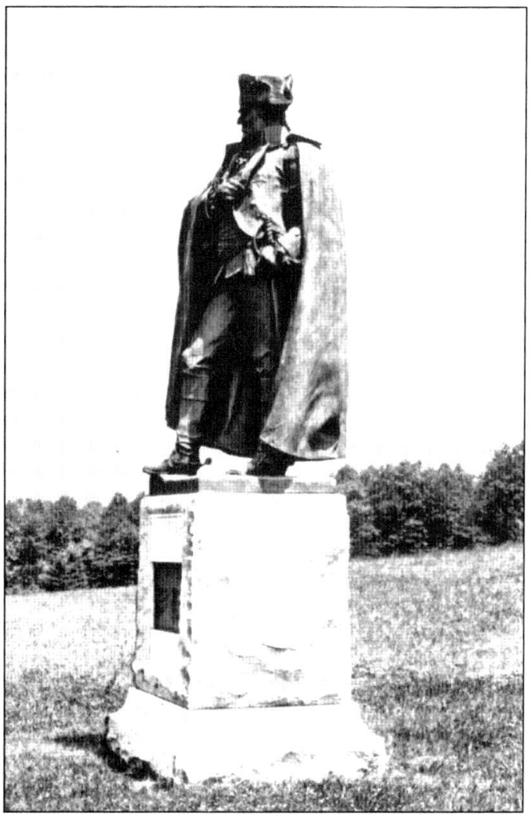

Corning is in Steuben County. It is one of 62 counties in New York State and is named after Friedrich Wilhelm von Steuben. Steuben was a Prussian officer who served as inspector general and major general of the Continental army during the American Revolution. He is credited with teaching the Continental army the essentials of military drill and discipline, helping to guide it to victory. This 1950s postcard shows a statue of Steuben in Valley Forge National Historic Park.

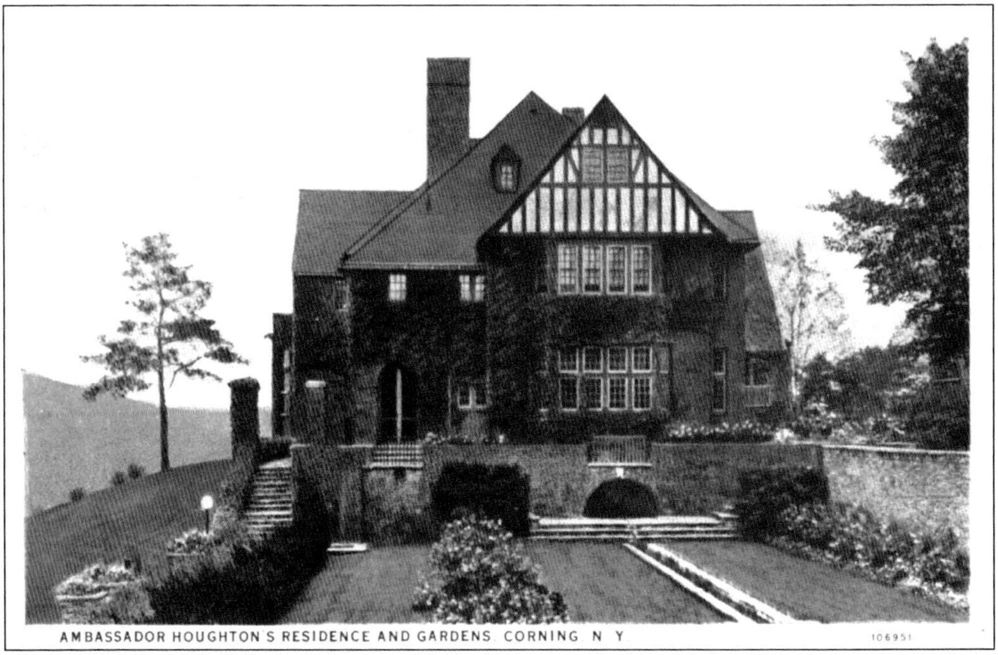

In 1918, Alanson B. Houghton was a two-term congressman who served on the Foreign Affairs and Ways and Means Committees. He resigned from Congress because he was appointed by Pres. Warren G. Harding as ambassador to Germany. In 1925, Pres. Calvin Coolidge appointed Houghton as the U.S. ambassador to Great Britain. In 1928, Houghton ran for a place in the U.S. Senate and lost. He is still remembered for serving as an ambassador.

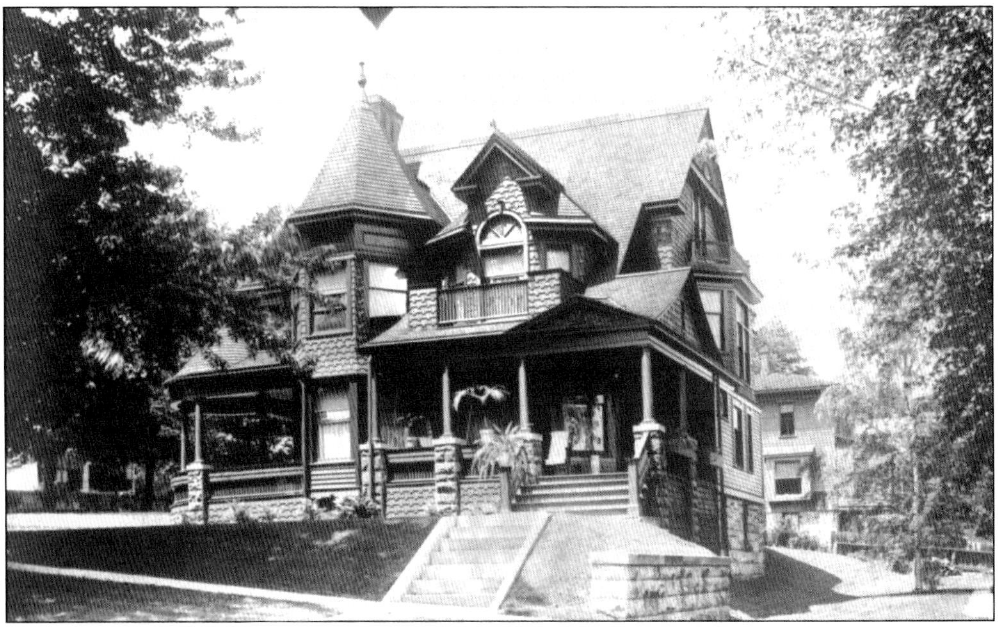

The back of this postcard identifies this as Corning's Wall Street and Rose and John C. Bradley's residence. John was born in Ireland. He was a contractor for the railroad companies and later a general contractor. The Bradleys had no children. The house is still there and looks much the same.

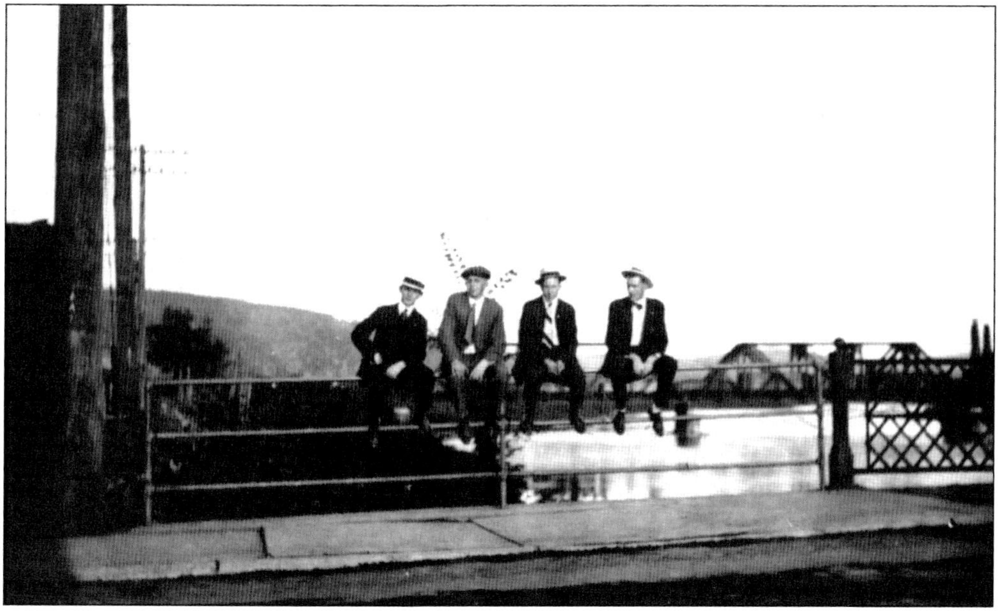

This postcard was mailed from Corning in July 1918 to Pvt. Alfred Bayer in the 152 Depot Brigade, 4th Platoon, Company 12, at Camp Upton on Long Island. The railroad bridge and two smokestacks from Corning Glass Works can be seen in the background.

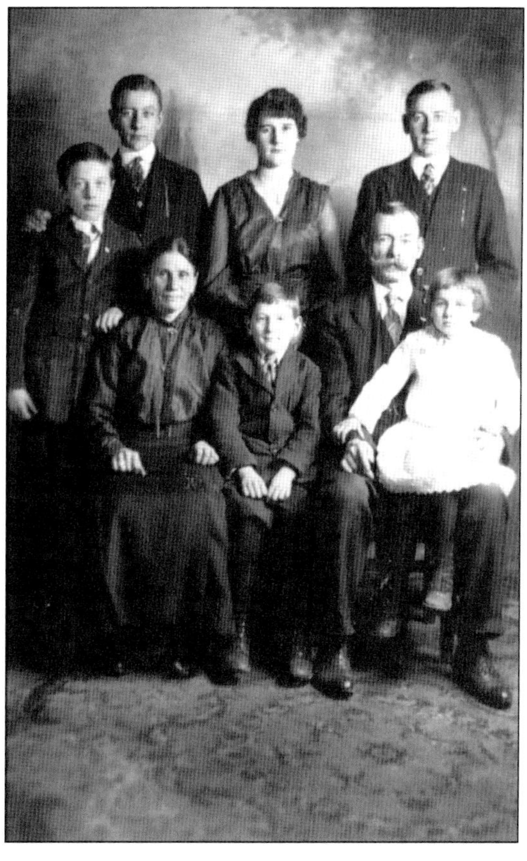

At the height of real-photo postcards' popularity, many families and individuals had their photographs put on them. This postcard, from the second decade of the 20th century, shows John Buchinger (1840–1919), a glassblower, with a child on his knee, and John Buchinger Jr. (1870–1946) standing behind him. They lived at 262 Washington Street.

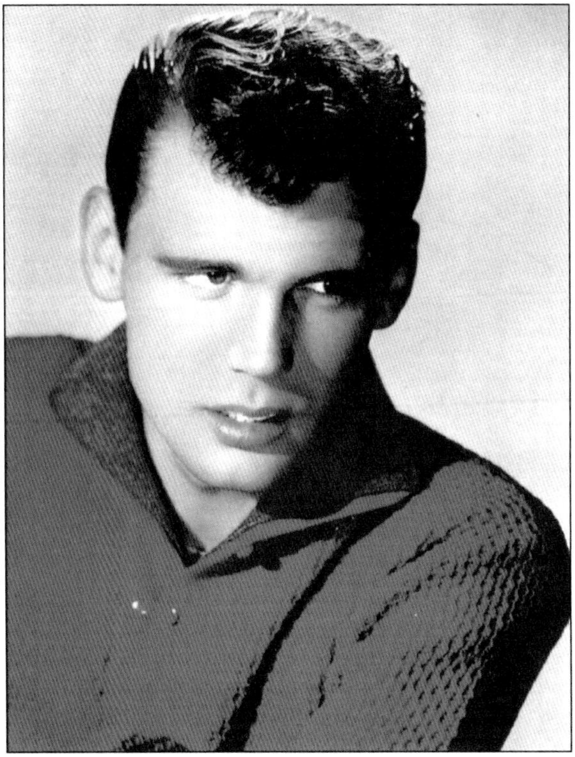

Grammy award–winning guitarist and member of the Rock and Roll Hall of Fame, Duane Eddy was born in Corning on April 26, 1938. On November 11, 1937, his parents, Lloyd Eddy and Alberta Granger, married at the Towanda Episcopal Church and then moved to Corning. Lloyd worked for the Corning Baking Company, which was at 110–125 Conhocton Street.

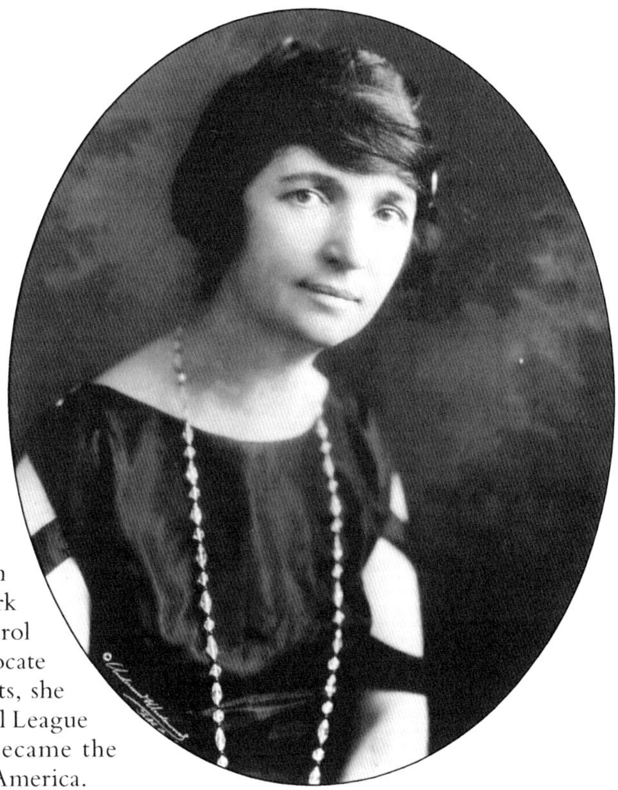

Margaret Sanger was born on September 14, 1879, as the sixth child of an Irish immigrant father and a devout Catholic mother. Her father opened a marble and stone-cutting business in Corning. Sanger later left Corning to be a nurse in the poor neighborhoods of New York City and founded the first birth control clinic in the country in 1916. An advocate for birth control and women's rights, she founded the American Birth Control League in 1921. Later the organization became the Planned Parenthood Federation of America.

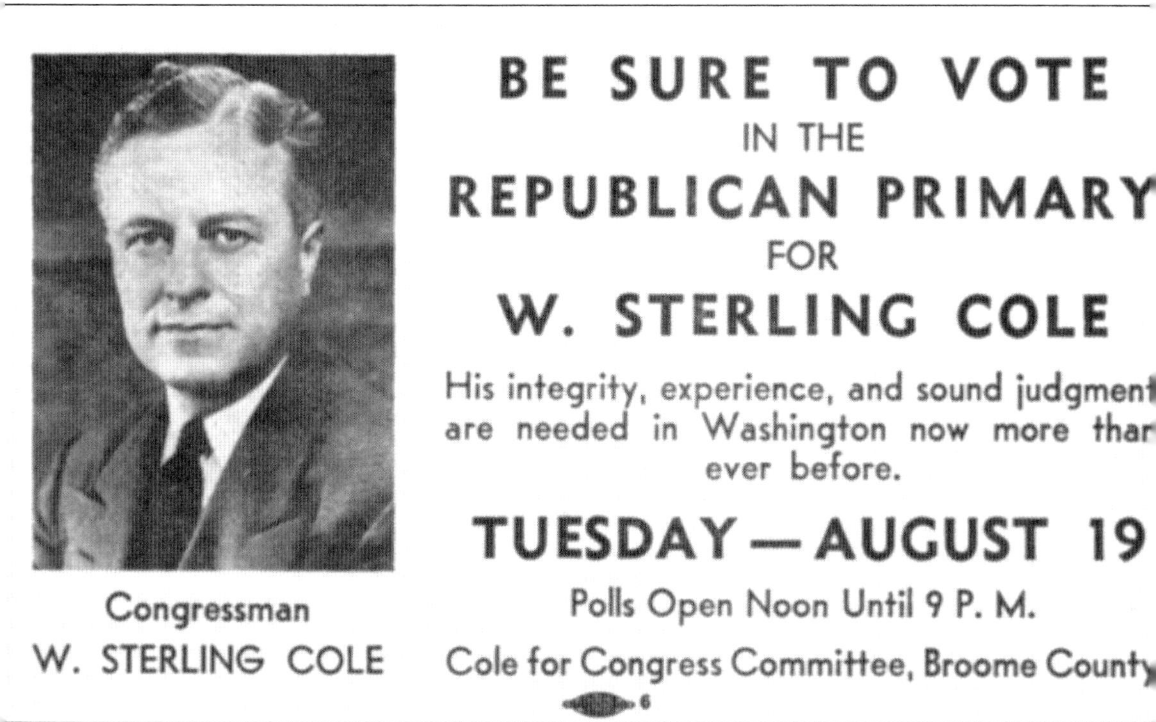

William "Sterling"" Cole was born in Painted Post on April 18, 1904. Later he was a teacher in the Corning Free Academy in 1925 and 1926. After being elected to his first term in Congress, he was reelected 11 straight times. This postcard is from his campaign in 1952.

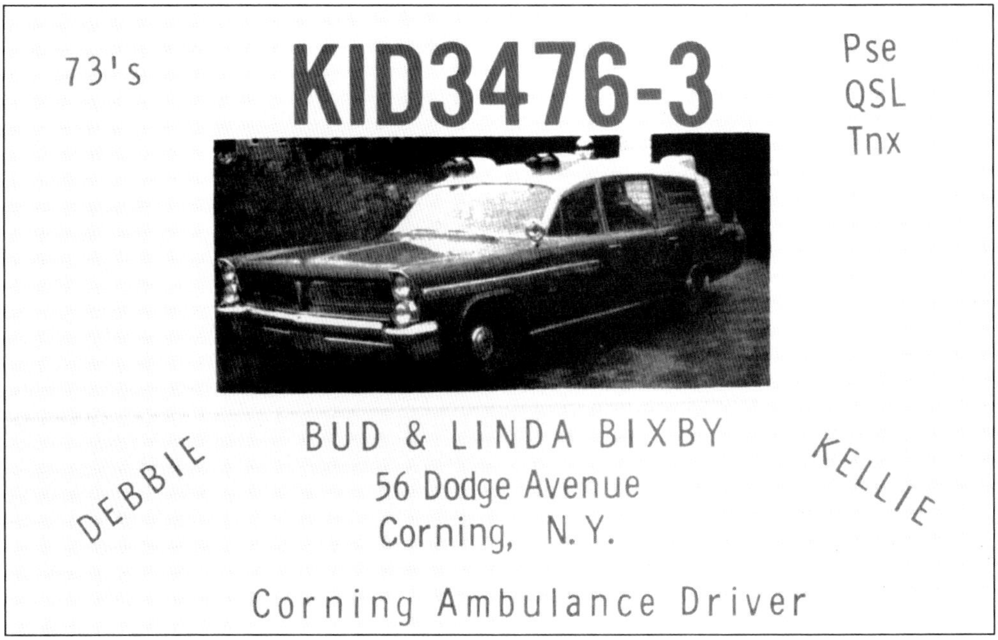

QSL postcards like these two were mailed to someone to confirm a radio reception from a distance away. QSL cards were first used in 1919 and are still actively used and collected by amateur radio operators from all over the world. These are from the 1960s and belonged to people in Corning.

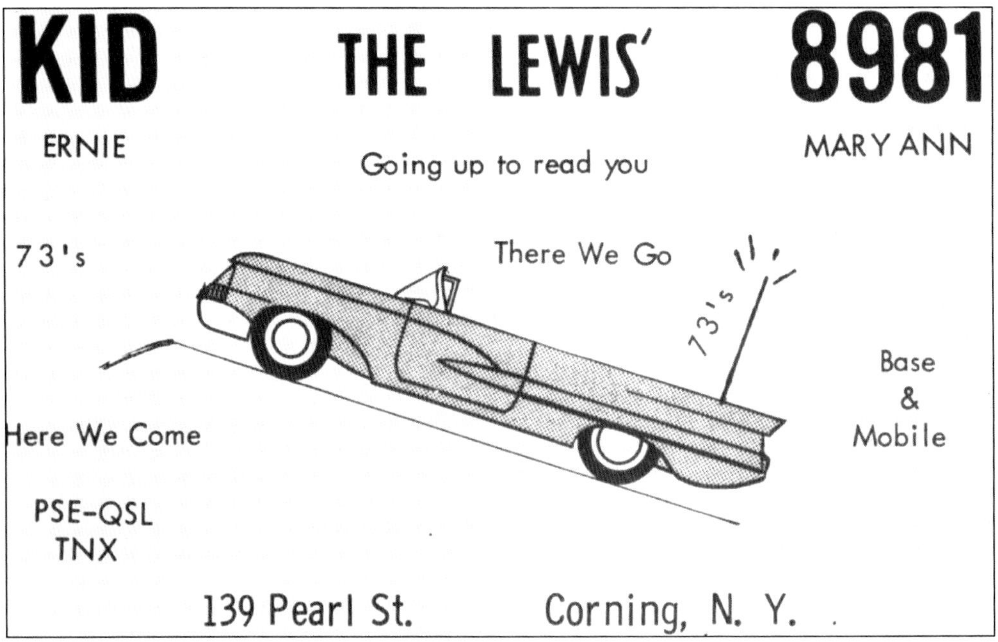

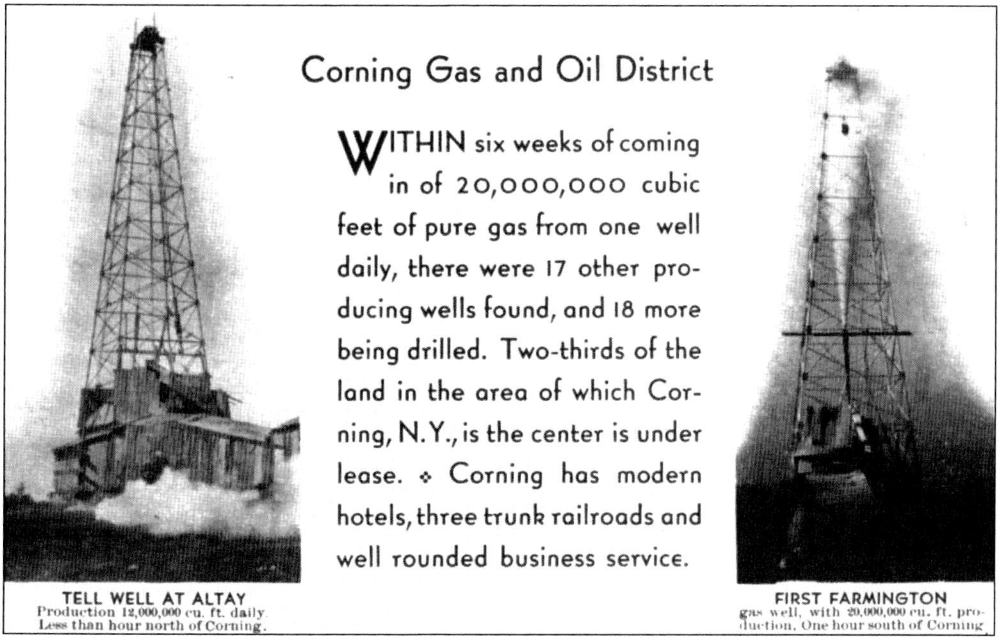

Natural gas was discovered at Farmington Field near Sabinsville in Tioga County, Pennsylvania, in September 1930 by the Allegany Gas Company. Since the year 2000, many natural gas deposits have been found in outlying areas of Corning, such as Hornby and Gibson, as well as other parts of Steuben and Chemung Counties.

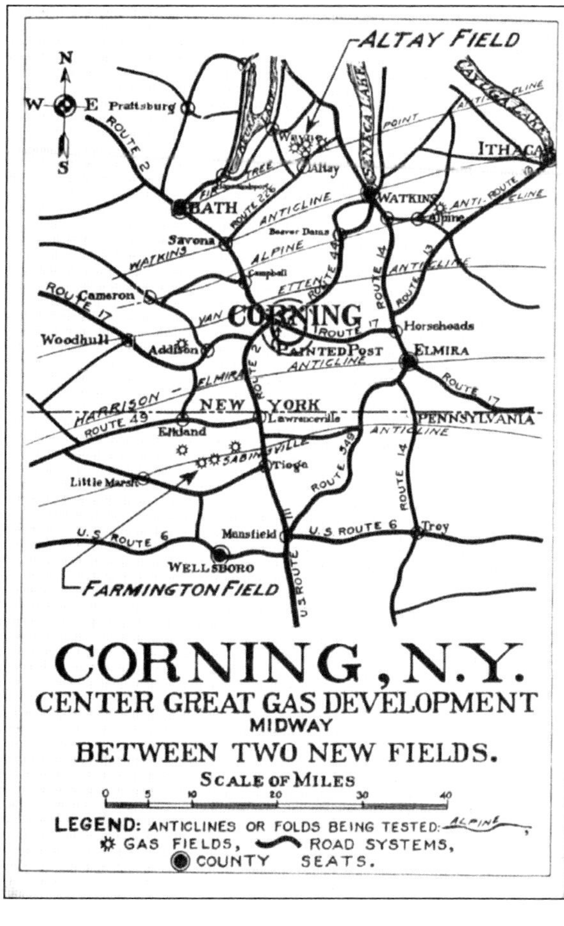

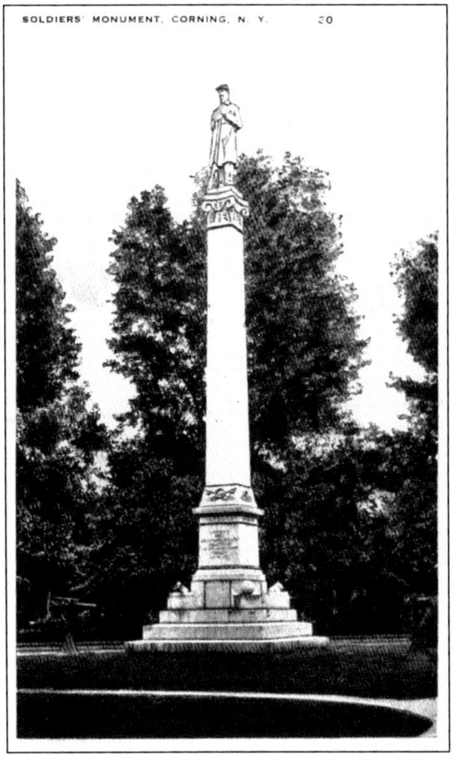

About 10,000 people gathered for the dedication of this monument on Memorial Day in 1911. This monument is 45 feet high and weighs over 56 tons. It is still on the corner of Park Avenue and First Street. One side near the bottom has the words, "Erected by the Patriotic Organizations and Citizens of Corning MCMXI [1911]." Another side reads, "In memory of those who served their country during the war for preservation of the union."

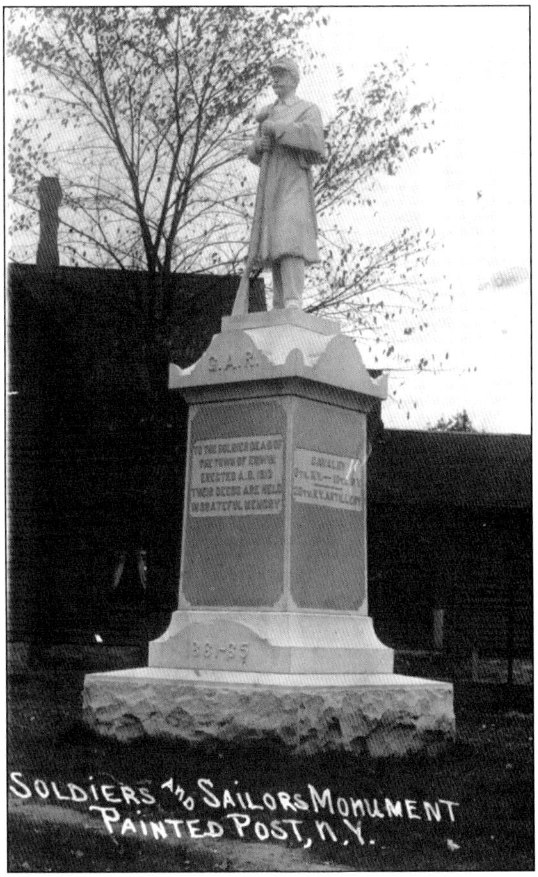

This statue was erected in 1909 in Painted Post and has the inscription, "To the dead of the town of Erwin, Their deeds are held in great full memory." The three other sides of the monument list the New York State regiments that had members from this area. Today the monument is beside the Painted Post Post Office.

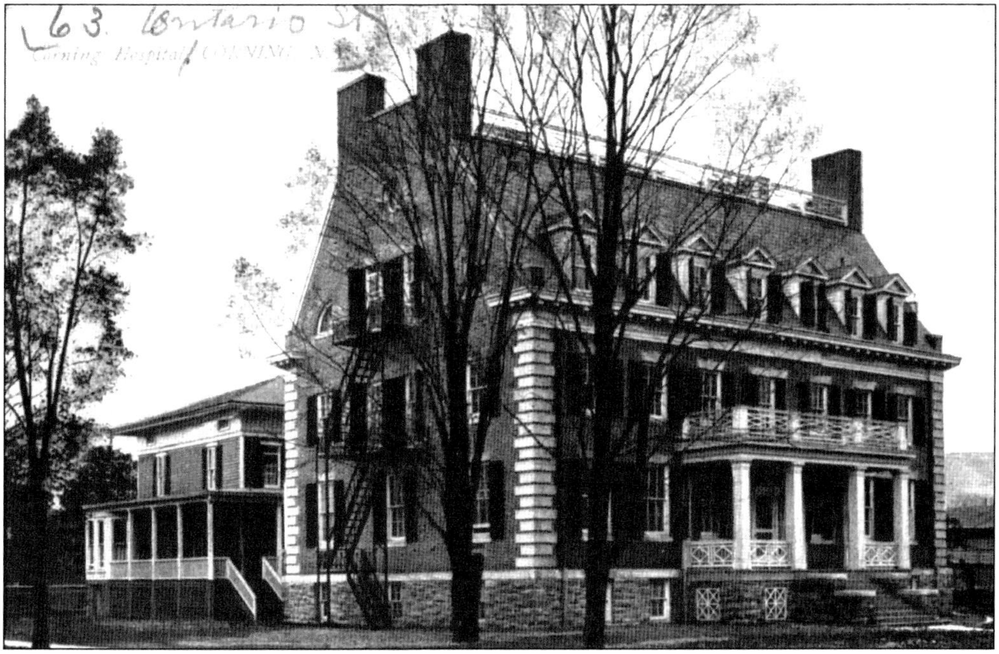

This early version of the Corning Hospital was opened on October 10, 1905. It stood where the Corning Hospital is now.

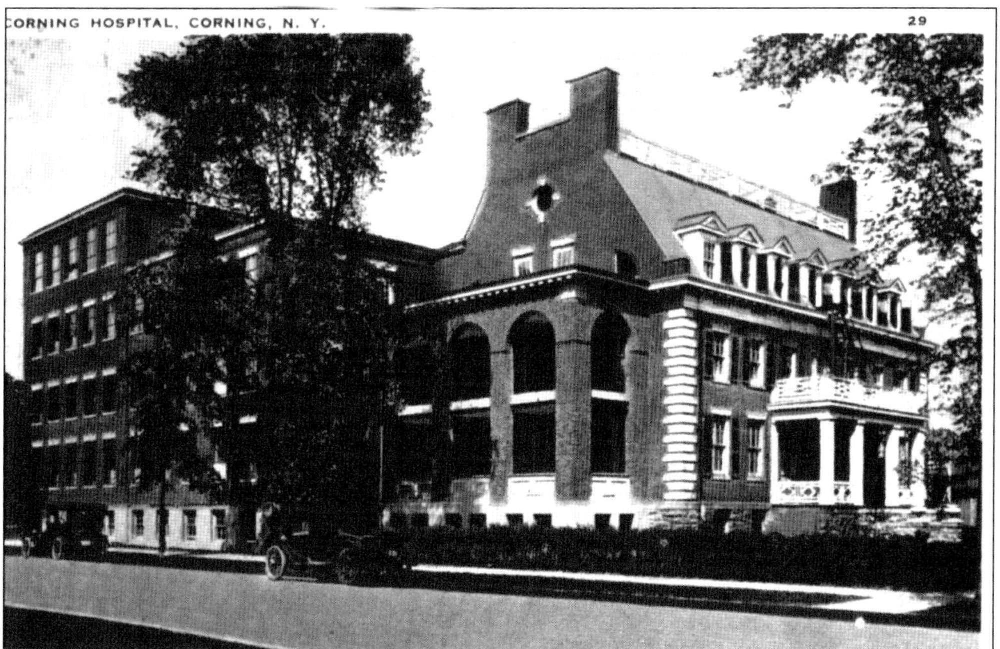

The year 1924 saw a significant change to the Corning Hospital campus. A new brick building was added to the back of the hospital. With the new building, opened on April 5, capacity was up to 75 beds.

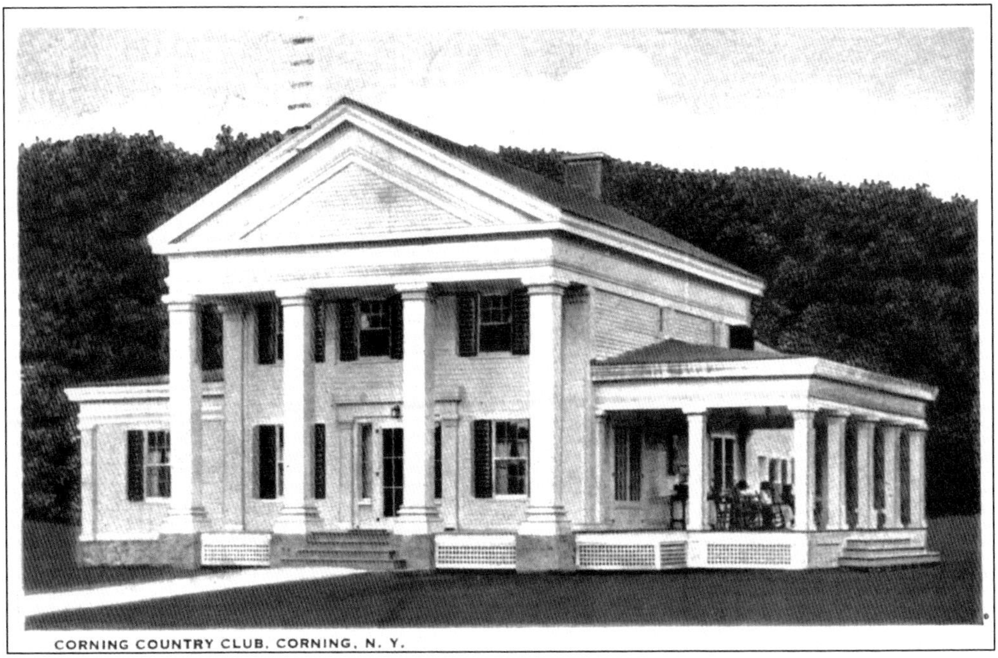

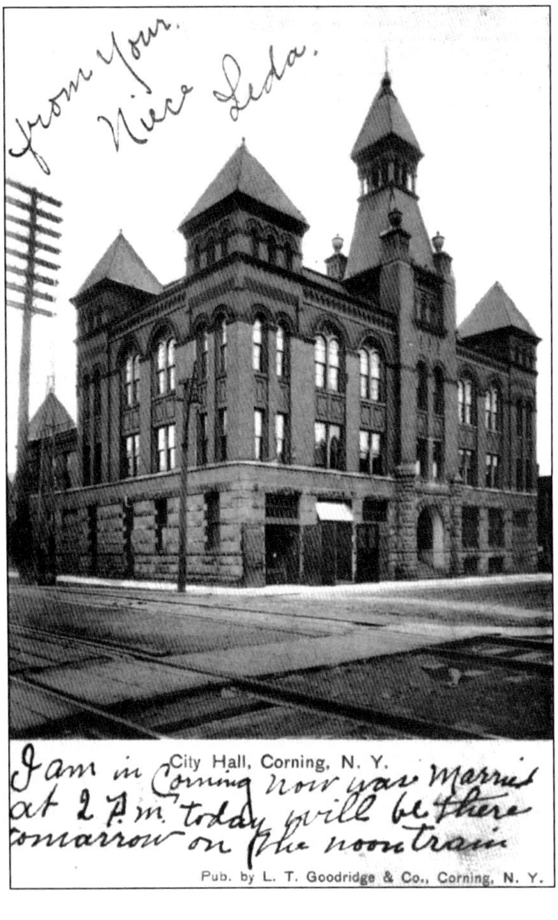

The Corning Country Club was established in 1919 outside of Gibson. The land that was acquired for the golf course was well situated, being surrounded by rolling hills and including a farmhouse. The farmhouse structure was modified and became the first clubhouse. In 1951, the clubhouse was destroyed by fire. A second clubhouse was built on a different site and was opened to rave reviews in July 1952.

City hall was located at 113–123 Cedar Street. It contained offices for many civic groups. The city chamberlain, city water works, fire department, mayor, police headquarters, and the superintendent of public works all had offices here. Today this renovated building is a museum.

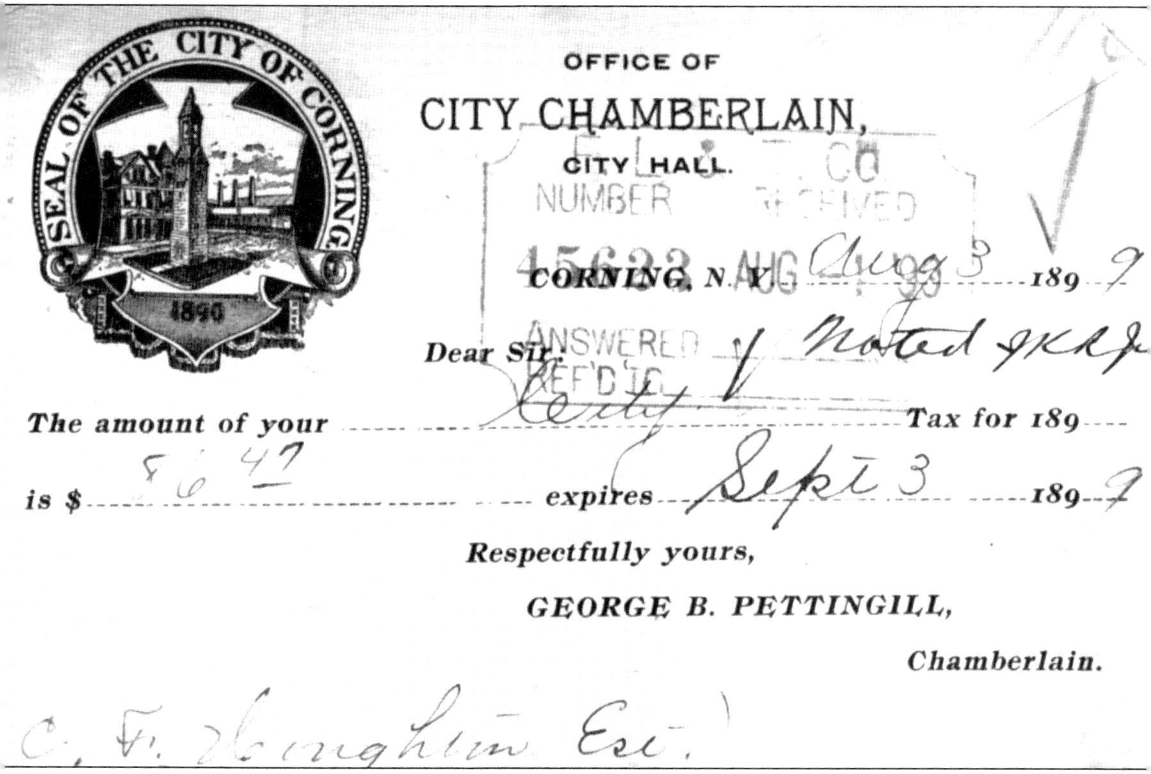

SEAL OF THE CITY OF CORNING
1890

OFFICE OF

CITY CHAMBERLAIN,

CITY HALL.

NUMBER RECEIVED

15623 AUG

CORNING, N. Y. Aug 3 189 9

ANSWERED

REF'D TO

Dear Sir: Noted

The amount of your City Tax for 189

is $ 86 47 expires Sept 3 189 9

Respectfully yours,

GEORGE B. PETTINGILL,

Chamberlain.

On March 20, 1890, Gov. David Hill signed the act that created the city of Corning. This merged together the villages of Corning and Knoxville. City planners chose to put the clock tower in the design of the city seal that is shown on this card from the city chamberlain. It was mailed to the Farmers Loan and Trust company in New York City to inform them that they owed $86.47 in taxes.

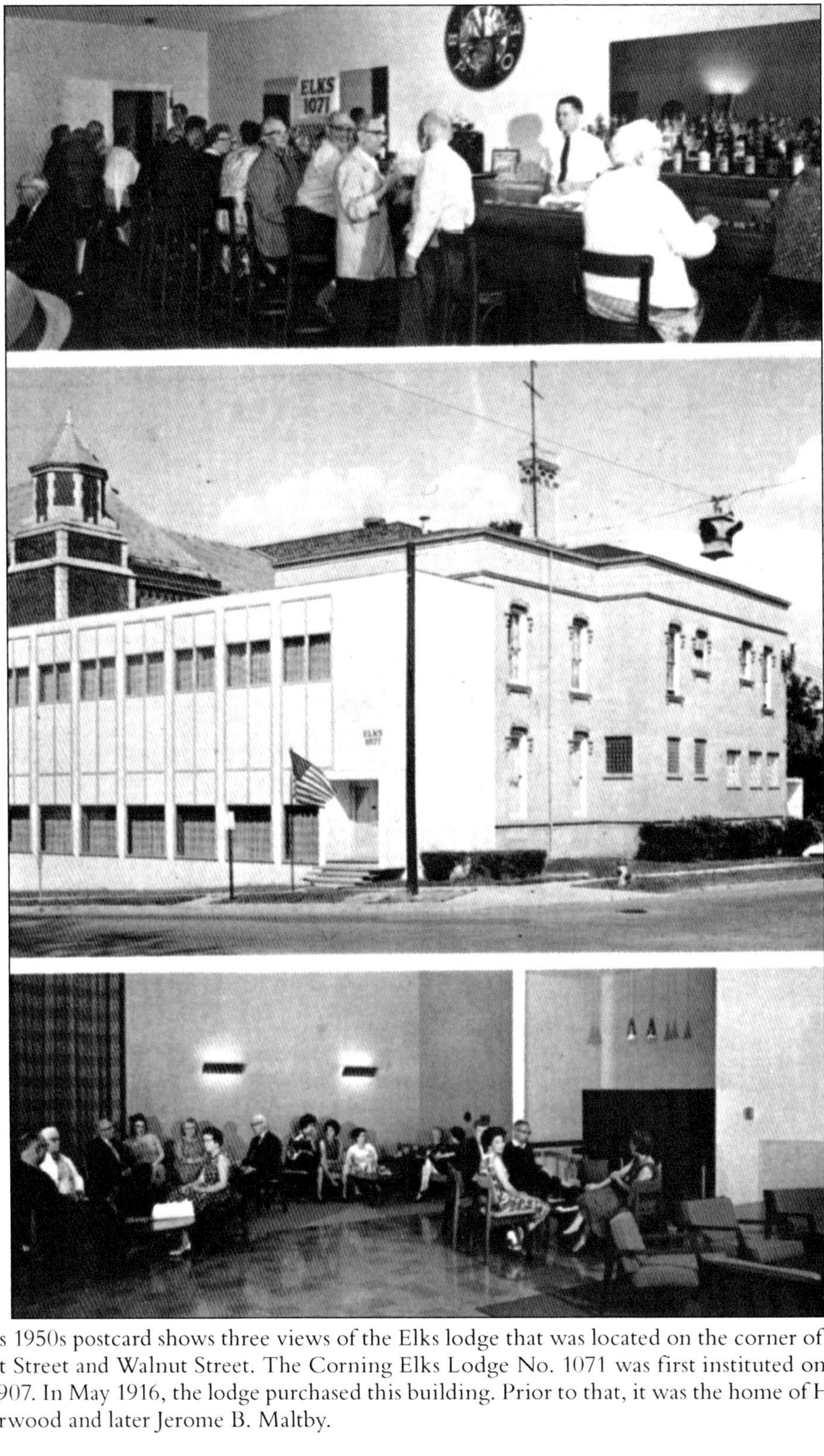

This 1950s postcard shows three views of the Elks lodge that was located on the corner of West First Street and Walnut Street. The Corning Elks Lodge No. 1071 was first instituted on May 9, 1907. In May 1916, the lodge purchased this building. Prior to that, it was the home of Henry Sherwood and later Jerome B. Maltby.

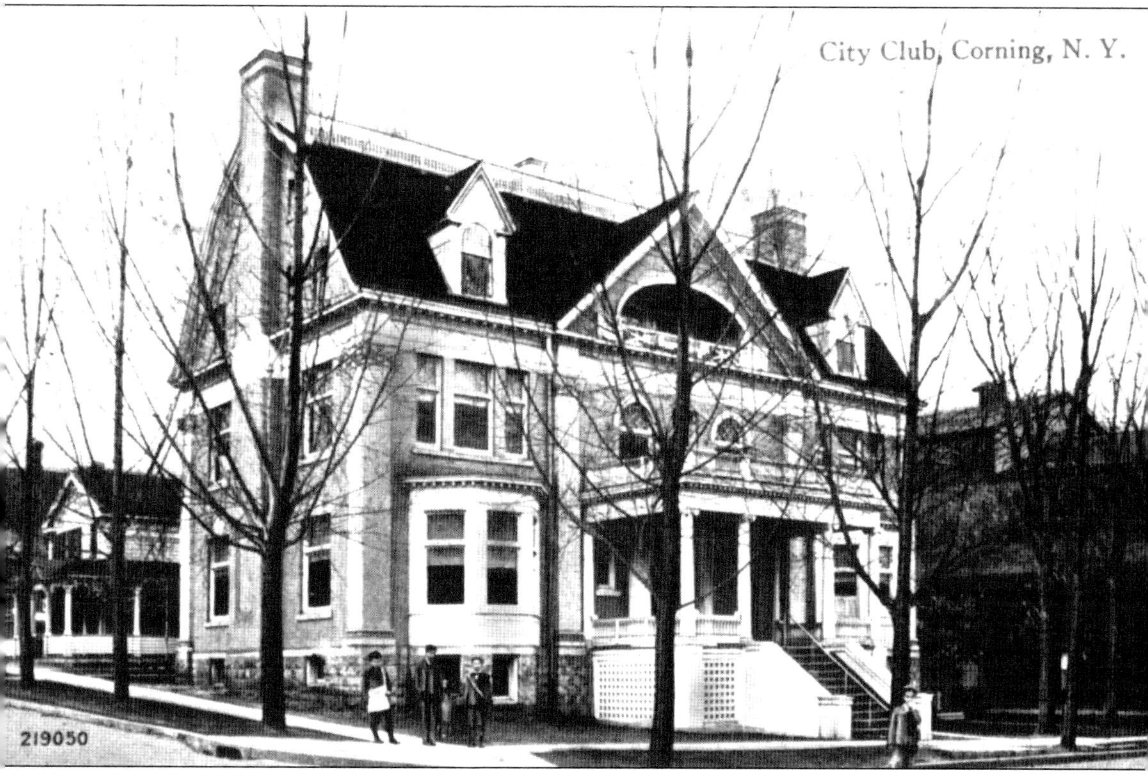

The City Club was opened in 1898 in this building at 149 Pine Street. In 1926, the inside of building was damaged by fire. The City Club decided not to rebuild and started having its meetings in the Baron Steuben building until the club broke up in 1938.

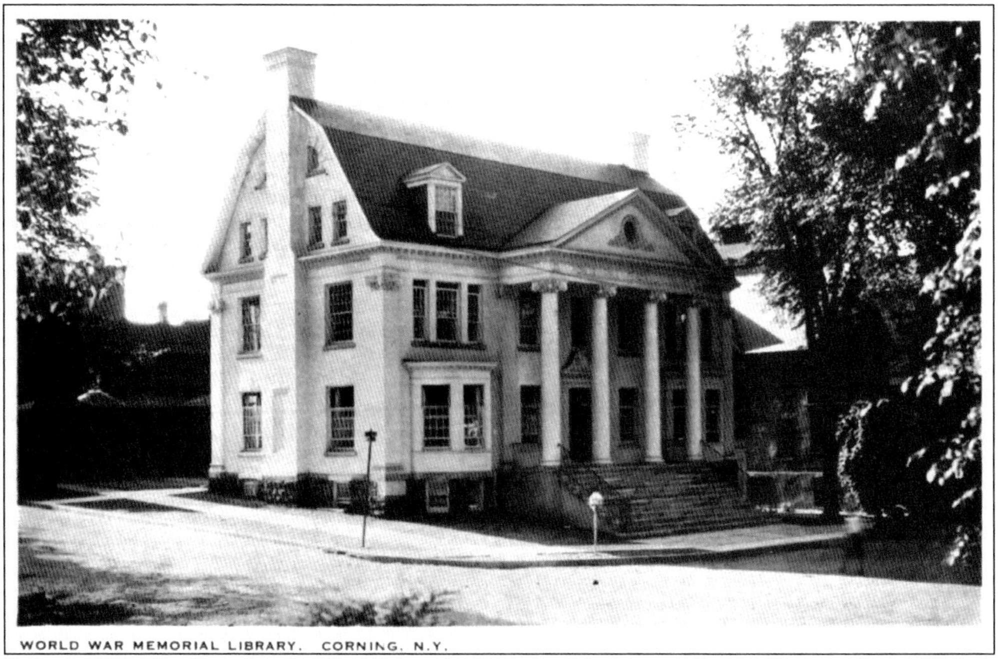

Before 1930, the Corning Public Library had one main room and a small room for children's books in the city hall building. Citizens raised money for repairs and improvements after the 1926 fire in the city club building, and the War Memorial Library was opened in 1930. Famed glass designer Fredrick Carder created a custom glass panel with the names of Corning's 30 locals who died during world wars. Those names included Carder's own son Cyril.

Corning, Dec. 12, '88.

DEAR SIR:

The annual meeting for election of officers of the Mutual Vigilance Society of Steuben, Schuyler and Chemung Counties N. Y. and Tioga County Pa., will be held in G. A. R. Hall, corner Market and Cedar Sts., Corning, on Saturday Jan. 12, 1889, *at one o'clock in the afternoon.*

President, Vice-President, Treasurer, Secretary and three Managers to be elected, at which time the annual dues of one dollar are to be paid. See article 25 *of by-laws.* *J. PRATT, Sec'y.*

The Mutual Vigilance Society was formed in 1886 to protect citizens from horse thieves. The society helped set up a $100 reward for their capture. In 1895, the society had 400 horse-owning members in five counties in New York and Pennsylvania.

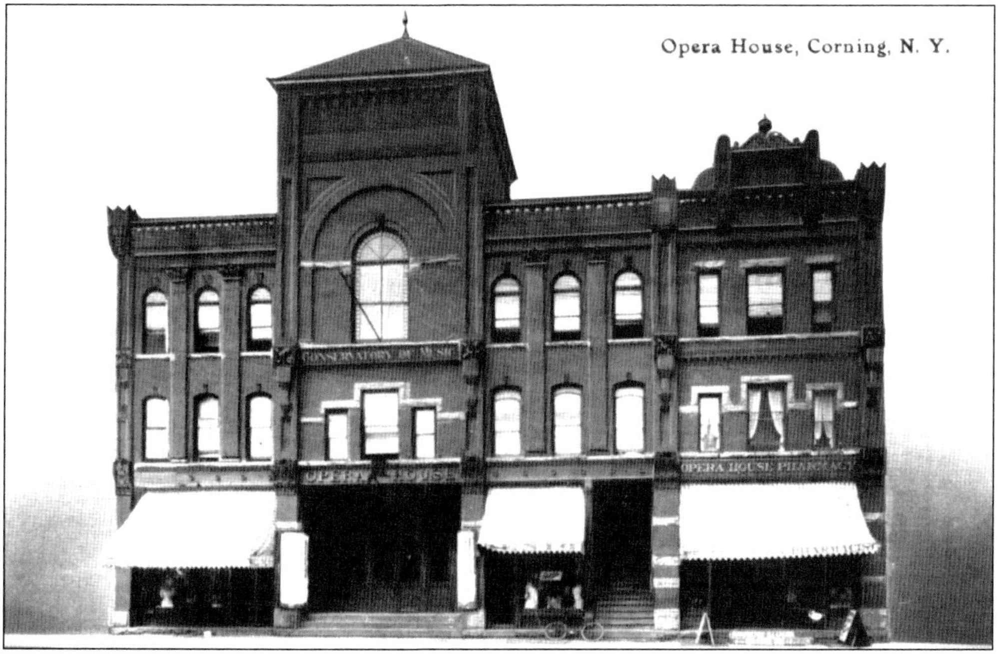

This theater building was constructed in 1891 by the H. O. Dorman Company for a little over $33,000. It was on Pine Street between Erie Avenue and First Street. Opening night, October 8, 1891, was a great success, with the play *Dorothy's Dilemma* taking in over $1,200 in ticket sales. Phonographs were played there in 1893. Moving pictures and later talking pictures were shown here as well.

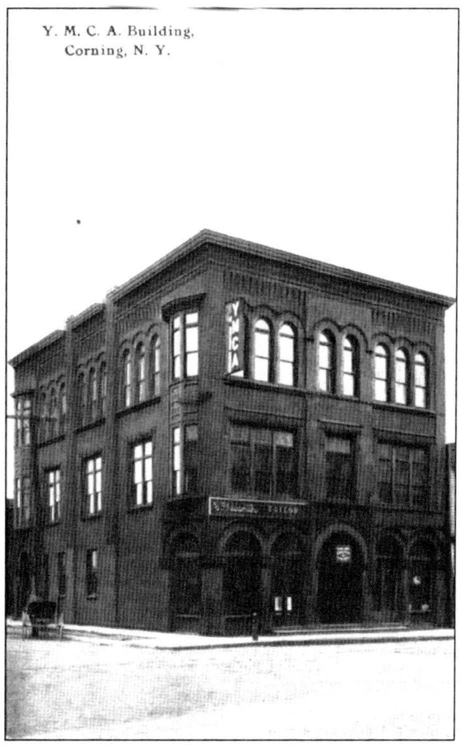

The YMCA was dedicated on May 8, 1892, on the northeast corner of Market and Cedar Streets by the Reverend B. I. Ives of Rochester. In 1907, it built two bowling alleys. Fred Wuersmith had a tailor shop in the building in the second decade of the 20th century. His sign can be seen on the lower corner. The 1916 message on the back was written in German and mailed to a music company in Chicago.

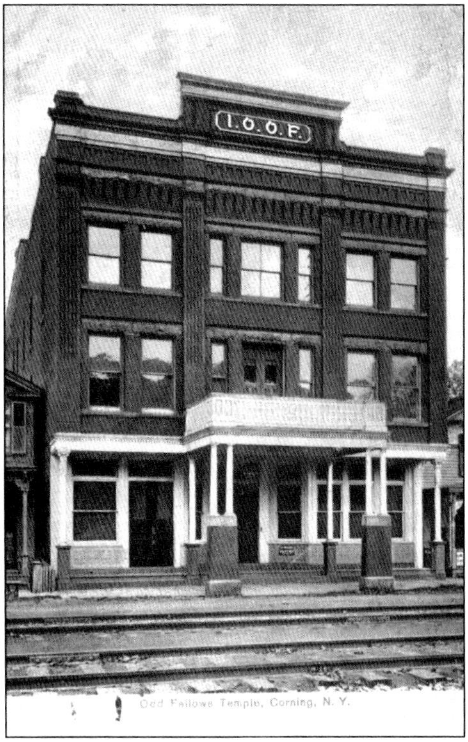

The Independent Order of Odd Fellows is a fraternal organization that was formed in England in the 1700s. John Hoare, the cut glass designer, was an Odd Fellow as well as a Mason.

The city of Corning is named after a man that had a great mind. Erastus Corning served as mayor of Albany, was a member of Congress, and later became president of a railroad. Corning was also an investor in several early banks. The Bank of Lansingburgh was incorporated on March 19, 1813. This early document shows his signature on a transaction where he was investing in a bank in 1823.

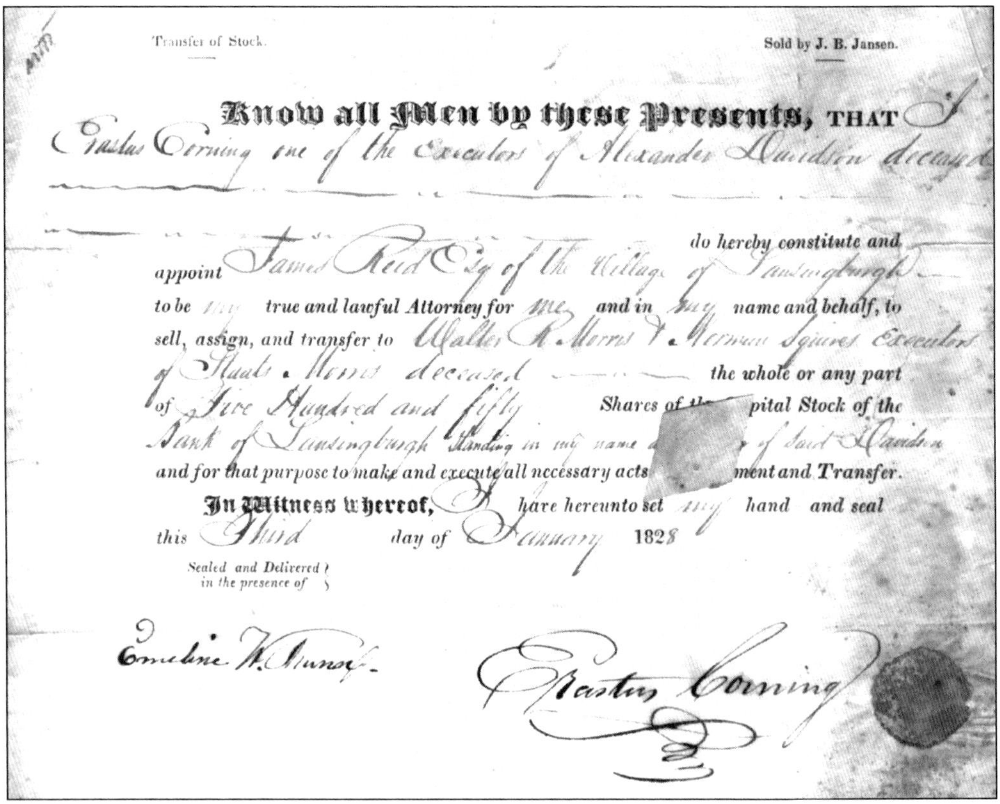

Transfer of Stock.

Sold by J. B. Jansen.

Know all Men by these Presents, THAT I Erastus Corning one of the Executors of Alexander Davidson deceased

do hereby constitute and appoint James Reed Esq of the Village of Lansingburgh to be my true and lawful Attorney for me and in my name and behalf, to sell, assign, and transfer to Walter R. Morris & Herman Squires Executors of Staats Morris deceased the whole or any part of Five Hundred and fifty Shares of [illegible]pital Stock of the Bank of Lansingburgh standing in my name [illegible] of said Davidson and for that purpose to make and execute all necessary acts [illegible]ment and Transfer.

In Witness whereof, I have hereunto set my hand and seal this Third day of January 1823

Sealed and Delivered in the presence of

Emeline W. Munsey

Erastus Corning

Six

Parks and Recreation

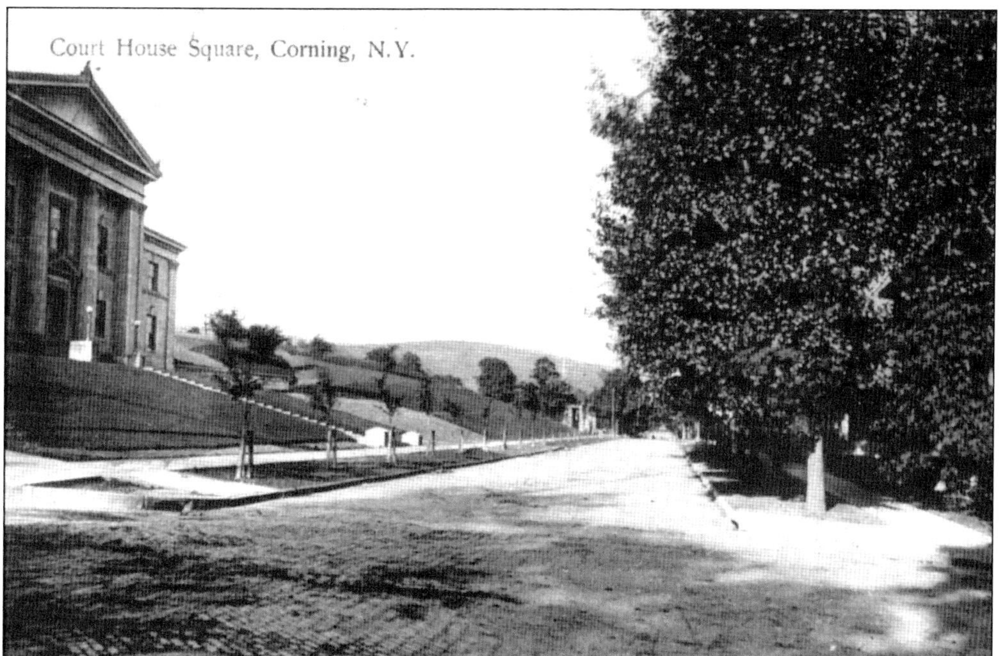

This postcard shows the view from First Street and the courthouse square. This block still looks mostly the same.

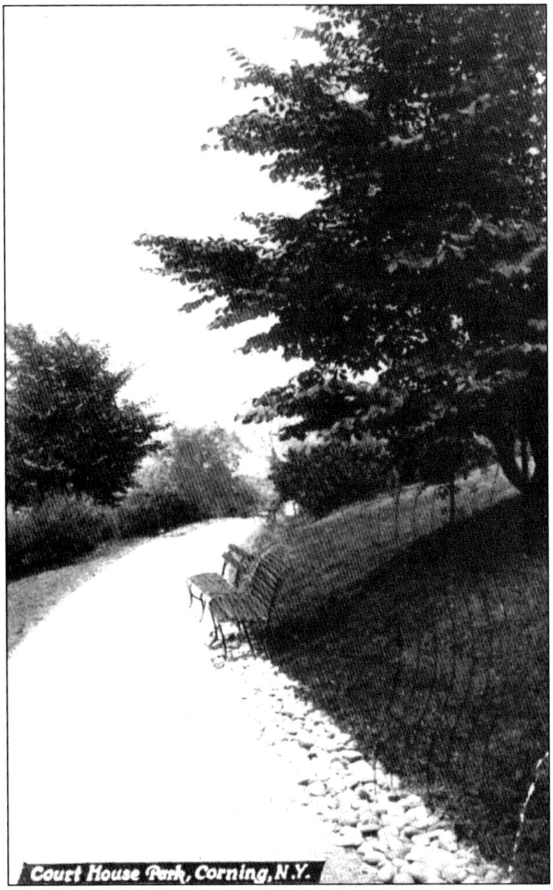

In 1905, R. H. Canfield drew up plans to turn the area around the courthouse into Courthouse Park. Later this park came to be called Canfield Park.

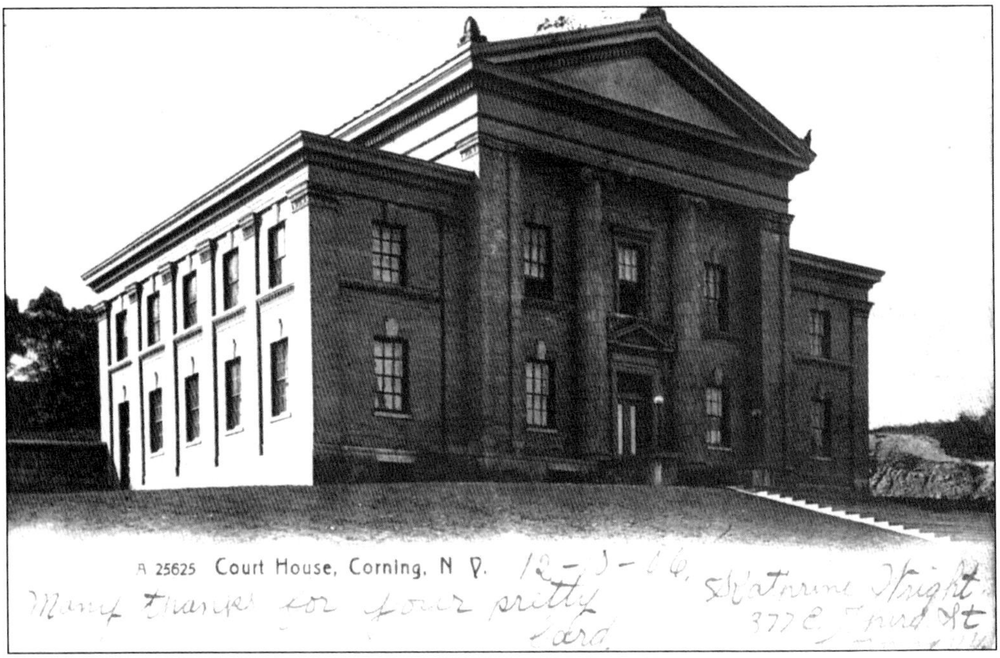

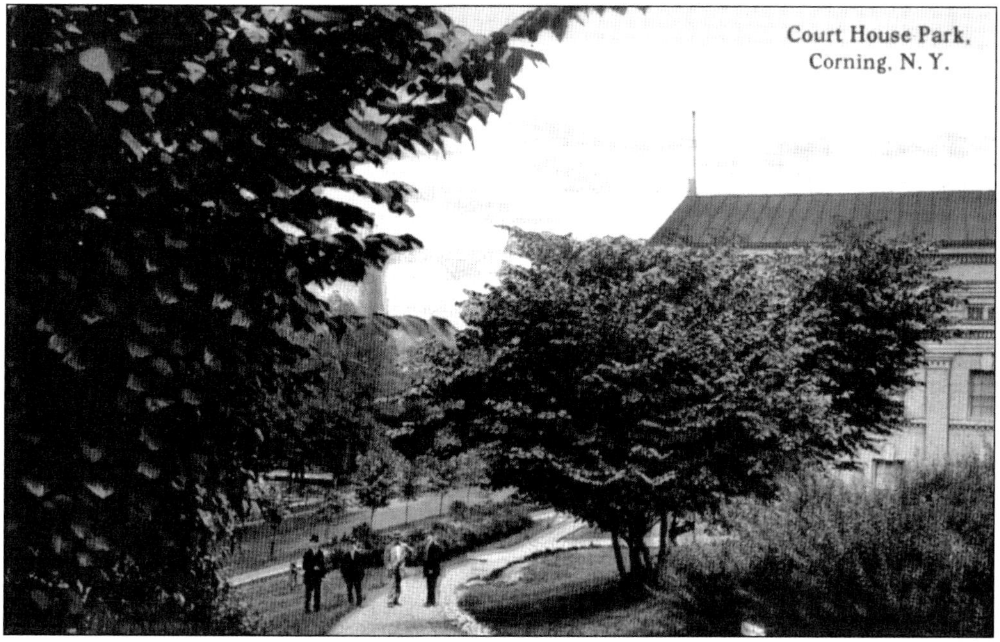

The remains of the walking paths in this park are still visible. Places can still be seen that were paved with coal cinders.

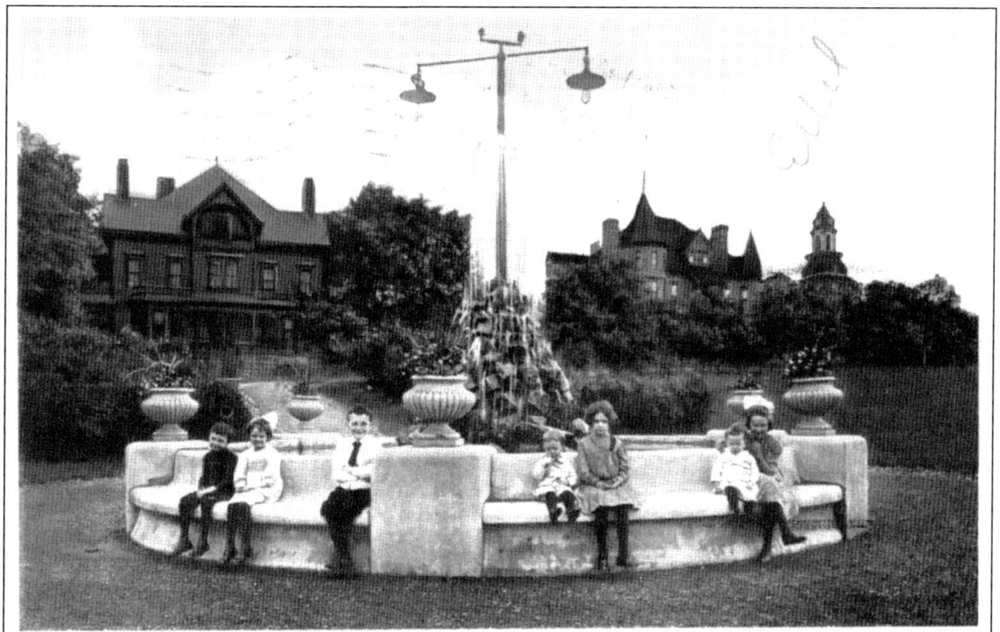

This fountain was added to the park in 1909. In the background are the Hawkes house, the Drake house, and Corning Free Academy.

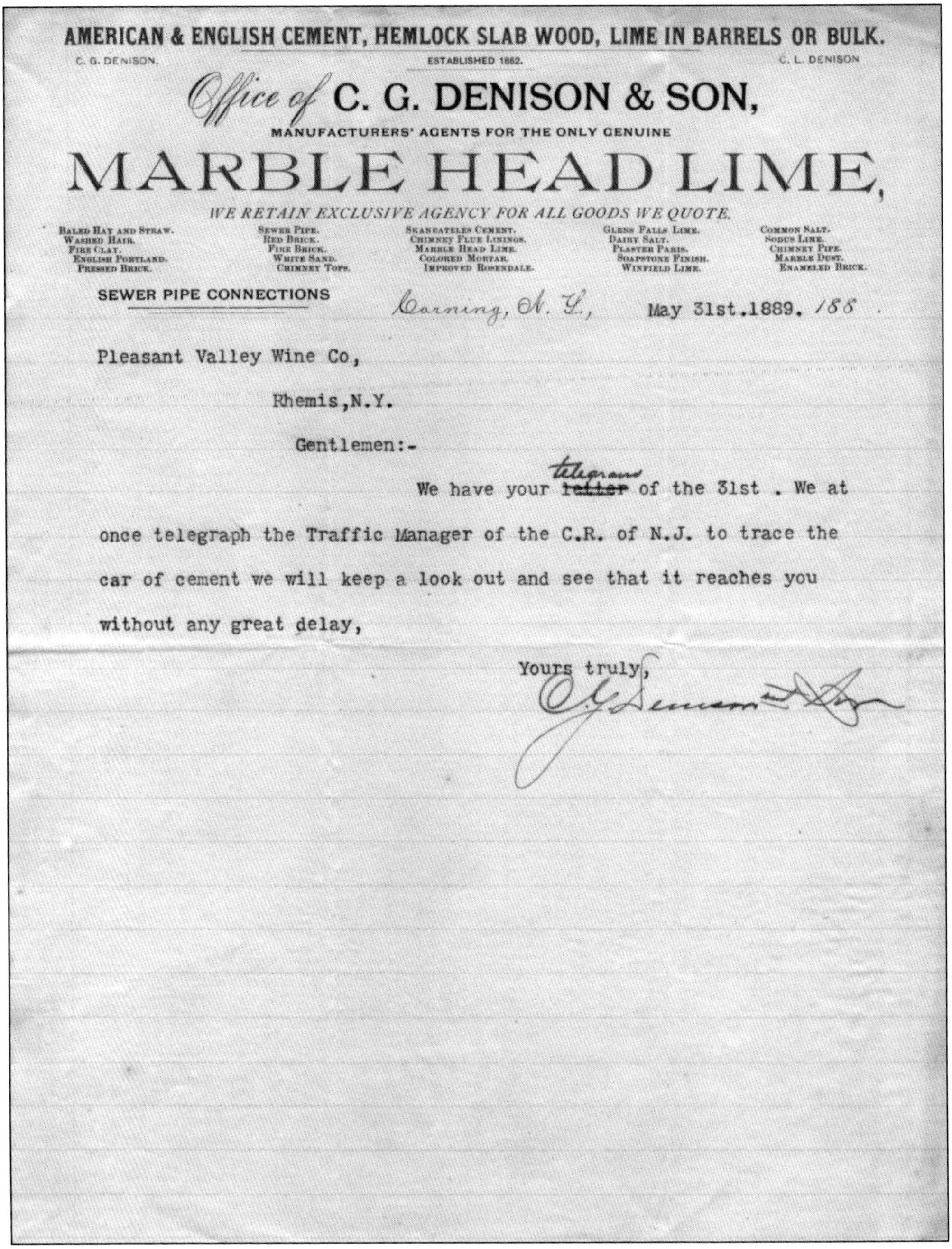

AMERICAN & ENGLISH CEMENT, HEMLOCK SLAB WOOD, LIME IN BARRELS OR BULK.

C. G. DENISON. ESTABLISHED 1862. C. L. DENISON

Office of C. G. DENISON & SON,

MANUFACTURERS' AGENTS FOR THE ONLY GENUINE

MARBLE HEAD LIME,

WE RETAIN EXCLUSIVE AGENCY FOR ALL GOODS WE QUOTE.

Baled Hay and Straw. Washed Hair. Fire Clay. English Portland. Pressed Brick.
Sewer Pipe. Red Brick. Fire Brick. White Sand. Chimney Tops.
Skaneateles Cement. Chimney Flue Linings. Marble Head Lime. Colored Mortar. Improved Rosendale.
Glens Falls Lime. Dairy Salt. Plaster Paris. Soapstone Finish. Winfield Lime.
Common Salt. Sodus Lime. Chimney Pipe. Marble Dust. Enameled Brick.

SEWER PIPE CONNECTIONS

Corning, N. Y., May 31st.1889. 188 .

Pleasant Valley Wine Co,

Rhemis,N.Y.

Gentlemen:-

We have your ~~letter~~ telegram of the 31st . We at once telegraph the Traffic Manager of the C.R. of N.J. to trace the car of cement we will keep a look out and see that it reaches you without any great delay,

Yours truly,

C. G. Denison & Son

This bill head is from a group of many Corning businesses that was mailed to Pleasant Valley Wine Company. Charles G. Denison was a community leader who was elected five times as trustee of the village of Corning in 1863, 1871, 1872, 1877, and 1880. Denison Park was later named after him.

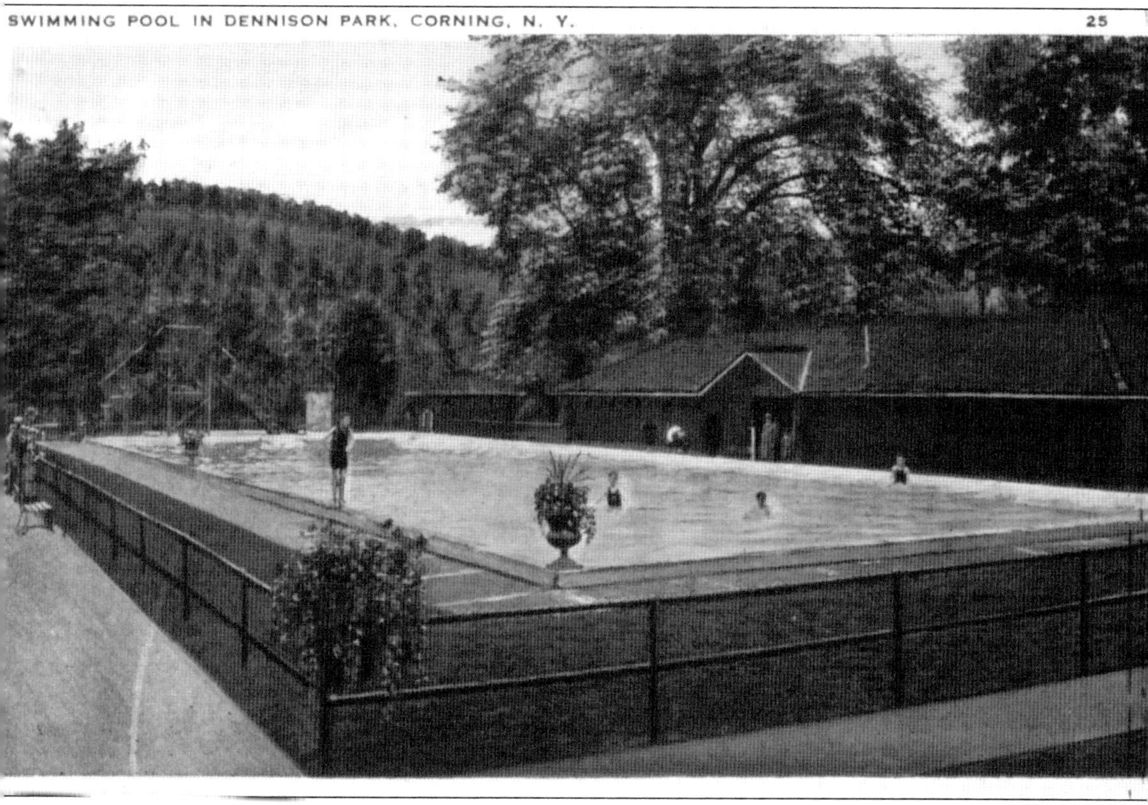

The building of this pool was started in 1919. In 1921, Charles L. Denison gave Denison Park a chlorinator for its pool. Because of water supply problems, it was not always possible to fill the pool. (Courtesy of Diane Gardner.)

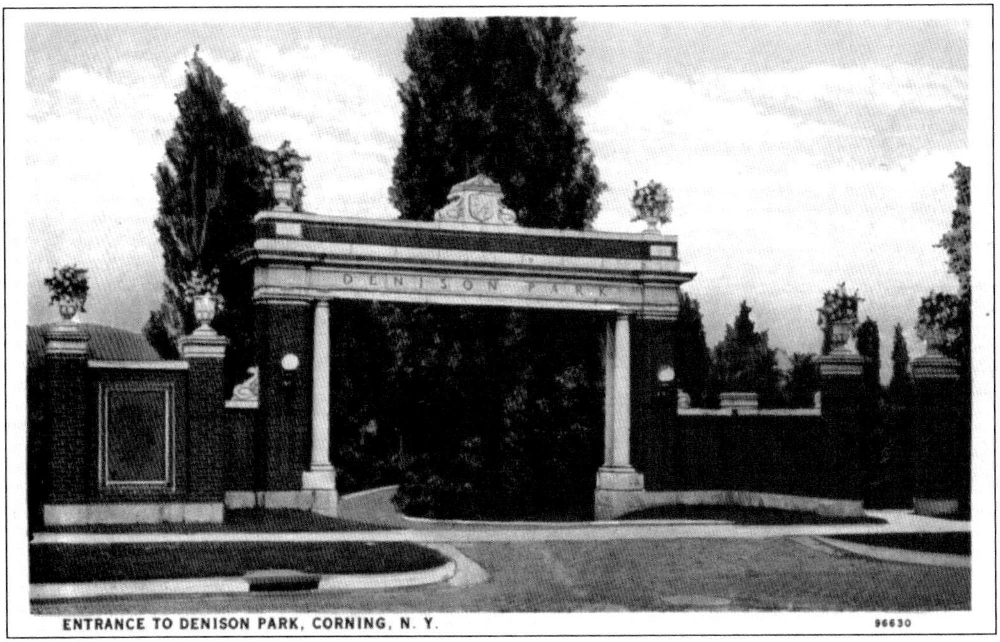

This arched brickwork still exists but is no longer the main entrance for the park. The brass plaque on the left reads, "Erected by the citizens of Corning, New York in memory of C. G. Denison the father of C. L. Denison a true friend of Corning whose bountiful gift made the park possible."

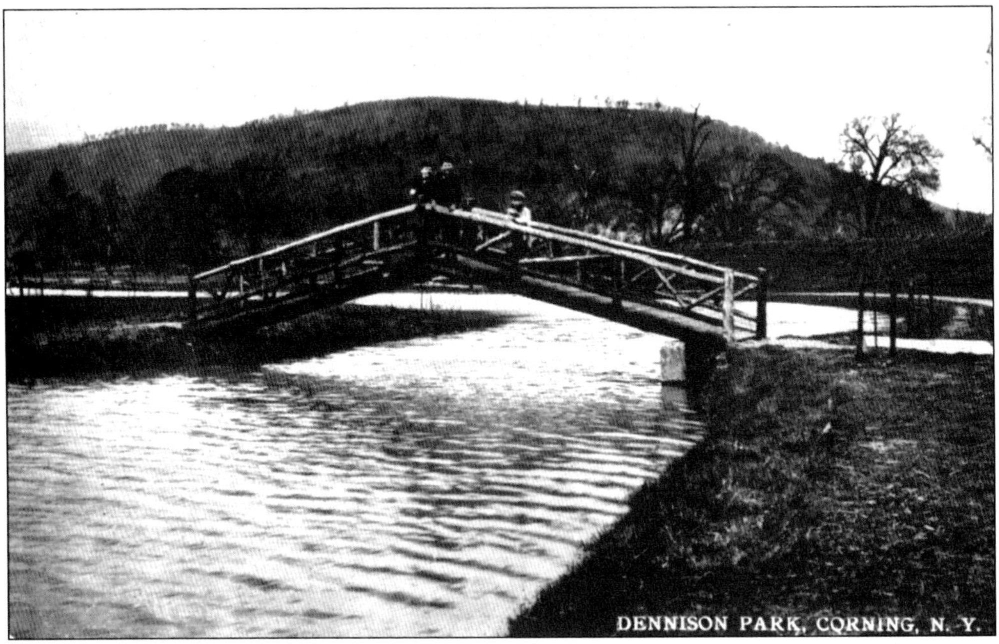

Children enjoy the view of the water. The river may have been closer than it is now. There were no dykes back then, and the water in Denison Park was likely always higher than now.

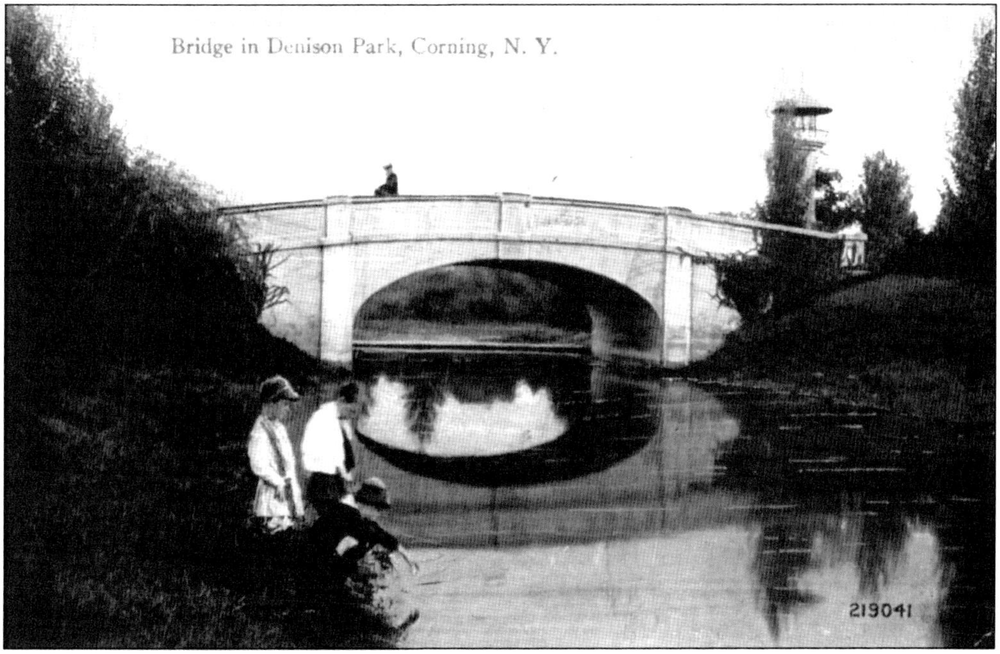

Denison Park got its name when, in 1908, Charles L. Denison gave a large amount of money to construct the park in memory of his father, Charles G. Denison, who was a lifelong resident of Corning. Pavilions were built in 1910, and that same year, the concrete bridge was designed by R. H. Canfield. In 1919, Charles L. Denison gave money to build a heated swimming pool, which was opened on May 30, 1921.

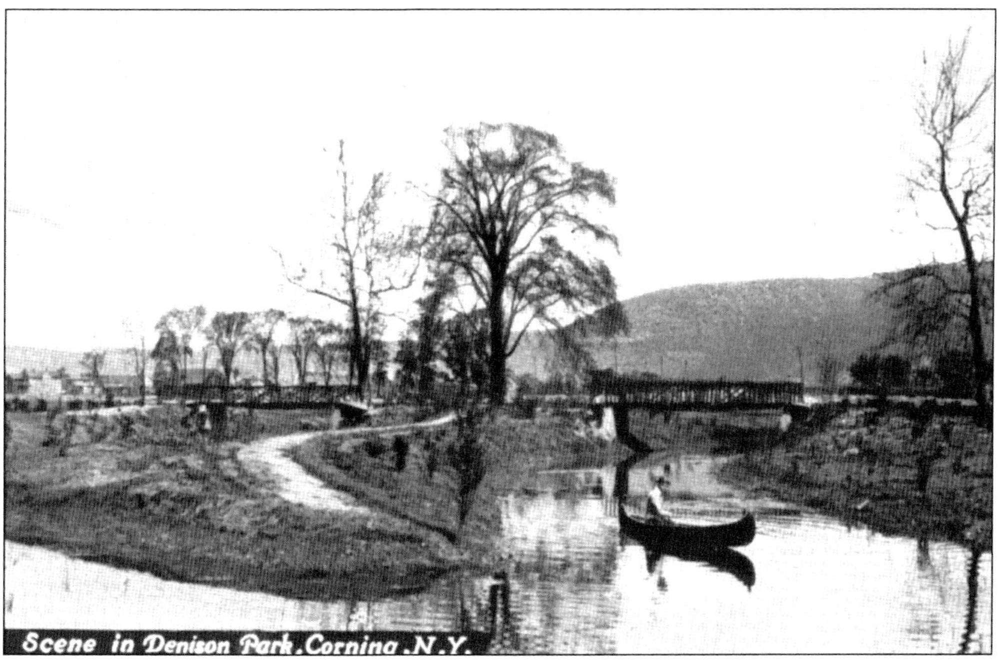

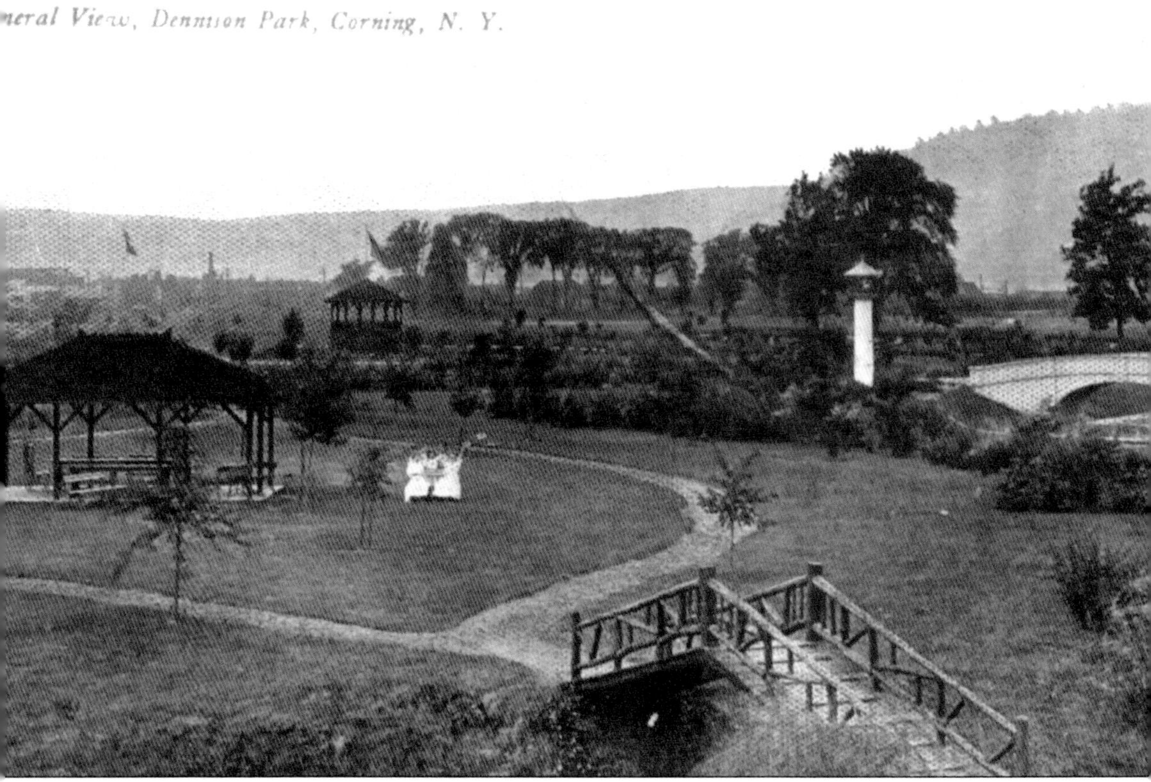

Both the stone bridge and the wooden bridge can be seen in this postcard. There were probably at least two waterways circulating through the park to the river.

Play Grounds, Dennison Park, Corning, N. Y

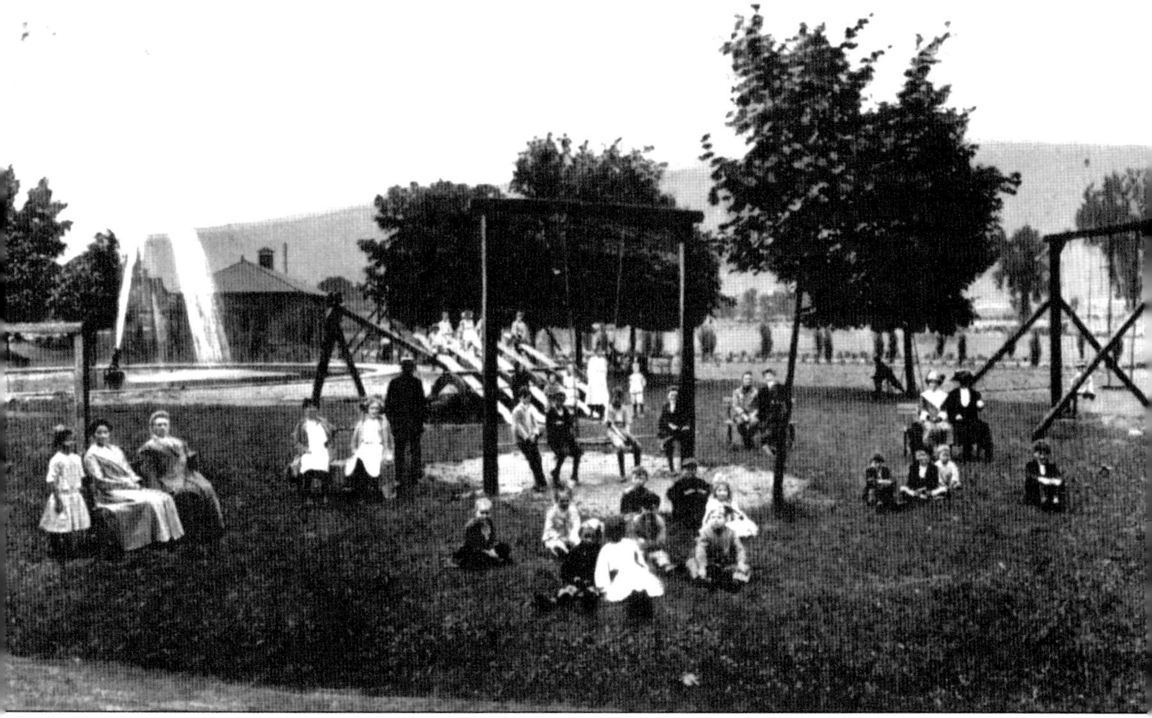

The buildings and everything in this postcard are long gone. They have been replaced by modern swings and slides for children to play on.

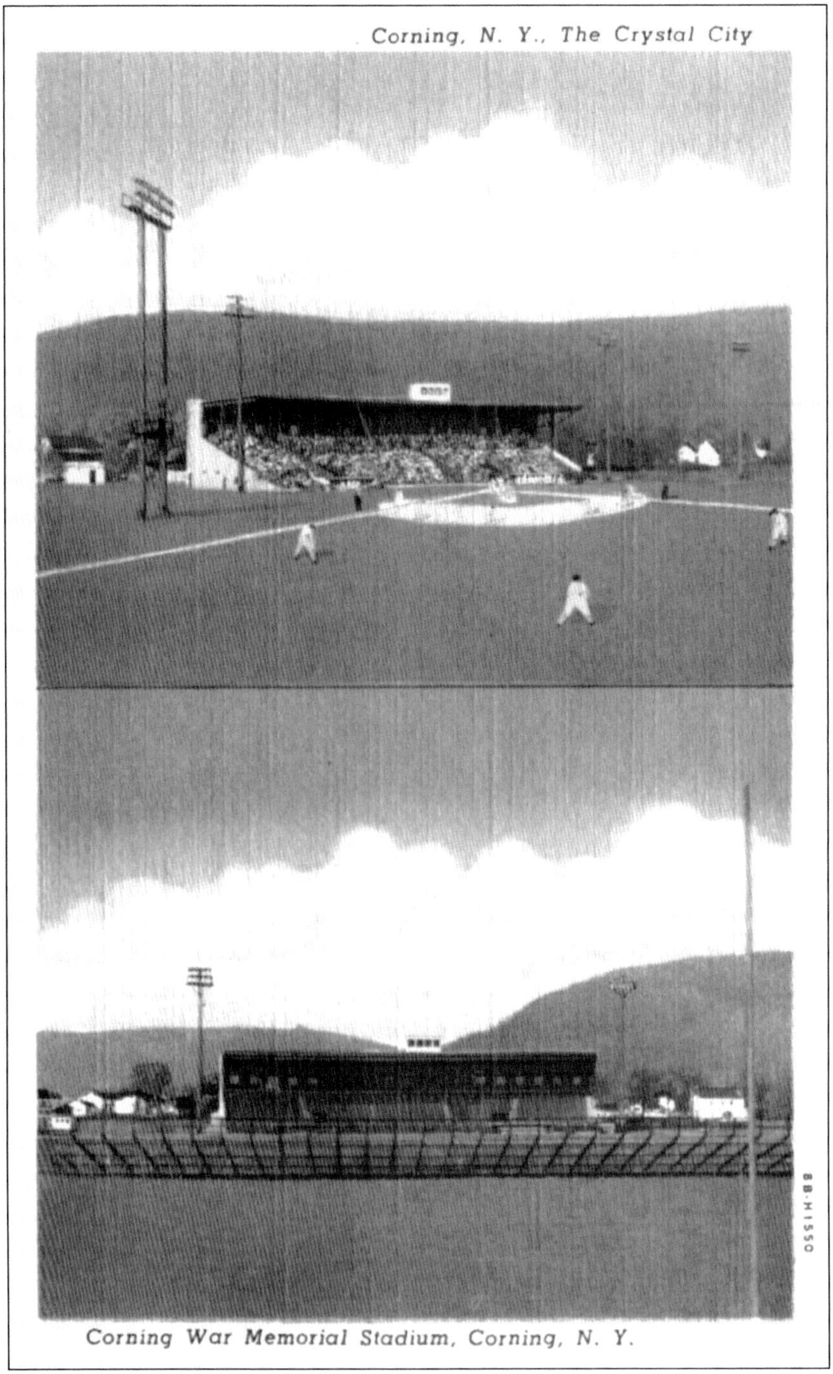

Dwight D. Eisenhower was here for the opening dedication of this stadium before he became president. In the past, Corning hosted several minor-league baseball teams. They are listed as follows: Corning A's, PONY League (1951–1952); Corning Independents, PONY League (1953); Corning Red Sox, PONY League (1954–1956); Corning Red Sox, New York–Penn League (1957–1958, 1960); Corning Cor-Sox, New York–Penn League (1959); and the Corning Royals, New York–Penn League (1968–1969).

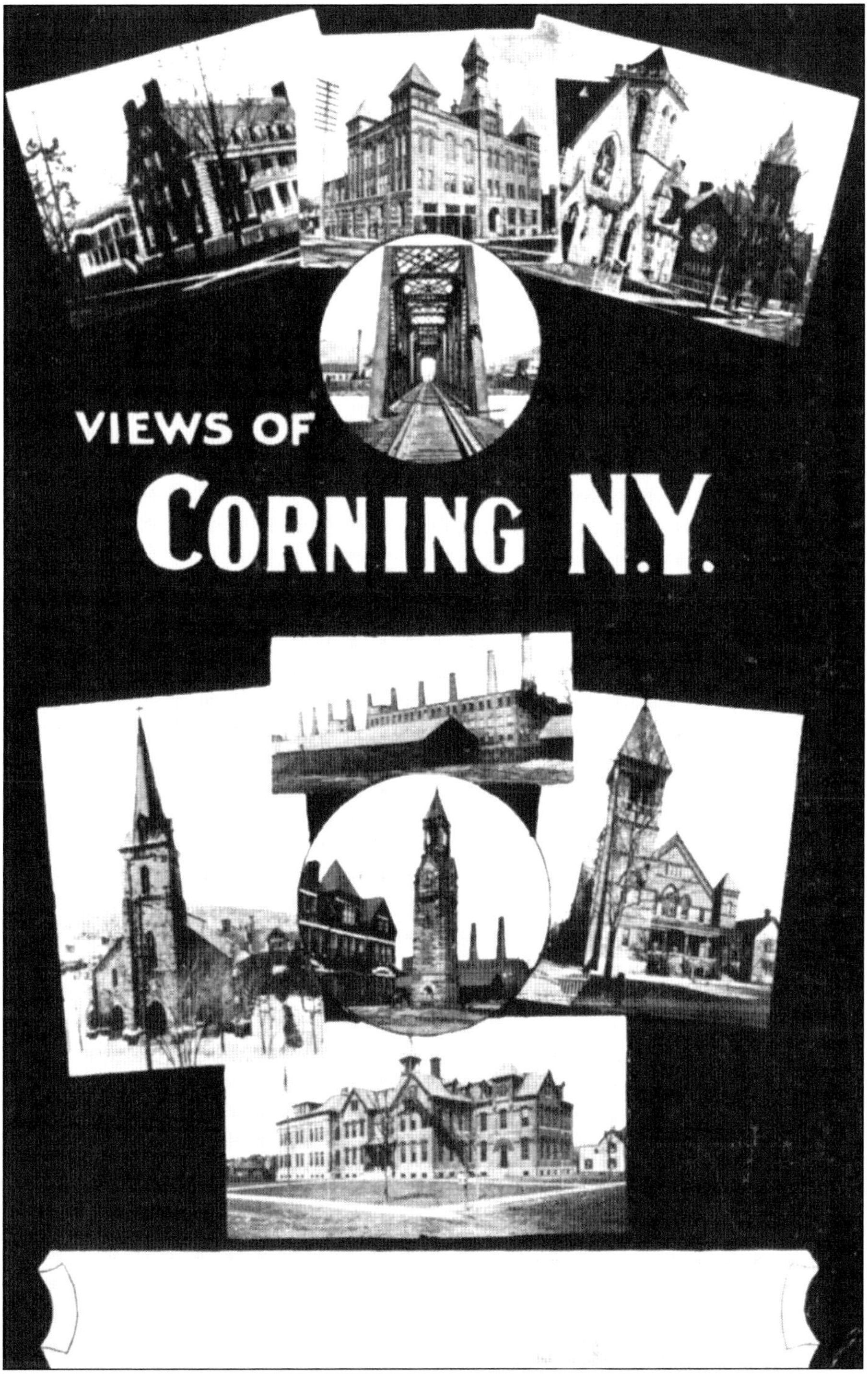

This multi-view card shows nine Corning postcards from about 1908. They are listed from left to right and from top to bottom as follows: Corning Hospital, city hall, Christ Church and Methodist Church, bridge, Corning Brick Works, First Presbyterian Church, clock tower, First Congressional Church, and North Side High School.